D1367416

LIBRARY IN A BOOK

POWER OF THE NEWS MEDIA

Harry Henderson

Facts On File, Inc.

To the young citizen-journalists

who are weaving new webs of media on the Internet

while sharing their understanding of the world

POWER OF THE NEWS MEDIA

Copyright © 2004 by Harry Henderson
Graphs copyright © 2004 by Facts On File

All rights reserved. No part of this book may be reproduced or utilized in any form or by any means, electronic or mechanical, including photocopying, recording, or by any information storage or retrieval systems, without permission in writing from the publisher. For information contact:

Facts On File, Inc.
132 West 31st Street
New York NY 10001

Library of Congress Cataloging-in-Publication Data
Henderson, Harry, 1951–
  Library in a book : power of the news media / Harry Henderson.
    p. cm.—(Library in a book)
Includes bibliographical references and index.
  ISBN 0-8160-4768-5 (acid-free paper)
1. Broadcast journalism—United States—History—20th century. 2. Press—United States—History—20th century. I. Title. II. Series.
  PN4888.B74H46 2004
  070.1′9—dc22   2003018900

Facts On File books are available at special discounts when purchased in bulk quantities for businesses, associations, institutions, or sales promotions. Please call our Special Sales Department in New York at (212) 967-8800 or (800) 322-8755.

You can find Facts On File on the World Wide Web at http://www.factsonfile.com

Text design by Ron Monteleone
Graphs by Dale Williams

Printed in the United States of America

MP Hermitage 10 9 8 7 6 5 4 3 2 1

This book is printed on acid-free paper.

PROPERTY OF THE LIBRARY
YORK COUNTY COMMUNITY COLLEGE
112 COLLEGE DRIVE
WELLS, MAINE 04090
(207) 646-9282

CONTENTS

PART I

OVERVIEW OF THE TOPIC

CHAPTER 1

THE DEVELOPMENT
OF THE NEWS MEDIA

It is useful to look at how the vast enterprise of American (and eventually global) media developed. In doing so, one finds important changes in media technology, the nature of the media's audience, and the role and purpose of journalism as seen by its practitioners.

THE ROOTS OF THE AMERICAN PRESS

Since its invention around 1450, printing has played an important role in the history of nations. The religious civil wars of the Reformation (16th and 17th centuries) were fought as much with pamphlets and handbills as by armies. In the emerging modern states in 17th and 18th centuries, in Europe, including Britain, the printing press was viewed as a technology that had to be tightly managed by the state to serve its purposes while preventing it from getting into the hands of dissidents. The norm in most countries was that printers were licensed and tightly controlled by the government.

However, as the movement toward rationalism and scientific inquiry began to take hold, a number of voices called for freedom of the press. In his 1644 work *Areopagitica*, English poet John Milton declared in favor of "free" (that is, unlicensed) printing:

> *And though all the winds of doctrin[e] were let loose to play upon the earth, so Truth be in the field, we do injuriously by licencing and prohibiting to misdoubt her strength. Let her and Falsehood grapple; who ever knew Truth to be put to the wors[e] in a free and open encounter.*[1]

About two centuries later John Stuart Mill in his essay *On Liberty* argued that while there was no guarantee that truth would prevail (or even that it could be completely ascertained), allowing censorship risks the people of being "deprived of the ability of exchanging error for truth."

3

However, in the new British America restrictions were often tighter than those back home—in part because British authorities from the very first were concerned that 3,000 miles of separation and the necessity for the colonists to be largely on their own was a recipe for eventual disunity. Thus the governors of the various American colonies received instructions in the late 17th century "to provide by all necessary orders that no person KEEP any press for printing, NOR that any book, pamphlet or other matters whatsoever be printed without your especial leave and license first obtained."[2]

William Berkeley, governor of Virginia, writing to his superiors in England in 1671 rejoiced that "there are no free-schools, nor printing; and I hope we shall not have, these hundred years. For learning has brought disobedience and heresy, and sects into the world, and printing has divulged them and libels against the best government: God keep us from both!"[3]

The first newspaper published in what would eventually become the United States, *Publick Occurrences, Both Foreign and Domestick* consisted of only four sheets of paper. The editor, Benjamin Harris, told his readers that he would take "what pains he can to obtain a Faithful Relation of all things; and will particularly make himself beholden to such Persons in Boston whom he knows to have been for their own use the diligent Observers of such matters."[4]

Harris planned to issue his newspaper at least monthly, or more often "if any Glut of Occurrences happen." Domestic news items included accounts of Christian Indians planning a Thanksgiving celebration, other American Indians kidnapping two white children, an ongoing smallpox epidemic, a fire in Boston, and other "occurrences." The main foreign news concerned the ongoing struggle of colonial forces against the French and their Indian allies in Canada.

However, only four days after the first issue of the paper was distributed, the colonial governing council of Massachusetts ordered it to cease publication. Under British law nothing could be printed without a government license, and the paper had none. Besides opposing "free printing," many of the more conservative members of the council had been angered by the unflattering portrayal of both military affairs and domestic scandals.

Nevertheless, a number of American printers managed to start newspapers. Benjamin Franklin in his article "Apology for Printers," published in the June 10, 1731, issue of the *Pennsylvania Gazette*, expressed a strikingly modern concern for objectivity when he explained that printers

are educated in the Belief that when Men differ in Opinion, both Sides ought equally to have the Advantage of being heard by the Publick. . . . Printers naturally acquire a vast Unconsernedness as to the right or wrong Opinions contain'd in what they print.

The Development of the News Media

In 1735 a newspaper called the *New-York Weekly Journal* published a satirical article ridiculing William Cosby, the colony's newly appointed governor. Cosby had the sheriff arrest and jail the paper's printer, John Peter Zenger, on charges of libel. At the time, a statement could be libelous even if true, and criticism of government officials was often considered libelous.

At trial Zenger's attorney, Andrew Hamilton, admitted that the article's author, James Alexander, had indeed written the words in question, and Zenger had printed them. As far as the judge was concerned, that was the end of the case, but Hamilton boldly addressed the jury and asked them to acquit his client because he had the right to print the truth:

> *Every man who prefers freedom to a life of slavery will bless and honor you as men who have baffled the attempt at tyranny; and by an impartial and uncorrupt verdict, have laid a noble foundation for securing to ourselves, our posterity, and our neighbors that to which nature and the laws of our country have always given us a right—the liberty—both of exposing and opposing arbitrary power . . . by speaking and writing truth.*[5]

The jury acquitted Zenger to the applause of the courtroom audience. Although this would not be the end of confrontations between newspapers and the government, the case of John Peter Zenger would become a symbol of the freedom of the press and of the growing American spirit of opposition to arbitrary rule.

As the 18th century progressed dozens of small newspapers sprang up. Their reporting gradually shifted from consisting mostly of foreign news taken from British papers to including more local events and to interpreting foreign events in terms of their local effects (as on colonial trade, or on conflicts such as the French and Indian War). This, too, reflected the growing consciousness of "Americanism," or American identity.

The press played an important role in the American Revolution, from the pamphlet *Common Sense* by Tom Paine to the spreading of news about the movements of British troops. When the revolution had been won and the movement began to replace the makeshift Articles of Confederation with a constitution specifying a stronger central government, the insistence on making sure fundamental rights were secured led to the adoption of the Bill of Rights in 1791. Its first article, or amendment, specified:

> *"Congress shall make no law respecting an establishment of religion, or prohibiting the free exercise thereof; or abridging the freedom of speech, or of the press, or the right of the people peaceably to assemble, and to petition the Government for redress of grievances."*

However, only seven years later, with war with France looming and fear of French revolutionary zeal in the air, the Federalists in control of Congress passed the Alien and Sedition Acts of 1798. Among other things, this law made it illegal to publish "any false, scandalous, or malicious writing or writings against the Government of the United States, with the intent to defame . . . or to bring them into contempt or disrepute."

Fourteen people were convicted under this sedition provision. In an example case, Matthew Lyon, congressional representative from Vermont, was charged for writing that President John Adams and his administration showed "an unbridled thirst for ridiculous pomp, foolish adulation, and selfish continual grasp for power." He was convicted, jailed for four months and fined $1,000—a substantial sum at the time. Anthony Haswell, editor of the *Vermont Gazette*, defended Lyon as a victim of "the oppressive hand of usurped power." Haswell in turn was fined $200 and sentenced to two months in prison.[6]

A modern reader is likely to wonder why the Supreme Court did not promptly declare this provision to be in violation of the free speech and free press guarantees of the First Amendment. It should be noted that the Supreme Court's role as an arbiter of the Constitution that could overturn federal laws would not be established until Justice John Marshall and a unanimous Court majority first undertook that role in *Marbury v. Madison* (1803). Instead, Thomas Jefferson and James Madison led the fight against the law in the political arena, authoring the Kentucky and Virginia Resolutions in 1798. The Kentucky Resolution took the position that the sedition law encroached on the rights of the states under the Tenth Amendment, including "the right of judging how far the licentiousness of speech and press might be abridged without lessening their useful freedom." In the Virginia Resolution, Jefferson further declared that the Sedition Act and similar measures were "leveled against the right of freely examining public characters and measures, and of free communication among the people thereon, which has ever been justly deemed the only effectual guardian of every other right." When Jefferson won the presidency in 1800, the Alien and Sedition Acts was allowed to lapse.

THE "PENNY PRESS" AND THE RISE OF POPULAR JOURNALISM

By the beginning of the 19th century there were about 200 regular newspapers being published in the United States. Despite the sentiments of Benjamin Franklin as quoted earlier, newspapers in the young republic did not embrace objectivity in the modern sense, where political advocacy is relegated to editorials and opinion pieces. Most newspapers belonged to one or the other of the factions that were gradually coalescing into modern political parties. Jefferson himself was the target of a typical partisan blast in the Federalist *New-England Palladium:*

> *Should the infidel Jefferson be elected to the Presidency, the seal of death is that moment set on our holy religion, our churches will be prostrated, and some infamous prostitute, under the title of the Goddess of Reason, will preside in the Sanctuaries now devoted to the worship of the Most High.*

For a time, Jefferson's advocacy of free speech was replaced by a measure of cynicism. Writing to 17-year-old John Norvell, who had asked him about the prospect of a career in journalism, Jefferson replied that "Nothing can now be believed which is seen in a newspaper. Truth itself becomes suspicious by being put into that polluted vehicle."

In the end Jefferson returned to his ideals. Near the end of his life, writing to his old friend the marquis de Lafayette, Jefferson insisted that "the only security of it all is a free press. The force of public opinion cannot be resisted, when permitted freely to be expressed. The agitation it produces must be submitted to. it is necessary, to keep the waters pure."[7]

By the 1830s the newspaper business was in high gear. Andrew Jackson had won the presidency in 1828 by conducting a new-style populist campaign in which he deliberately sought newspaper editors and fed them speeches and news. Before this time newspapers were mainly of interest to the small political and intellectual elite and to businesspeople who needed news of market prices. In 1833, however, Ben Day founded the *New York Sun,* the first of the "penny papers." Unlike the five or six cents charged by other papers (which was a good part of a working person's daily wage), the *Sun* could be afforded by the working class. The *Sun* had features that appealed to a popular audience, including reports of crime and trials, which are still a major source of media fodder today. Day also invented a new moneymaking device: the small "want ad."

The following year the *Sun* had a competitor, the *New York Herald* of James Gordon Bennett, which, unlike the *Sun,* took a substantial interest in politics. As more of the new penny papers began to cover political issues, this reinforced the role of the larger electorate that now had to be addressed by candidates. Meanwhile, New York's status as the newspaper capital of the United States was further reinforced in 1841 by Horace Greeley, who founded the *New York Tribune.*

In the coming decades newspapers would be embroiled in contentious issues such as tariffs, the war with Mexico in 1846, and most important of all, slavery. The growing abolitionist movement gained a powerful voice when

William Lloyd Garrison founded the *Liberator* in 1831. Most southern states passed laws banning publication or possession of any writing that could be interpreted as encouraging a slave rebellion. Penalties ranging from whipping to imprisonment up to death were specified. The Rev. Elijah Parish Lovejoy, publisher of the abolitionist *St. Louis Observer,* was killed in an armed confrontation with a mob seeking to destroy his press . . . for the third time.

As the nation grew, so did the need for timely news and market information. In 1844 the *New York Sun* reported on the development of a technological solution to this problem:

> *MAGNETIC TELEGRAM—The new invention is complete from Baltimore to Washington. The wire, perfectly secured against the weather by a covering or rope yarn and tar, is conducted on the top of posts about twenty feet high and one hundred yards apart. The nominations of the [Democratic National] convention this day are to be conveyed to Washington by this telegraph, where they will arrive in a few seconds. . . . At half past 11 A.M. the question being asked, what was the news at Washington, the answer was almost instantaneously returned: "Van Buren Stock is rising." That is indeed the annihilation of space!*

NEW FRONTIERS IN JOURNALISM

The newspaper industry continued its strong growth at midcentury. In addition to the telegraph, newspapers in the larger cities had new steam-powered presses with much greater production capacity. The nation's growing railroad network made it practical to send correspondents to a story in a few days rather than weeks.

By 1860 the U.S. Census had reported 276 daily newspapers in the North, what would become the Union in the Civil War—the economically much poorer Confederacy had only 69. The war brought many new challenges to journalists. The major papers, particularly those in New York, sent correspondents into the field (the *New York Herald* alone had more than 60).

It was not clear what sort of information journalists would be allowed to report, and newspapers often featured speculative articles (complete with maps) showing where they thought the armies were marching next. Gradually, however, the military instituted censorship on the telegraph lines. Meanwhile, in border states such as Maryland and Missouri Union authorities often simply shut down newspapers that had pro-Southern, or "Copperhead," sentiments. In the South, the problem faced by newspapers was less censorship and government heavy-handedness than a worsening shortage of basic supplies, including paper and ink.

The Development of the News Media

Battlefield reports could be vivid and moving, as in this dispatch by Ned Spencer of the *Cincinnati Times* following the Battle of Shiloh:

> *As I sit tonight, writing this epistle, the dead and wounded are all around. The knife of the Surgeon is busy at work, and amputated legs and arms lie scattered in every direction. The cries of the suffering victim, and the groans of those who patiently await for medical attendance, are most distressing to anyone who has any sympathy with his fellow man. All day long they are coming in. . . . I hope my eyes may never again look upon such sights.* [8]

The stark camp and battlefield photography of Mathew Brady could not yet be reproduced in newspapers, but illustrators could make woodcuts based on photos, and the war also gave a boost to illustrated newspapers and newsmagazines such as *Harper's*.

Despite the horrendous losses of life and resources from the war, both the U.S. economy and the press continued to grow in the last third of the 19th century. Much of that growth would be in the newly opened West. The 1850 census had counted only 11 newspapers in the far western states and territories. By 1860 there were 285, and by 1890 there were more than 1,000 newspapers, serving a western population of about 3 million people.

Running a newspaper was expensive—telegraph charges in particular were very high. Many newspapers failed, only to be replaced by equally short-lived successors. However, some new technologies and journalistic practices helped small-town newspapers. "Ready-print" and feature syndication companies began to offer ready-made pages of national and world news that small papers could reproduce and combine with their local news. Press associations and cooperatives gave access to news to papers that could not afford to have their own correspondents in places like New York and Washington, D.C.

Newspapers played an important role in the growth of small-town economies. Often land speculators and builders subsidized newspapers as a form of "boosterism." Newspaper editors in turn extolled the climate, farming productivity, and economic opportunity available in the community.

Meanwhile in big cities such as New York, the population was swelled by a growing stream of immigrants from Ireland, Germany, Italy, and other countries. At least for the first generation or two, immigrants tended to settle in their own ethnic communities and these, too, supported vigorous newspapers.

Journalists in the elite newspapers began to have a growing sense of their craft. The basic journalistic techniques still used today began to be taught in college courses. For example, the uncertainty of war and the expense of the telegraph began to encourage a tighter, more organized style of writing.

Stories were expected to have a strong lead sentence and opening paragraph summarizing the story, which would then be fleshed out by paragraphs containing supporting details. Reporters were taught that their stories should answer the classic questions: who, what, when, where, why, and how. Reporters were also reminded to look for a "hook"—some aspect of the story that had great human interest and would grab the reader's attention. Increasingly structured ways of gaining information were also employed. Starting in the 1870s, reporters began to interview public figures rather than wait for them to say something.

THE PRESS IN THE TWENTIETH CENTURY

Toward the end of the 19th century a new generation of newspaper publishers built their enterprises on a larger corporate scale. They also ratcheted up the populism and sensationalism of their publications. By now presses had not only become faster; type could be set at a Linotype keyboard instead of by hand. Further, newspapers could use multicolored inks and print engravings and halftone photographs. Joseph Pulitzer's *New York World* used all these techniques to create a new, visually compelling popular press. Another of his innovations was the comic strip, of which the *World* had one called the Yellow Kid (because of the color of his shirt). He became the icon of what came to be known as yellow journalism.

When revolution broke out in Cuba in the late 1890s, Pulitzer and his competitor, a wealthy young heir named William Randolph Hearst, were ready to highlight Spanish atrocities and agitate for U.S. involvement in the conflict. When Hearst's illustrator in Cuba, Frederic Remington, cabled back to headquarters that nothing was happening and he and his colleague wanted to go home, Hearst famously replied "Please remain. You furnish the pictures and I'll furnish the war." Combined with the mysterious explosion of the battleship *Maine*, yellow journalism soon furnished the war.

Early in the 20th century, the growth of large corporations (including in the newspaper industry) began to provoke a reaction in the form of journalists who used the newly refined tools of their craft to investigate the effects of that corporate power and the persistence of crushing poverty in American cities. They would become known as muckrakers. They included Josiah Flynt (pen name of Josiah Frank Willard) who began a series in 1900 called "True Stories of the Underworld." But the foremost muckraker was probably Ida Tarbell, already pioneering as a woman general reporter, whose exposé attacked the powerful Standard Oil Company of John D. Rockefeller for its monopolistic practices. Other prominent muckrakers included Lincoln Steffens, whose pieces such as "The Shame of Minneapolis" attacked corruption in American cities. Muckraking combined with a new interest in social problems, highlighted by the photojournalism of Jacob August Riis.

The muckrakers struck a chord with the American public and helped boost both newspaper and magazine sales and the efforts of the political movement called Progressivism, which worked for such reforms as an end to child labor, eight-hour workdays, and pure-food-and-drug laws.

As the century progressed, the popular press began to include more weekly news magazines, such as *Reader's Digest* (1922), *Time* (1923), the *New Yorker* (1925), *Fortune* (1930), *Newsweek* (1933), *U.S. News* (1933), *Life* (1936), and *Look* (1937). By then photojournalism had emerged as a distinct profession, and most of these magazines used photography extensively. A related development, the newsreel film, became a common accompaniment to a night at the movies. In the pretelevision age illustrated magazines and newsreels would be the main medium for conveying images such as the trenches of World War I and the breadlines of the Great Depression of the 1930s.

Although newspapers continued to be economically successful, conditions often required merging competing newspapers for efficiency and to secure a large enough readership. The development of radio and especially television (following World War II) cut into newspaper advertising revenue. Another factor was the spreading out of populations from central cities to suburbs that could not be served efficiently by city newspapers.

Starting in the 1970s newspapers used new technology to cut labor costs, often against the staunch resistance of unions. With computerized typesetting, the keystrokes made by a reporter could find their way to the printed page by way of an editor's screen, with human printers no longer needed to compose the pages.

Even innovations such as Al Neuharth's *USA Today*, a colorful paper that organized stories into bite-sized pieces suitable for an audience raised on television, could not arrest the gradual decline in newspaper circulation. In 1970 about 77 percent of the adult population read newspapers regularly; by 1994 this had fallen to 67.5 percent. Newspapers fought back with a growing emphasis on local and "human interest" stories as well as trendy features, but the long-term prospects were troubling—in particular because many young people growing up in the 1980s and 1990s did not acquire the daily habit of reading a newspaper at the breakfast or dinner table.

The latest attempt to graft new growth onto newspapers is to put them on the Internet. Starting in the mid-1990s newspapers began to create online editions, both to encourage prospective readers and to tie into additional advertising and revenue sources. Today just about every newspaper of any size has a web site.

RADIO: SPARKING A NEW MEDIUM

Radio dates back to the last years of the 19th century, but until the 1920s it functioned mainly as a wireless equivalent of the telegraph, such as for linking ships at sea. However, inventors gradually mastered the techniques of carrying voice and sound rather than just the dots and dashes of Morse code. This in turn opened the possibility that programs could be broadcast to a suitably equipped audience of ordinary people.

Many historians consider KDKA in Pittsburgh, Pennsylvania, to be the nation's first commercial radio station. One of its first broadcasts was live coverage of the returns in the 1920 presidential election, in which Republican Warren G. Harding defeated Democrat James W. Cox. Radio soon caught on. According to radio historian Fred MacDonald:

> *Radio aerials now began to clutter the skyline, and people shopping for new homes began looking for locales with good reception. Since early 1922, a daily radio log listing programs for the day became a regular feature of most newspapers, and by the end of the year twenty-seven [radio show] fan magazines were being published in the United States.[9]*

It was not immediately clear who would pay for radio broadcasting. In 1920, Herbert Hoover, then secretary of state, proposed that the sellers of radio receivers be assessed a fee to pay for broadcasting. (In Britain, owners of radios and television sets would be charged an annual license fee and, until the 1970s, broadcasting would essentially be a government monopoly.) However, the model of paying for broadcasting by carrying commercials soon became standard in the United States.

By 1930 there were 618 radio stations in the nation, serving 13,750,000 households. By then the problem of stations broadcasting too close together on the dial and interfering with one another had been addressed by the federal Radio Act of 1927, which gave out licenses to radio stations and assigned their frequency and conditions of operation. This law signaled an important fact: because of the nature of the technology, broadcasting would require a kind of regulation not needed by print media.

Radio first gained real political significance in the depths of the Great Depression, when newly elected president Franklin D. Roosevelt used the medium as an effective means of direct communication with the people. He not only began the practice of holding regularly broadcast press conferences but also sent his voice into the nation's living rooms with occasional "fireside chats." Demagogues, such as Huey P. Long of Louisiana and Father Charles Coughlin, found radio to be an effective tool, as indeed would the rising fascist and communist dictators abroad.

At first the newspapers tried their best to keep radio out of the news business, fearing the loss of advertising revenue. The American Newspaper Publishers Association urged the large news services that served newspapers not to provide their news feed to radio stations. For much of the 1930s, radio news would be limited to the reading of short bulletins.

However, by the time World War II began the big radio networks whose names are still familiar today, such as NBC, CBS, and ABC, had become powerful economic forces in their own right. They trained a worldwide network of news correspondents as well as commentators. The dean of radio commentators is generally thought to be Edward R. Murrow. Broadcasting from London during the Blitz, Murrow brought the agony of Britain under the onslaught of German bombers directly to American homes—and, not incidentally, helped push Americans toward giving greater aid to that beleaguered nation. Here is an excerpt from one such broadcast:

> *Just straightaway in front of me the searchlights are working. I can see one or two bursts of antiaircraft fire far in the distance. Just on the roof across the way I can see a man wearing a tin hat, a pair of powerful night glasses to his eyes, scanning the sky. Again, in the opposite direction, there is a building with two windows gone. Out of one window there waves something that looks like a white bed sheet, a window curtain swinging free in this night breeze. It looks as though it were being shaken by a ghost. There are a great many ghosts around these buildings in London.*[10]

THE AGE OF NETWORK TELEVISION

Electronic television was invented more or less simultaneously by Philo T. Farnsworth and Vladimir Zworykin in the late 1920s and mid-1930s. By the end of the latter decade there was a tiny television industry consisting of a few stations broadcasting a few hours a day to a few hundred sets. The coming of World War II essentially put the development of television on hold. After the war, however, growth was rapid. The 8,000 sets in 1945 grew to a million in 1949 and jumped to 10 million in 1951. By 1960, 45 million sets would bring television into about 90 percent of the nation's homes.

The journalists who began to broadcast television news not surprisingly started with the procedures that had become familiar from radio. In 1941 the announcer on CBS's experimental New York television station WCBW simply sat at a desk facing the camera and read wire service dispatches.

After the war, as television grew, its news techniques also changed. Gradually the CBS and NBC television news staffs began to make better use of the medium's ability to transmit pictures. The networks equipped their overseas radio bureaus with movie cameras so they could film events as they occurred. The film could then be flown back to the United States and shown on television. Gradually, television cameras were set up at sites where news was constantly made (such as in Washington, D.C.) and mobile units were developed, although the latter would be hampered by the very bulky, power-consuming camera and lighting equipment of the time.

The documentary was developed as another way to take advantage of television's ability to show pictorial news in depth. Here, too, Edward R. Murrow became a pioneer. His documentary series *See It Now* broadcast an investigation of communist-hunting Senator Joseph McCarthy in March 1954. The program's devastating look at McCarthy's tactics did much to put that witch hunt out of business. Another Murrow documentary, *Harvest of Shame* (1960) revived the muckraker tradition by exposing the horrible conditions suffered by migrant farmworkers.

Meanwhile, the nightly network newscasts grew in sophistication and innovation. The famous NBC team of Chet Huntley (in New York) and David Brinkley (in Washington, D.C.), along with Walter Cronkite, helped establish the role of the news anchor, whose familiar voice of authority would create a bond with the audience. The network coverage of the major party political conventions also began to change those events from contentious arenas for debating platform issues and selecting nominees to the highly produced political infomercials that they are today.

The other significant political impact of early television was the first televised presidential debate, which pitted Democrat John F. Kennedy against Republican Richard Nixon in 1960. Nixon, awkward, sweaty, and devoid of makeup, contrasted poorly with the young, confident Kennedy. Indeed, while radio listeners when surveyed considered Nixon to be the winner of the debate by a small margin, television viewers greatly preferred Kennedy. Although the presidential debates would not be held again until 1976, politicians were now on notice that they would have to look and sound good on television in their live appearances and ads.

TUMULTUOUS TIMES:
THE MEDIA IN THE 1960s AND 1970s

The 1960s can well be considered to be the most explosive decade in U.S. political and social history. In 1963 both CBS and NBC expanded their evening news broadcasts from 15 minutes to half an hour. They were just in time to cover the growing tempo of the civil rights struggle, which culminated in Martin Luther King, Jr.'s march on Washington, D.C., in August. Three months later, for the first time in history, television would run continuous news coverage without any commercials—responding to the assassination of President Kennedy and its aftermath.

The social upheavals continued with the Watts riot of 1965, the assassinations of Martin Luther King, Jr., and Robert Kennedy in 1968, and the growing Black Power and antiwar movements. For the first time the devastation and casualties of war could be seen not through delayed newsreels but on nightly television news broadcasts.

As the Vietnam War dragged on into the early 1970s, newspapers, not television, would take center stage in exposing an explosive political scandal that began with the seemingly ordinary burglary of the Democratic National Committee headquarters in the Watergate complex in Washington, D.C., on June 17, 1972. Since it did not appear particularly newsworthy at first, the *Washington Post* assigned two young reporters, Bob Woodward and Carl Bernstein, to the story. But by March 1973, long after Nixon had won the presidential election over Senator George McGovern in a landslide, evidence emerged that the burglary had been covered up by three of Nixon's top advisers—H. R. Haldeman, John Ehrlichman, and presidential counsel John Dean. When the existence of an incriminating tape recording also emerged, Nixon's house of cards began to crumble; the House Judiciary Committee voted to impeach the president, and the Supreme Court ruled that he had to turn over the tapes.

The result was Nixon's resignation—and fame for Woodward and Bernstein, who had uncovered much of the skullduggery, with the aid of a mysterious source known as Deep Throat. Their book *All the President's Men* was a best-seller, and it inspired a new generation of self-conscious "investigative reporters."

Besides investigative journalism, the 1960s and 1970s would also spawn somewhat peripheral but interesting new styles of writing—the countercultural "underground newspapers"/alternative press and the blend of journalism and surrealism of Hunter S. Thompson, which would become known as "gonzo journalism."

NEW KINDS OF NEWS

By the late 1960s documentary programming had mostly disappeared from the commercial television networks. However, the Edward R. Murrow tradition reemerged in a somewhat different form in 1968 as the television program *60 Minutes*. This hour-long format, which became known as the television newsmagazine, featured two or three stories and some stand-alone commentary. In 1978 ABC introduced a similar program, *20/20*. Besides introducing new personalities to regular television viewers, the newsmagazines could, at their best, produce relatively in-depth and hard-hitting stories about important matters. However, competitive pressure more often than not led to stories featuring the travails of celebrities or sometimes rather one-sided exposés of allegedly dangerous products.

Debating the value of television newsmagazines, Neal Shapiro of NBC's *Dateline*, itself a TV newsmagazine, insists that they are a good thing:

> *I think "Dateline" has really pushed the genre, I think in a very good way. I think "Dateline" has said, you don't have to be predictable. I think we're the ones who can say, this story is worth an hour. Let's do it, or tonight you're going to get six different stories. Tonight you're going to get two different stories.*

Media reporter Marc Gunther points out the strong economic motive for networks to put on this type of program:

> *What has changed is the opportunities for news have arisen as the economics of the rest of the television business have gone south. It's hard to find hit shows, the costs of Hollywood are expensive, news programming can be put on more economically and as a result the corporate owners of the networks are coming to the news division and saying "give us more news." . . . "Dateline", because it's on so often, probably makes 100 million dollars a year. That's a very substantial number when you realize that the NBC network as a whole is making about 500 million dollars a year. So "Dateline" alone would account for 20 percent of NBC's profits.[11]*

Meanwhile, out in radio land, a new phenomenon was emerging. With most people relying increasingly on television for their news and recordings for their music, radio was facing tough economic challenges. By the 1980s, however, an increasing number of radio stations were discovering that people were willing to spend hours listening to their neighbors calling in and talking about the news of the day. Although talk shows at first were not particularly political (because of the Federal Communications Commission's (FCC) Fairness Doctrine, which required equal time for opposing views), the lapsing of this regulation in 1987 left an opening for explicitly political, opinionated talk radio hosts.

The best known of these is Rush Limbaugh, who appealed to millions of listeners who believed that the national media was dominated by liberals. Limbaugh gave his legions of self-identified "ditto-heads" an affirmation for their views while launching humorous barbs at liberals such as Bill and Hillary Clinton. Limbaugh probably peaked in influence in 1994, when he was credited with mobilizing many of the voters who gave the Republicans control of Congress.

Another kind of "talk show" is the television political pundit show, such as ABC's *This Week* and *Fox News Sunday*. These shows have tended to focus on "insider" politics and competing "spin doctors" who are deployed each time a major legislative initiative is launched in Congress. Media critic James Fallows views these shows negatively, as not really contributing much to the public's understanding of significant issues:

> *The discussion shows that are supposed to enhance public understanding may actually reduce it, by hammering home the message that issues don't matter except as items for politicians to fight over. Some politicians in Washington may indeed view all issues as mere tools to use against their opponents. But far from offsetting this view of public life, the national press often encourages it. As Washington-based talk shows have become more popular in the past decade, they have had a trickle-down effect in cities across the country. In Seattle, in Los Angeles, in Boston, in Atlanta, journalists gain notice and influence by appearing regularly on talk shows—and during those appearances they mainly talk about the game of politics.[12]*

Relatively few people actually watch the political pundit shows. More popular fare usually focuses on celebrities and scandals. Taking its name from the supermarket tabloid newspapers, these programs are often called "tabloid television." *Washington Post* reviewer Peter Carlson declared the 1990s to be the "decade of airing dirty laundry." The examples he gives include:

> *Joey Buttafuoco, John Wayne Bobbitt, Tonya Harding, O.J., the Menendez Brothers, Heidi Fleiss, JonBenet Ramsey, Anna Nicole Smith, Hugh Grant . . . And the "fun couples" of the decade: Woody and Mia, Clarence and Anita, Chuck and Di, Chuck and Camilla, Di and Dodi, Bill and Gennifer, Bill and Paula, Bill and Monica. . . .*

Carlson concludes: "It's a decade characterized by Mike Tyson's ear-biting, Marv Albert's back-biting, Dick Morris's toe-sucking, Monica Lewinsky's . . . well, you get the idea. . . . This *is* the Tabloid Decade. . . . It's not just the plethora of cheesy characters and sleazy deeds . . . it's the unprecedented way that the media, high and low, have publicized every seedy detail of their tawdry shenanigans."[13]

Journalist and sociologist Todd Gitlin suggests that there is a deeper impulse behind the growth of this type of pseudonews, using the Clinton-Lewinsky scandal and its inordinate media coverage as the ultimate example:

> *It's a culture of confession. It's a culture of a sort of striptease. We have a president who is reckless. We had a [Kenneth] Starr inquisition that was unstoppable.*

We had the press that was in collusion with him to leak and leak and leak and leak and carry water again and again. And, not least, we have a profit-minded juggernaut of the president and a pack mentality that inhibits people who should know better in the media from just saying no, from the moment that the network anchors left Havana more than a year ago, left the story of Cuba and the pope to come back to America to drop everything and to run away with this galloping story, it's been very hard to find journalists who would simply say no.[14]

With the media intensely competitive, the result is often what is known as "pack journalism"—swarms of reporters or photographers converging on the same story, camping out and broadcasting incessant, repetitive reports.

NEW MEDIA TECHNOLOGIES: CABLE AND INTERNET

Cable television began in the 1950s simply as a way to get signals to remote communities or those that lacked good over-the-air reception. In the mid-1970s, however, satellites became available for distributing programming to cable systems, and systems began to offer not only premium movies through services such as HBO but also original programming. Entrepreneur Ted Turner and his WTBS "superstation" pioneered the supplying of whole channels of original programming to local cable systems, essentially creating a new form of television network.

Besides now offering subscribers from dozens to hundreds (with digital) of channels, services such as Cable News Network (CNN) have become major competitors of traditional broadcast network news. Today the vast majority of homes have access to cable or satellite television services, and the broadcast networks are now only a small (though still significant) portion of the stream of news and entertainment.

By overcoming the physical scarcity of broadcast channels, cable has led to a great proliferation of specialty channels for everything from golf to Chinese drama. Cable has vastly increased the diversity of programming, but at the same time the most popular channels are controlled by increasingly large conglomerates.

The same cable that carries television signals is also one of the main ways to bring the Internet into the home. Even more so than cable, the Internet overcomes physical scarcity by allowing virtually anyone to distribute words or images to anyone in the world. Unlike cable, the Internet is an interactive medium, with the ability of users to find, sift, and retrieve desired information from any source, as well as to communicate with other users through e-mail, chat, Netnews, and other types of forums.

The Development of the News Media

As mentioned earlier, most print newspapers and magazines now have web sites. There are also a large number of Internet-only, fully electronic publications. In the late 1990s two web sites, Slate.com (run by political commentator Michael Kinsley and owned by Microsoft) and Salon.com, pioneered the idea of high-quality Internet presentation of news, syndicated columnists, and other resources. Taking advantage of the online medium, the sites offered their users ample opportunity to comment on the events of the day and the ideas of the featured columnists, as well as to debate issues with one another. However, purely Web-based news sites have struggled to remain afloat since the bursting of the "Internet bubble" in 2001–02. The sites most likely to survive seem to be those that are spinoffs or subsidiaries of traditional media companies that can subsidize their online operations.

The ability to get at vast quantities of information without intermediaries and to distribute information virtually instantaneously has challenged traditional journalistic standards and practices. Online journalist Matt Drudge first surfaced in the public mind when he and his host, America Online (AOL), were sued in the summer of 1997 by Sidney Blumenthal, a White House aide, for posting allegations that Blumenthal had been guilty of spousal abuse. Drudge had reported what turned out to be a false rumor; he retracted it the next day but to no avail. In 1998 AOL was let off the legal hook when a federal court ruled that the Communications Decency Act of 1996 specified that online service providers would not be held responsible for their users' content. However, the judge also said that "Drudge is not a reporter, a journalist, or a newsgatherer. He is, as he admits himself, simply a purveyor of gossip."

Drudge saw the use of the Internet in more positive terms, as potentially making everyone their own journalist:

> We have entered an era vibrating with the din of small voices. Every citizen can be a reporter, can take on the powers that be. . . . The Net gives as much voice to a thirteen-year-old computer geek . . . as to a c.e.o, or Speaker of the House. We all become equal. . . . Now, with a modem, anyone can follow the world and report on the world—no middle man, no big brother.[15]

Starting around 2000 a new Internet phenomenon began to appear: the weblog, or "blog." A blog is a regularly posted series of commentaries on a personal web site. The writings can be about whatever interests the writer— movie reviews, cultural criticism, or politics, for example. In 2003 blogs were used both to report news and to comment on the news media. During the second U.S. war against Iraq, a blogger named "Salam Pax" posted from Baghdad until his power went out. Another example in how blogs made news was when they picked up the originally local story of Republican senator Trent Lott of Mississippi making comments favorable to the idea of voting for segregationist candidate Strom Thurmond in 1948. The quotes were not picked up by the regular media until they had been relayed and amplified by a growing number of blogs. Following several weeks of uproar and attempted apologies, Lott then stepped down from his position as Senate majority leader.

One of the most popular media-related web sites is hosted by James Romenesko. Because its news is about the insider developments in the media itself, it is particularly popular with journalists, who in May 2003 followed the meltdown of the *New York Times* editorial staff that resulted from the revelation that a young reporter, Jayson Blair, had extensively fabricated his news stories.

An important feature of blogs is that they encourage readers to post their own comments, as well as including links to other blogs that the author finds to be of interest. One blog reader said that "I like weblogs because you get sophisticated political commentary in bite-sized chunks. And together with that, you get the opportunity to correspond in real time with writers. I think the whole process is just terrific."[16]

MEDIA TRENDS IN THE TWENTY-FIRST CENTURY

As the first years of the new century unfold, the media in general and the news media in particular continue to undergo rapid but often contradictory changes. Technologically, the trend called "digital convergence" continues, with traditionally separate forms of media being merged and combined in new ways.

Newspapers and magazines can now be delivered in paperless online form, while radio and television broadcasts are "streamed" over the Internet. Programming is essentially available anywhere and at any time, delivered not only to personal computers but to personal digital assistants (PDAs) and even enhanced cell phones. Emerging digital video recording technology (such as TiVo) will also increase the control media consumers have over what they see and when they see it. Thus, besides providing great flexibility in how people access news and other media, the emerging technology also allows for a great deal of personalization. Each individual can choose the channels, programs, or even types of stories that will appear on the screen.

This emerging media cornucopia presents serious challenges, however. The 21st-century media consumer who also wants to be an informed, active citizen can no longer rely on a few trusted voices of authority. News is no longer a common narrative shared by millions of viewers but rather, a roiling sea of fact and speculation that changes from hour to hour. Evaluating the credibility of often obscure sources can be difficult. People thus need a greater understanding of the many forces that shape media content work, and they must explore issues that once were only the professional concerns of journalists.

[1] John Milton, *Areopagitica: A Speech for the Liberty of Unlicensed Printing to the Parliament of England*, 1644.

[2] Quoted in Margaret A. Blanchard, editor. *History of the Mass Media in the United States*. Chicago: Fitzroy Dearborn, 1998, p. 224.

[3] Quoted in Blanchard, p. 79.

[4] Blanchard, pp. 544–545.

[5] Quoted in Blanchard, p. 711.

[6] Blanchard, p. 218.

[7] These quotes are cited in Blanchard, editor, p. 285.

[8] Quoted in Blanchard, p. 141.

[9] J. Fred Macdonald. *Don't Touch That Dial! Radio Programming in American Life from 1920 to 1960*. Chicago: Nelson-Hall, 1979, p. 12.

[10] Edward R. Murrow, *This Is London* (CBS broadcast), September 22, 1940.

[11] Both quotes from Terence Smith. "News Magazines." PBS Online NewsHour. Available online. URL: http://www.pbs.org/newshour/media/newsmags/newsmags_1-13.html. Posted on January 13, 1999.

[12] James Fallows. "Why Americans Hate the Media," *Atlantic Monthly*, February 1996, p. 45ff.

[13] Peter Carlson, "The Decade of Dishing Dirty Laundry," *Washington Post*, February 2, 1999, p. C2.

[14] Todd Gitlin, quoted in Terence Smith. "Lowering the Bar?" PBS Online News Hour. Available online. URL: http://www.pbs.org/newshour/bb/media/jan-june99/tabloid_2-3.html. Posted on February 3, 1999.

[15] Quoted in Tom Goldstein, "Drudge Manifesto," *Columbia Journalism Review*, vol. 39, January 2001, p. 76.

[16] Terence Smith. "Weblogging." PBS Online NewsHour. Available online. URL: http://www.pbs.org/newshour/bb/media/jan-june03/blog_04-28.html. Posted on April 28, 2003.

CHAPTER 2

PERSPECTIVES AND ISSUES

Depending on how far back one's memory goes, one might recall an urgent voice on the radio sounding far away as bombs rained on London—or the sudden announcement on a Sunday morning that Pearl Harbor had been bombed. The early memories of the next generation encompass a television screen that transfixed viewers as Soviet missiles in Cuba and a confrontation at sea threatened to trigger a world holocaust. Also during the 1960s a president, a national civil rights leader, and a promising candidate were all assassinated, ghettos erupted in flames, demonstrators and police battled in the streets, a flag was planted on the Moon, and the body bags kept piling up in Vietnam.

The news media continued to create searing images in the national consciousness as new wars were fought in El Salvador, Nicaragua, Grenada, Afghanistan, Panama, and the Persian Gulf. There was a succession of terrorist attacks, hostage crises, summit meetings, the collapse of the Soviet Union, the celebration of the new millennium—and then the burning towers and the gaping hole in the Pentagon and a frightening, perplexing new war.

For many people, the media was also detailing too much about other things, such as the O. J. Simpson trial, the life and death of Princess Diana, and the Bill Clinton–Monica Lewinsky scandal. Out of this torrent of stories, all delivered in about the same tone of importance, it has become hard to tell what really *is* important.

The news media has become a 24-hour presence, endlessly streaming and pumping images and information through the air, beaming it down from space, pushing and pulling it through cables and phone lines across the Internet. For consumers, today's news media is dominated by television newscasts and pundit shows, although the major national and metropolitan newspapers still matter, especially for policy makers and the political elite. Radio fills important niches—local news, talk shows—and the Internet is threatening to rewrite the rules of journalism.

All these channels of information can be tapped by people interested in persuading other people. Perhaps the most telling testimony about the power of the media to determine voters' political choices is the hundreds of millions of dollars spent on television and radio ads during each election cycle. As much as politicians may decry their incessant need to raise funds, today's reality is that they have to pay if they are going to be in play.

Other professions and institutions spend much of their time working with the media. A legion of public relations professionals seek to "manage" the news and turn it to their corporate clients' benefit. "Spin doctors" ply a similar trade in the political arena. Activist groups increasingly know that they, too, must master sophisticated techniques in order to get their message out into the public discourse. Meanwhile, courts try to balance the rights of freedom of the press, national security, access to information, the protection of privacy, and the right to a fair trial. No one can afford to ignore the news media.

The news media, for all its great power and influence, finds itself under siege. Newspapers and broadcasting are increasingly dominated by huge conglomerates that buy hundreds of outlets and marry together networks, cable systems, media producers, and online services. Beleaguered television and newspaper news departments often face great pressure to conform to corporate strategies seeking to maximize revenue while cutting costs.

Public attitudes toward the news media reflect growing ambivalence and uncertainty. A Gallup survey taken in 2000 found that only about half of the respondents had "a fair amount" or "a great deal" of confidence that the news was being reported "fully, fairly, and accurately."[1]

The situation appeared even more dismal in a 1997 Roper Center survey. It asked whether people agreed with various characterizations of the news media and the behavior of journalists. Large majorities of respondents felt that "reporters were insensitive to people's pain when covering disasters and accidents," that "reporters focus too much on the private lives of public officials," and that the news was manipulated by a variety of powerful interest groups, including elected officials, big business, corporate media owners, and advertisers. Most respondents also thought that the news was a victim of media companies' desire for profit.

At the same time that substantial majorities found fault with the work of journalists and the independence of the media, 80 percent of the survey respondents agreed that "the press is crucial to the functioning of a free society."[2] This suggests that people are not very happy with the media, but would want to fix it, not abandon it.

PERSPECTIVES ON THE MEDIA

A good start in considering ways of understanding what the news media does (and why it does it) is to look at the word *media* itself. In physics, a *medium* is something through which waves, such as light or sound, pass. Physical media have relatively simple, predictable effects on the quality of the energy that passes through them, such as sound traveling at different speeds in materials of different density.

A naive view of the news media is that it is like a physical medium—a sort of passive conduit through which ideas can be communicated or events seen. But clearly even at the physical, technological level, the media is not a mere transmitter. Consider some characteristics and features of modern video and computer editing technology as described by communications scholars G. Ray Funkhouser and Eugene F. Shaw:

- altered speeds of movement, either slow or fast motion
- reenactments of the same action (instant replay)
- cutting instantaneously from one scene to another
- excerpting fragments of events
- juxtaposing events widely separated in time or space
- shifting points of view, via moving cameras, zoom lenses, or multiple cameras
- combining sight from one source and sound from another (such as background music, sound effects, dubbed dialogue)
- merging, altering or distorting visual images, particularly through computer graphics techniques and multiple-exposure processing
- manufacturing "events" through animation or computer graphics.[3]

According to Funkhouser and Shaw, a documentary or even an ordinary news report is a "synthetic experience." The media diet of such "synthetic experiences" has created several problematic tendencies in the contemporary public: "Low tolerance for boredom or inactivity . . . heightened expectations of perfection and of high-level performance . . . expectation of quick, effective, neat resolutions of problems . . . misperceptions of certain classes of physical and social events (such as automobile collisions or fights) . . . limited contact with, and a superficial view of, one's own inhabited environment."[4]

These technical manipulations are near the end of the process of creating media content, but many other things must happen before a story is produced. Since the 1950s, media theorists have developed the concept of "gatekeeping" to explain how reporters and editors select the stories to be pursued and the aspects of those stories to be featured. Many factors can influence the decisions made by the media gatekeepers—personal values and ideals, the interests of the media owners, concerns of advertisers, material provided by outside groups and sources, and so on. From this point of view, the media is not a neutral channel but a "mediator" or "intermediary" that negotiates with different interest groups in society to obtain information, makes decisions about how to shape and present that information, and then feeds it back into society, creating a sort of circulation of ideas within the body politic.

Another way to look at the media gives it an even more active role than that of gatekeeper. The decisions made by the media about what issues and events are important are also communicated to society. In 1972 two researchers, M. E. McCombs and D. L. Shaw, interviewed a sample of undecided voters to see what issues they were most concerned with—in other words, a representation of the public agenda. They concluded that there was a strong correlation between the public agenda and the media's agenda, or the issues it spent the most time covering. Issues identified as being on the media's agenda were likely to show up soon in the public agenda. Since then a number of studies have found similar correlations.

Agenda setting does not mean that the public or all segments of the public simply move in lockstep with the media. There is a system of constant feedback in which public response in turn exerts pressure on the gatekeeper for making future selections of material. Foreign policy expert Bernard Cohen believes that

> *the press functions in the political process like the bloodstream in the human body, enabling the [policy] process that we are familiar with today to continue on, by linking up all the widely-scattered parts, putting them in touch with one another, and supplying them with political and intellectual nourishment.*[5]

As a result of the gatekeeping and agenda-setting functions of the media, Cohen concludes that the press:

> *may not be successful much of the time in telling people what to think, but it is stunningly successful in telling its readers what to think about. . . . The world will look different to different people depending . . . on the map that is drawn for them by writers, editors, and publishers of the papers they read.*[6]

This process suggests yet another meaning for the word *medium*—in biology, a culture medium is a mixture of nutrients that enables an organism (such as bacteria) to flourish. The collective effort of journalists, therefore, by selecting certain issues and rejecting or deemphasizing others, plays an important role in deciding which will flourish as part of the public discourse. As with gatekeeping, however, this is a process that is subject to feedback. For example, in 1992, when Ross Perot, who had the means to get his ideas before the public independently of the media gatekeepers, injected the issue of world trade agreements into the election campaign, the media had to respond by paying more attention to that issue. (Terrorists rely on another means—violence—to inject their ideas and demands into the public discourse.)

But what is the ultimate purpose of the media? According to the libertarian theory, with its roots in the Enlightenment, poet-philosopher John Milton, and philosopher John Locke in the 17th and 18th centuries, the purpose of having a free press is to facilitate people's rational decision-making by providing a "marketplace of ideas." If anyone is free to publish without government interference, then rational human beings will find and adopt the best solutions to governance.

By the 1940s, however, many political thinkers had a less sanguine view based on a world where powerful totalitarian systems had apparently flourished despite the supposed inherent human tendency toward liberty and rationality. Looking at the role of the media in the modern world, these thinkers suggested that in a complex society where the democratic process must somehow deal with powerful, conflicting forces and people have a limited ability to process information, the media cannot simply provide a marketplace of ideas. It must proactively try to ensure that people get the information they need for democratic decision-making.

This "social responsibility" theory of the media was embodied in an influential 1947 report entitled *A Free and Responsible Press*, which was the work of the Hutchins Commission, sponsored by Henry Luce, founder of *Time* magazine. The report summarized the duties of journalists as follows:

1. To provide a truthful, comprehensive, and intelligent account of the day's events in a context that gives them meaning.
2. To serve as a forum for the exchange of comment and criticism.
3. To provide a representative picture of constituent groups in society.
4. To present and clarify the goals and values of society.
5. To provide citizens with full access to the day's intelligence.[7]

Many journalists and other people would agree that a media that met these objectives would serve people well. However, there are many problems and challenges in fulfilling them. How does one provide events with "a context that gives them meaning" if one has only 20 seconds of television time? How does a newspaper or broadcast station ensure that the many different groups identifiable by race, ethnicity, gender, age, or special interests are adequately and fairly represented? And when presenting and clarifying the goals and values of society, just what are those common goals and values in an increasingly diverse society?

Walter Lippmann, the pioneering columnist and scholar of public opinion, suggested back in 1922 that such an ambitious program of reconciling society with itself was too much to ask of the press as an institution:

If the press is not so universally wicked, nor so deeply conspiring . . . it is very much more frail than the democratic theory has as yet admitted. It is too frail to carry the whole burden of popular sovereignty, to supply spontaneously the truth which democrats hoped was inborn. And when we expect it to supply such a body of truth we employ a misleading standard of judgment. We misunderstand the limited nature of news, the illimitable complexity of society; we overestimate our own endurance, public spirit, and all-round competence. We suppose an appetite for uninteresting truths which is not discovered by any honest analysis of our own tastes.[8]

ISSUES FOR THE NEWS MEDIA

The editors, producers, and journalists working in the news media face a number of pressures, conflicting interests, and other challenges. One of the most powerful forces that affect decision-making in the news media is the changing nature of media ownership and control.

CORPORATE DEMANDS VERSUS JOURNALISTIC VALUES

Although the variety of media available in print, cable, and the Internet is constantly growing, the media channels through which most people get most of their news are increasingly controlled by a few very large conglomerates.

Starting in the mid-1980s as the broadcasting networks were swallowed up in media megamergers, the number of employees working in the news divisions was cut drastically, in some cases by as much as half. This trend was accelerated by the passage of the Telecommunications Act of 1996, which removed all restrictions on a single company owning television and radio stations, except for a limit on the total reach of all stations not exceeding 35 percent of the nation's households. The further relaxation of FCC rules in 2003 (if it survives some opposition in congress) will allow for even greater concentration of ownership, including cross-ownership between broadcasting outlets and newspapers.

A similar situation has occurred with regard to newspapers. William Randolph Hearst, Joseph Pulitzer, and the Scripps family built the first big newspaper chains around the turn of the 20th century. In the past 50 years the portion of the nation's daily newspapers belonging to large chains has risen from about 20 percent to almost 90 percent. Today, a single chain, Gannett, pulls in about $10 billion in annual revenue, operating newspapers in 45 states as well as several foreign nations. Today, there are only about 25 cities that still have at least two competing daily newspapers.

A sort of chain reaction of media mergers precipitated itself in the 1990s. Consider the following:

- General Electric bought NBC.
- Westinghouse bought CBS and later sold it to Viacom for $46 billion. Viacom now includes MTV, VH1, Nickelodeon, Paramount, Blockbuster, Simon and Schuster, and Spelling Entertainment.
- Disney Corporation bought ABC.
- Westinghouse/CBS merged with Infinity Broadcasting, creating the world's largest radio chain.
- Time/Warner (already a huge conglomerate) bought Turner Broadcasting, including the WTBS "superstation," CNN, and TNT.
- America Online merged with Time/Warner in a $115 billion deal.
- MCI bought a 13.5 percent interest in the News Corporation (the parent company of Fox Television).
- Microsoft and NBC created a joint multimedia venture, MSNBC.

When media critic Ben Bagdikian published the first edition of *Media Monopoly* in 1984, he identified about 50 companies as being overly influential and threatening excessive control of the U.S. media. By the time of the fifth edition, in 1997, Bagdikian's list was down to about 10; today, it is arguably about five. But even in 1984, Bagdikian pegged the "number of media corporations with dominant power in society" at closer to 10. The "new communications cartel," he wrote, has the power to "surround almost every man, woman, and child in the country with controlled images and words." With that power comes the "ability to exert influence that in many ways is greater than that of schools, religion, parents and even government itself."[9]

In an opposing view, Robert Samuelson suggests that economic concentration does not necessarily translate into unified control of media content, especially because of the multiplicity of media channels available:

> *The notion of a media elite, if ever valid, requires that people get news and entertainment from a few sources dominated by a handful of executives, editors, anchors, reporters, and columnists. . . . As media multiply, the elite becomes less exclusive. Smaller audiences give them less prominence and market power (i.e. salaries).*[10]

A more radical view is held by linguist and political theorist Noam Chomsky and his followers. They argue that the media explicitly serves the function of maintaining and reinforcing the economic, social, and political agendas of privileged groups. Their "Propaganda Model" seeks to explain how the various functions of the media, including the cultivation of pundits and experts, all reflect these agendas and serve to keep the public discourse within controlled bounds that do not challenge the power elite.

Even if one does not accept the idea of tightly focused corporate control on media content, it seems undeniable that the changing economic incentives in a media world dominated by conglomerates have important effects on the news end of the business. Reporter Ken Auletta describes how the growing economic coordination between news divisions and the rest of their parent company works:

> *Synergy, Tribune-style, occurs in the Washington office, when James Warren, bureau chief for the Chicago Tribune, and Cissy Baker, bureau chief for Tribune Broadcasting, attend one another's story conferences. Synergy occurs when Baker feeds the same TV story to her 16 stations . . . when a TV or radio station, or 24-hour cable news channel, or one of the online publications, uses a story from the Tribune newspapers . . . when Tribune reporters "extend the brand" by appearing in different media. . . .[11]*

The bringing together of many diverse companies under one roof can lead to pressure on journalists to moderate their news coverage of those companies. For example, ABC News and Disney are part of the same conglomerate. In 1998 ABC News killed a story on its *20/20* newsmagazine about convicted pedophiles found working in Disney theme parks.

The defensiveness that many large companies have about litigation can also inhibit investigatory journalism. Thus in 1995 CBS canceled a *60 Minutes* segment that included explosive statements by a high executive who had worked in the tobacco industry, because the network's higher-ups feared an expensive legal onslaught.

Journalism professor Neal Hickey gives a litany of bad effects of enhanced corporate control and commercialism on the news process:

> *[A]s mainstream print and TV news outlets purvey more "life-style" stories, trivia, scandal, celebrity gossip, sensational crime, sex in high places, and tabloidism at the expense of serious news in a cynical effort to maximize readership and viewership . . . editors collude ever more willingly with marketers, promotion "experts," and advertisers . . . editors shrink from tough coverage of major advertisers lest they jeopardize ad revenue; . . . news executives cut muscle and sinew from budgets to satisfy their corporate overseers' demands for higher profit margins each year.[12]*

Hickey goes on to say that this process of wearing down the creative process of journalism to fit a uniform agenda can be subtle:

News coverage is being shaped by corporate executives at headquarters far from the local scene . . . It rarely involves killing or slanting stories. Usually it is by the appointment of a pliable editor here, a corporate graphics conference there, that results in a more uniform look, a more cookie-cutter approach among the chain's newspapers, . . . As papers become increasingly shallow and niggardly, they lose their essentiality to their readers and their communities. And this is ultimately suicidal.[13]

This uniformity and "cookie-cutter look" can also be seen in local television news. While production is generally of high quality, stories tend to all be covered in the same way, with predictable "person in the street" comments and other familiar elements. Increasingly, local news stations have also adopted a certain artificial sense of drama. They tease viewers with "breaking news" timed to coincide with the beginning of a broadcast and often featuring events such as crime, fires, or accidents. While these events certainly are tragedies for the people they involve their prominent placement gives a misleading impression of their real importance compared to the economy, foreign conflicts, and even significant issues within the local community.

IS THE MEDIA BIASED?

While some critics focus on the negative effects of corporate concentration in the media, others debate the question of whether ideological bias skews news coverage.

Bernard Goldberg, former senior CBS producer and author of the book *Bias*, has asserted that the culture of the elite national media is relentlessly and pervasively liberal. He suggests that this is seen in a number of factors and practices:

- Conservative organizations or persons are routinely identified as such, but liberal figures are seldom so identified.
- Belittling adjectives are often applied to proposals from conservatives, such as describing a "flat tax" proposal as "wacky."
- The broadcast media generally looks to the elite print media—such as the liberal *New York Times* and *Washington Post*—for cues on how to handle political stories.
- The coverage of issues such as homelessness and AIDS is driven by a narrow range of liberal activist groups.

Supporters of the liberal bias theory often cite surveys about the voting behavior and attitudes of journalists. They often cite a 1981 study by S. Robert

Lichter and Stanley Rothman that found, among other things, that of 240 "elite" journalists surveyed, 81 percent had voted for the Democratic candidate in every presidential election from 1964 to 1976. A survey by the Freedom Forum published in 1996 suggested that this pattern continued: 89 percent of Washington-based reporters surveyed said they had voted for Bill Clinton in 1992; 7 percent voted for George H. W. Bush; 2 percent voted for Ross Perot. Since in most presidential elections the margin between the Democrat and Republican votes is usually less than 10 percent (often much less), this might suggest that liberals predominate in the elite media.

However, besides raising questions about the sampling techniques used in these often less-than-rigorous polls, critics of the liberal bias theory also question the equation of "liberal" with "voting Democrat." They point out that many of the Democratic candidates (including Clinton) might better be described as centrist than liberal. Also, in what is essentially a two-party system, voting for Clinton only suggests that the voter is more liberal than Bush, but gives no indication of *how* liberal the voter might be.

Self-identification might provide a more useful indication. In a 2001 poll by the Kaiser Family Foundation on "the role of polls in policymaking," policy makers and media professionals were asked to characterize themselves as conservative, moderate, or liberal. Fifty-nine percent of the participating journalists considered themselves to be moderate, 25 percent liberal and only 6 percent conservative. Similarly, the journalists broke down as 27 percent Democrats, 55 percent independents, and only 4 percent Republicans.

However, this still leaves the question of how partisan allegiance or statements of general ideological orientation might translate to positions on particular issues. A survey by FAIR (Fairness and Accuracy in Reporting) concluded among other things that:

- On select issues from corporate power and trade to Social Security and Medicare to health care and taxes, journalists are actually more conservative than the general public.
- Journalists are mostly centrist in their political orientation.
- The minority of journalists who do not identify with the "center" are more likely to identify with the "right" when it comes to economic issues and to identify with the "left" when it comes to social issues.[14]

This last point may be a key to a more nuanced understanding of media bias. Rather than concluding that the media as a whole has a liberal or conservative bias, it may be better to suggest that the media has a number of possibly competing biases. The powerful corporate interests in the modern media might tend to shape coverage and priorities in an economically

31

conservative direction that furthers corporate interests. At the same time, the generally liberal background and worldview of the majority of the media elite raises the possibility of liberal bias operating with regard to social issues. And when one travels from the realm of policy to that of "horse race" electoral politics, yet another kind of bias might come into play—bias in favor of the winning candidates and party, who can control the public agenda and access to policy makers.

THE MEDIA AND POLITICAL CAMPAIGNS

The single most important fact about the intersection between political campaigns and the media is that the former give huge amounts of money to the latter every two or four years. The amount being spent has grown rapidly starting in the mid-20th century. Thus in the 1956 election, out of a total of about $155 million in campaign spending, only $9.8 million (about 6.5 percent) was used for radio and TV advertising. Just 12 years later, in the 1968 election, total spending had nearly doubled to $300 million and, at $58.9 million, spending on broadcast media had soared to 20 percent.

The potentially corrupting effects of all this money caught the attention of activists seeking to reform the campaign finance system. In 1971 the Federal Election Campaign Act (FECA) was passed. Since broadcast media was the fastest-growing campaign expense, limits were placed on how much candidates could spend on TV and radio: a maximum of $50,000 or $0.10 times the voting-age population of the relevant district. Further, no more than 60 percent of the media spending could be on broadcast as opposed to print media. There were also tighter rules requiring that the source of political contributions be disclosed.

However, the limits on spending by candidates were declared to be unconstitutional in *Buckley v. Valeo* (1976). The Supreme Court, by a narrow 5-4 majority, ruled that spending was, given modern realities, essential to sending a political message to the public. Thus "a restriction on the amount of money a person or a group can spend on political communication necessarily reduces the quantity of expression by restricting the number of issues discussed, the depth of their exploration, and the size of the audience reached."

In 2002 Congress made another attempt at campaign finance reform. The Bipartisan Campaign Reform Act (BCRA) does not limit spending on media as such. Rather, it seeks to cut off the flow of undisclosed, unregulated "soft money" from interest groups, and the use of thinly disguised political attack ads.

Political money buys ads. Ads, in turn, help buy public and news media attention for the campaign, which in turn, for a successful campaign, creates a sense of electoral legitimacy. As part of this cycle, journalists tend to reinforce rather than investigate what the campaign is doing. Summarizing the conclusions of researchers in politics and the media, communications professor Philip Patterson and journalism professor Lee Wilkins note that

> *Study of media coverage of political campaigns has uncovered some disturbing trends. Journalists function as a pack; there is seldom any really distinctive political reporting during elections. . . . However campaign assignments remain sought after by members of the national press corps for reasons of personal prestige. The person who covers the winning candidate for the network will almost assuredly become the White House correspondent for the next four years, a guarantee of celebrity status, increased income, and, many would argue, real political power. The journalists covering a national election have almost as much at stake as the candidates they cover.*
>
> *Further, journalists treat front-runners differently than they do the remainder of the candidate pack. . . . Front-runners are the subject of closer scrutiny, but those examinations are seldom about issues, even though it is issue-oriented reporting that tends to provoke political interest and public participation. . . . Instead, electoral reporting focuses on personality, a key component of political leadership, but certainly not the only one.*[15]

Another facet of modern campaign coverage is the focus on the "horse race"—who is winning, and discussion of tactics rather than the issues on which the candidates are presumably campaigning. Editor and commentator James Fallows gives the following as one of many examples of "why Americans hate the media":

> *Midway through the interview [Democratic candidate Bill] Bradley gave a long answer to the effect that everyone involved in politics had to get out of the rut of converting every subject or comment into a political "issue," used for partisan advantage. Let's stop talking, Bradley said, about who will win what race and start responding to one another's ideas.*
>
> *As soon as he finished, [CNN interviewer Judy] Woodruff asked her next question: "Do you want to be President?" It was as if she had not heard a word he had been saying—or couldn't hear it, because the media's language of political analysis is utterly separate from the terms in which people describe real problems in their lives.*[16]

In recent years a movement called civic journalism or public journalism has tried to address the failure of journalists to engage the truly important public issues. It takes the social responsibility theory of journalism a step farther. Instead of seeing the journalist as simply a passive chronicler of political affairs, civic journalism seeks to involve the journalist actively in the process of helping the community discuss political issues. According to civic journalism proponent Jay Rosen, the goals of civic journalism are to:

1. address people as citizens, potential participants in public affairs, rather than victims or spectators;
2. help the political community act upon, rather than just learn about, its problems;
3. improve the climate of public discussion, rather than simply watch it deteriorate; and
4. help make public life go well, so that it earns its claim on our attention.[17]

Another advocate, Carl Sessions Steppe, gives a concrete example of civic journalism:

One newspaper implementing a civic journalism agenda has hosted town hall meetings, sent reporters knocking on doors canvassing the public's ideas for issues to cover, sponsored a yearlong literacy project, and teamed with state public television for a series on Hispanics in Nebraska. During last year's city election, [editor David] Stoeffler presided over meetings in city council districts in which citizens were asked about their priorities, candidates were quizzed on the issues, and the paper focused its ongoing coverage on those areas.[18]

Stoeffler wants "people thinking differently about the newspaper's role in the community." In particular, he is aiming to be more "solution-oriented."[19]

Civic journalism has its critics, who point to a conflict between the objectivity needed for fair, balanced news coverage and the emotional and even political involvements into which a civic-minded journalist will inevitably be drawn. If that happens, they say, how can the public trust the journalist to be objective?

COVERING WAR AND TERRORISM

If the media does not effectively discuss the underlying issues in political campaigns, it also has trouble reporting on major crises. The aftermath of the terrorist attacks of September 11, 2001, did lead to at least a temporary improvement in public attitudes toward the news media. There was a sense that the media was helping to bring people together in the face of a common threat. The role of the media in conveying vital information was also appreciated. People depended on the media to know what local security measures were being enforced, when they could fly again, and how they could help with the recovery efforts in New York and Washington. In the first weeks and months after September 11, most in the media, like politicians, seemed to have suspended their usual adversarial role. Many commentators who were usually seen as cynical critics of government policies seemed to be perfectly willing to share in the upsurge in expressions of patriotism.

As the immediate crisis subsided and the question became how to pursue the war on terrorism at home and the ensuring of homeland security, thoughtful media critics began to ask whether the media had become too closely allied to the government. Had necessary "critical distance" been lost in covering issues such as the threat to civil liberties of new homeland security policies and the justification for attacking Iraq?

A primary purpose of terrorism is to gain media attention. This can be seen particularly in the actions of small groups such as the Earth Liberation Front (ELF), which sponsor relatively limited attacks such as arson of research facilities. These attacks are obviously newsworthy, but in covering them, the media becomes the "medium" by which the terrorists can achieve at least part of their goals.

Many journalists have had to struggle to find an objective place for the competing agendas of critics who saw the terrorist attack as a wake-up call for a problematic foreign policy and administration supporters who were trying to marshal patriotic sentiment. Among the latter is former senator Alan Simpson:

> *Well, [the media are] not there to be cheerleaders. We wouldn't expect that of them. But they're there to replace one ism with another ism. They're there to replace skepticism with patriotism. . . . I think as a media person or as a human being, think of the people who are serving our country. Do you want them injured? Do you want them maimed? Do you want them killed? Because some of the questions they ask in this situation are so stupid as to, you know, "where will [the military] attack? What will they use?" And they seem to have kind of rocks for brains when they don't understand that [the enemy is] watching everything that comes over our television.*

However, journalism critic Geneva Overholser wants journalists to stick to their traditional role as trusted interpreters rather than participants:

> *I think American journalists are best patriotic when they retain their skepticism. That isn't cynicism. But we need to think about whether the public more needs a flag-waving journalist who says "I'm here because I'm mostly an American and not a journalist" or whether they need good, reliable, solid information. . .* [20]

As an indication that the media may be returning to a more objective stance, in response to a survey taken almost a year after the September 11 attacks, the popular feeling that the press "stands up for America" had jumped from 43 percent to 69 percent in the wake of the attacks, but by summer 2002 they had fallen back to 49 percent.

When the "war on terrorism" turned into a real shooting war in Afghanistan and then in Iraq, the physical and professional difficulties of journalists in covering armed conflict came to the fore. During World War II there was little conflict in outlook among Americans about the rightness of the war, and journalists had a supportive rather than adversarial relationship with the military. During the Vietnam War the perception that the U.S. government was hiding bad news, as well as a growing opposition to the war, put journalists more at odds with the Pentagon. Many conservatives and military people would later blame the media (particularly television) for turning Americans against the war.

In the 1991 Gulf War, the military attempted to control the media by restricting battlefield access to a small pool of journalists who would be allowed to make their reports available to their colleagues. There was exciting footage of bombs and cruise missiles in "precision strikes" on targets, as well as Peter Arnett of CNN broadcasting live from Baghdad as the sky lit up with antiaircraft tracer fire. As the *New York Times* noted "Some potential travelers are riveted to their television sets, captivated by the constant news reports about the war, a condition that some people are calling the 'CNN Effect."[21] However, after the war, 17 news executives representing the major networks, news services, and newspapers signed a report complaining that "By controlling what reporters saw and when they saw it, the military exerted great power to shape and manage the news."[22]

During the 2003 Iraq War the military tried a different approach. Instead of controlling the journalists through the pool system, they allowed journalists to live and travel with military units full time. These reporters became known as "embedded journalists." On the one hand, television viewers were able to see a soldier's life and the reality of a firefight close up. However, the embedded journalist was frequently isolated from the overall flow of the war, unable to see the larger context of troop movements and the struggle for overall control of the country. CBS anchor Dan Rather wryly remarked later that "there's a pretty fine line between being embedded and being entombed."[23]

There have also been questions of how to sort out the actual events from the spin and embellishments. On April 1, 2003, Private Jessica Lynch, who had been part of a group of support soldiers captured by Iraqi fighters, was rescued in a night raid by Special Forces troops who extricated her from an Iraqi hospital. After the military released information about the operation, the picture of her being carried out on a stretcher provided a boost to morale during a period in which U.S. forces, while successful in their overall campaign, had met unexpectedly tough pockets of Iraqi resistance.

However, the story seemed to undergo rapid embellishment based on what the media learned from various off-the-record government sources. Lynch was said to have fought fiercely against the Iraqis until she ran out of ammunition. She supposedly suffered several gunshot wounds, was possibly stabbed, denied prompt care, and may have been abused by her captors. However, as the media began to hear conflicting reports (such as by Iraqis who had been at the hospital), it began to investigate the story further. Although much would remain unclear, it now seemed that Lynch had not had a prolonged gun battle with the Iraqis, she had not been shot or stabbed, and she had been given proper medical care by the Iraqis. Her injuries had probably arisen from the crash of her vehicle.

JOURNALISTS, SPIES, AND SECRETS

As with the military, the special needs and agenda of intelligence agencies make for, at best, an uncomfortable fit with journalism. From the cold war through the early 1970s, cooperation between journalists and intelligence agencies such as the Central Intelligence Agency (CIA) was fairly common. Reporting jobs were sometimes used as "cover" for agents working in foreign countries, with some publications (such as the *New York Times*) explicitly providing such cooperation. Such use of journalists can make all journalists more vulnerable in parts of the world (such as much of the Middle East) where American journalists are already viewed as being spies or agents by the more militant people (as shown by the kidnapping and brutal murder of *Wall Street Journal* reporter Daniel Pearl in Pakistan in 2002, journalism in the world's trouble spots can be very risky.)

Sometimes, false stories planted in the foreign media by intelligence agencies can be picked up by the domestic media and publicized in the United States. This is called "feedback" or "blowback." Sometimes this was unintentional, but at any rate there was no system in place to warn American media outlets that the stories were false.

During the 1977–78 hearings by the House Select Committee on Intelligence, a number of prominent journalists testified about (and in opposition to) these practices. Stuart Loory of the *Chicago Sun-Times* warned that "The danger of blowback is you feed propaganda to a foreign journalist and the first thing you know you are reading it in the *Chicago Sun-Times*. . . . I think there are extreme ethical and moral problems involved in polluting the information network."[24]

Some of the most controversial stories in journalism involve allegations of secret operations by the CIA, the military, or other agencies. One prominent example is when *San Jose Mercury News* investigative journalist Gary Webb was offered contact with a source who claimed to have worked for years dealing drugs for the CIA on behalf of the anticommunist contra forces in Nicaragua—thus playing a major role in introducing powerfully addictive crack cocaine to the streets of American cities. In August 1996 the *Mercury News* published Webb's three-part story about the contra drug-running. The story did not say the CIA was involved, but that was a reasonable implication. Although it was ignored by most of the established media, the story began to spread nonetheless, aided in part by the fact that the *Mercury News* had used its pioneering web site to good effect, preparing extensive online materials to release simultaneously with the printed story.

However, when other reporters, such as Robert Suro and Walter Pincus of the *Washington Post*, investigated the story, they could find no evidence that the CIA and the contras were connected with the crack cocaine epidemic. The *New York Times* and *Los Angeles Times* also investigated—the story itself now having become a story—and similarly found little corroboration.

The story tied in well with a longstanding suspicion of the CIA based on many earlier stories of its dubious activities at home and abroad. In particular, it fueled a powerful sentiment in parts of the black community that crack cocaine had been used by the CIA or other sinister forces to destroy their community and to prevent them from organizing politically.

Defenders of such "edgy" controversial stories point out that by their nature they implicate powerful, complex, hidden forces and involve sources that can be hard to verify. In presenting the Journalist of the Year Award of the Society of Professional Journalists (SPJ) to Webb, radio anchor Dave McElhatton noted that "Elements of the *Mercury News* series and presentation are open to dispute, as are criticisms of Webb's stories. A full airing is necessary and good for us all. But the [SPJ] chapter is convinced that the best journalism is that which is not afraid to venture into controversial areas of overwhelming national significance."[25]

Another firestorm erupted following the June 1998 release of a CNN story exposing alleged secret use of nerve gas by U.S. forces in Laos in 1970 during Operation Tailwind, which was said to have killed about 100 people, including some American GIs who had deserted and were living with local people. At first CNN, while admitting that there might have been errors, stuck by its story and said that it deserved further investigation. As pressure from the government and veterans' groups mounted, CNN finally retracted the story as "unsupportable," although an investigation did not find that the reporters had intentionally falsified anything in the story.

A subsequent article in the *Columbia Journalism Review* identified 10 mistakes that CNN and *Time* made in handling the Operation Tailwind story. They include the rush by CNN to develop a blockbuster story to introduce its *NewsStand* program into a highly competitive market, failure to perform sufficient independent fact-checking, and failure to consult the network's regular military consultant, who had extensive experience in Laos around the time of the alleged gassing. Higher-ups did not carefully review the script before broadcasting, and even those who had questions did nothing to delay the broadcast. Most remarkably, no one seemed to notice that the research for the story had not revealed any documents from the Laotian communist authorities referring to such an incident, even though it would have been in their interest to publicize it extensively. The article concluded that

> *The Tailwind reporting, in fact, was a chain reaction of three firecrackers sequenced to trigger a mega-explosion. Taken alone, each could have been containable: overzealous producers scrupulously supervised could have caused little mischief; veteran investigative reporters with no supervision similarly might have brought no grief; both of those factors, minus ratings pressure, could have spared CNN and Time the misfortune it suffered. But all three together created a morbific cocktail.[26]*

THE MEDIA'S GLOBAL MYOPIA

War and terrorism are guaranteed to receive media attention. However, many critics believe the media in the United States does a poor job of covering the more subtle developments in foreign affairs that might help people understand the roots of international conflicts and crises. Although the recent terrorist attacks have created at least a temporary increase in coverage of certain areas and types of foreign events, media scholars Philip Patterson and Lee Wilkins note that the general rule among network executives is that:

> *the public has an interest in only one foreign story at a time. So while the "pack" went first to the Persian Gulf and then to Somalia in the early 1990s, the continuing horrors of Bosnia and the killing fields of El Salvador went unreported or at best underreported. Similarly, events are reported more than processes. Stories written for the masses focus on quick-onset disasters such as Hurricane Andrew but not on the slow-onset disaster of global warming that may be spawning ever larger hurricanes.[27]*

If a media outlet does decide to cover a given foreign story, the results are likely to be expedient and superficial:

In terms of news content, "serious" items such as war, violence and human disasters are increasingly treated as entertainment. It is a widely held belief by those who compile news programmes that war and human disasters need to be covered "live". If a satellite link-up has been booked for prime time news bulletins it must be used regardless of whether or not the reporter on the ground has anything new to say. Editors claim that audiences expect a 20 second slot as close as possible to the action. Shots of a reporter ducking shrapnel (or an exocet missile) or being lowered into an earthquake rescue zone are seen as essential images in news agendas. Whether or not such images reveal anything more meaningful about a conflict or a human disaster that could not be reported further away from the bloodshed is open to question. These "action" shots are invariably provided more for entertainment than to inform.[28]

It is true that motivating a mass audience to watch in-depth stories on such subjects as the spread of AIDS in Africa or an assessment of the evidence for global warming can be difficult. Media outlets looking at the bottom line often resist attempts by conscientious journalists to "sell" such stories in editorial meetings.

PUBLIC RELATIONS AND THE MEDIA

As the media grew in power, so did public relations, or a PR, profession that seeks to manipulate the media on behalf of clients. Founded in the 1920s by pioneers such as Edward L. Bernays, the field today counts more than 200,000 PR professionals in the United States.

PR people and journalists depend on each other yet also have conflicting agendas. Journalists are supposed to determine the newsworthiness of events, but PR seeks to create events that have the appearance of newsworthiness.

Historian Daniel Boorstin coined the term "pseudo-event" to refer to things that would not have happened at all or would have happened in a substantially different form were it not for the media. He estimated in 1962 that as many as a quarter of all news items were really pseudo-events. Examples include press conferences, ceremonies, and even some kinds of demonstrations and strikes directed solely with an eye toward media coverage.

Perhaps the first pseudo-event was staged by John Adams—the Boston Tea Party. In 1889 George Westinghouse established what today would be called the first corporate PR department. The prolific inventor Thomas Edison was an equally energetic self-promoter—his announcement that he would be creating an incandescent lightbulb was taken by many to mean he had already invented it. The U.S. government itself increasingly adopted PR techniques starting in World War I. PR people see themselves as 'lawyers in the court of public opinion." A historian of the field notes that "the best PR ends up looking like news. You never know when a PR agency is being effective, you'll just find your views slowly shifting."[29]

Many PR news releases are distributed in the form of professionally produced audio and video segments (video news releases or VNRs), as well as prewritten articles and opinion pieces. The goal is to give hard-pressed media people something that will save them work and be ready to use. Often both a fully scripted and produced version and a "B-roll" of raw footage and supporting materials are provided. There are even companies that compile databases of the needs, interests, and preferences of thousands of journalists in order to help PR firms target them better.

As early as 1985 one company was telling PR firms: "Let us be your eyes and ears when the environmental media convene. . . . Gather vital information on key journalists. . . . Not only will you find news on journalists, we'll tell you what they want from you and what strategies you can employ with them to generate more positive stories and better manage potentially negative situations."[30]

PR materials might be viewed as a sort of virus that, when properly introduced to the news medium, is propagated to its audience. It not only serves as free advertising, it also has the advantage of not being *identified* as advertising or commercial speech. PR is not just a tool for corporations: it is also used by sophisticated activist groups and indeed by governments. Thus in 1990 the Kuwaiti government apparently fabricated reports of Iraqi soldiers removing infants from incubators in Kuwait hospitals and leaving them to die. They used PR-style production and distribution materials to get the story into the media in order to build support for U.S. intervention.

Politicians naturally make their own public relations efforts, working with their own corps of professional media manipulators. A first cousin to the PR professional is the "spin doctor," a specialist in framing issues in a way most favorable to a particular political interest. Failing that, the spin doctor will engage in "damage control," trying to minimize the significance of a threatening scandal or to deflect media attention to the foibles of an opponent.

These developments in public relations and media manipulation techniques confront readers or viewers with a challenge in determining the factuality or credibility of media content. Additionally, the traditional forms in which people receive information are being adopted for new purposes. Infomercials can look at first glance like documentaries, borrowing many of that genre's narrative and camera techniques. "Advertorials" look like newspaper editorials but represent a commercial interest; some newspaper ads are formatted like news stories, albeit with the word *advertisement* disclosed in tiny type. Many commercials use the same high-quality production values and effects as movies, and products in turn are embedded in movies in return for payment. "Reality TV" programs purport to represent real-life situations. The lines between news and advocacy and between fact and fiction are increasingly blurred.

The media consumer is not defenseless, however. He or she can still identify who is producing the content and determine their likely agenda. After identifying what overt or implied assertions are being made about a politician or a product, the consumer can take steps to further inform himself or herself about the issue.

THE MEDIA IN A DIVERSE SOCIETY

One of the most difficult problems for the news media is how to report fairly on events relating to racial and ethnic groups. In 1968 the Kerner Commission reported the results of its study of news coverage of riots in 15 cities. They suggested that the media had exaggerated the extent and severity of the violence. According to the commission, the mismatch between what had happened and what the media saw and reported was largely due to the fact that the national media was almost entirely white. Reporters who might understand and be able to properly interpret events in the black community were few and far between.

The record of the media with regard to race is mixed. The media did help the Civil Rights movement by exposing the nation to the kind of violence the movement faced and showing its nonviolent determination. There have been some gains in employment of minorities and women in mainstream media companies, but only after a prolonged struggle. During the 1970s women brought antidiscrimination suits against major media companies, including NBC, the Associated Press, the *New York Times*, and the *Washington Post*. The latter, ironically, was then headed by a powerful woman publisher, Katharine Graham.

On the other hand, as recently as 2000, CBS producer Bernard Goldberg took a sample of a month's program of the popular TV newsmagazine shows and found that in 51 stories from *Dateline* and *48 Hours* none featured black persons; *20/20* featured blacks in only two of 26 stories—and one was about Secretary of Defense William Cohen, who is white, and his wife, who is black. Only *60 Minutes* broke the pattern, with seven of 12 stories featuring African Americans. Often the word behind the scenes was that stories about blacks and other minorities were "not marketable." The self-justifying argument seems to be that blacks and other minorities generally do not watch the same shows that whites do (particularly news shows), so they cannot be marketed to advertisers as part of the mainstream audience.

African Americans have had an independent media since abolitionist days, and newspapers were founded in large urban black communities in the 1880s and 1890s. In 1905 the *Chicago Defender*, founded by Robert Sengstacke

Abbott, became the prototype for black community journalism in the 20th century. Today Hispanic Americans and Asian Americans, as well as African Americans, have their own broadcast stations and networks as well as newspapers.

Another group in U.S. society that has a problematic relationship to the news media is children. The majority of concern about television violence and its effects is focused on the entertainment side—most of the daily hours of television watched by children is not news or documentaries. However, news that focuses on crime, war, and other violent events might be expected to have similar negative effects on children—the repeated showing of the September 11, 2001, terrorist attacks troubled many young children and challenged their parents to try to put it in context.

The news media has also tried to deal with the lack of knowledge that many children have about current events, history, and science. Cable provides a steady diet of reasonably high-quality programming in those areas on such channels as the Discovery Channel and the History Channel.

Channel One is a newscast provided free to more than 350,000 classrooms in 12,000 schools (about 40 percent of U.S. students). However, it is a commercial product that includes two minutes of advertising, and critics decry it as an attempt to reach a captive audience in the schools with a commercial message.

Most elementary and high school curricula feature lessons on how to distinguish fact from opinion, how to detect bias in a news story, and so on. Some students may not grasp this material, leading to a failure to be able to confront the media critically. On the other hand, young people today have an unprecedented opportunity, thanks to relatively inexpensive computers, camcorders, digital cameras, and the Internet, to learn about modern media techniques firsthand.

PRACTICING BETTER JOURNALISM

Problems arise with the use of traditional journalistic tools and techniques, and some suggestions have been made to create ethical standards and practices for the profession.

ANONYMOUS SOURCES

Investigative journalism depends on the ability to strip away the layers of concealment, deception, or obfuscation used to enable powerful organizations and people to carry out agendas that would, if revealed, arouse public anger and possibly provoke reform. This generally means that the journalist must establish contact (or be contacted by) someone on the inside, such as "Deep Throat" of Watergate fame.

Because they often fear reprisals such as loss of employment or even physical violence, such sources agree to provide information to the journalist in exchange for the promise that their name and anything that might lead to their identity will not be revealed. The journalist in turn sometimes comes under pressure to reveal the source. Such demands generally do not come from government officials, but rather from court proceedings as the result of a subpoena by a prosecutor or defense attorney who considers the source's information or testimony to be important to his or her case.

In late 1999, for example, CBS was subpoenaed for the complete transcript of an interview Dan Rather had done with a Texas murder defendant in order to resolve apparent contradictions between the defendant's statements in an interview and statements he had given police. CBS refused to comply with the order; prosecutors also subpoenaed Rather and *60 Minutes II* producer Mary Mapes. Eventually CBS compromised: The network complied by giving the transcript to the court, but also published it on the Internet so it would be available to the public.

There is a simple reason why reporters and editors will fight so hard to avoid having to divulge confidential sources. As First Amendment lawyer Bruce Sanford notes:

> *[Journalists] don't take pictures or gather information and then trade it with the police or trade it with prosecutors. They don't do things like that, because, if they did, they would never get the interviews from whistle blowers, from watchdogs on government, from people who want to share information with them but who are terribly afraid of retribution by the government.*[31]

The root of this argument is that journalists ultimately serve the public and its institutions (including even law enforcement and the judiciary) only by being a completely independent entity whose mission is as important as that of the other fundamental institutions—and that can only be carried on if not subordinated to any other need of society. The opposing view is that law enforcement and the legal system are supreme in matters dealing with crime and that subject to due process all other institutions, including the media, must comply with the needs of justice.

The Supreme Court, although sometimes acknowledging that reporters have a legitimate need to use confidential sources in order to carry out their functions under the First Amendment, has not gone so far as to say that there is a First Amendment right to withhold sources. However, 43 states now have some form of "shield law" giving journalists the right to keep the names of sources secret and (in some states) to not be forced to turn over their notes or tapes.

In the political world, anonymous sources consist mainly of information given "on background" that is attributed only perhaps to "a senior State Department source."

Along with anonymous leaks, such sources frustrate the ability of the public to evaluate the reliability of the information presented. The public can only rely on the credibility of the media organization presenting the information. Since leaks are nearly always in the service of some institutional or political agenda, the media can in effect become an implicit partner in that agenda, and the credibility of the media itself can be threatened. To attempt to control abuses inherent in the use of anonymous sources, journalism professor David E. Boeyink suggests the following guidelines:

> Promises of anonymity must be authorized by the editor;
> Anonymous sources should be used only for a just cause;
> Anonymous sources should be used only as a last resort;
> Sources should be as fully identified as possible, with reasons for anonymity explained in the story;
> Editors should balance the potential harms and benefits in any use of anonymous sources;
> Anonymous sources can only be used with just intentions by the reporter, the media, and the source; and
> Use of anonymous sources requires independent verification by a second source.[32]

Sometimes anonymous leaks can have consequences that go far beyond journalistic ethics. In July 2003, Joseph Wilson, a former U.S. diplomat, wrote a commentary for the *New York Times* that criticized Bush administration claims that Iraq had tried to buy enriched uranium from Niger. Shortly thereafter, an anonymous source, presumably someone within the government, disclosed to columnist Robert Novak that Wilson's wife, Valerie Plame, was working undercover for the CIA. When Novak published this revelation, furious officials decried the leak as potentially threatening the safety not only of Plame but of other persons with whom she may have been working.

Many journalists would refuse to publish this type of information unless it bore upon a vital public interest. But the reality is that if the story is made available, someone probably will publish it. Generally, the journalist who receives and publishes the information is not subject to legal action, and the leaker's identity often remains unrevealed.

It should be clear that the use of anonymous sources is sometimes necessary but often problematic. Competitive pressures can lead to journalists being tempted to print or broadcast sensational material from an anonymous source or leak without engaging in proper verification procedures. Ultimately any restraint on the practice must probably come from within the cultures of journalism and politics, and from public demands for responsibility and accountability.

THE MEDIA VERSUS PRIVACY

Reporters often have to protect the privacy of sources. However, the quest for stories from reluctant subjects often leads the media to test the limits of personal privacy—and sometimes trespass beyond.

In general, invasion of privacy alarms and angers people. Whether they are on the Internet, spending some time at the mall, or just reading about the elaborate surveillance systems being deployed in the war against terrorism, most Americans have at least some degree of concern about threats to their privacy. For public figures, the media often figures in that concern, especially the fringe media, such as celebrity-chasing, camera-wielding paparazzi.

Paparazzi were initially blamed for the deaths of Princess Diana and Dodi al-Fayed in a 1998 car accident, although drunken driving was also implicated. Movie stars such as Alec Baldwin and his wife, Kim Basinger, in the mid-1980s, and Woody Harrelson and his daughter, in the mid-1990s were virtually stalked by paparazzi. Two photographers who used their cars to trap the vehicle containing Arnold Schwarzenegger and his wife, Maria Shriver, were eventually convicted in 1998 of false imprisonment and in the case of one of them, battery as well. They received brief jail terms.

A number of bills were proposed in response to the public outcry against paparazzi. One, by California state senator Charles Calderon (Democrat-Whittier) would require photographers to maintain a distance of at least 15 feet if requested. State senator Tom Hayden (Democrat-Los Angeles) wanted to include the use of "invasive technology" such as zoom lenses in the state's antistalking law. In 1998 a bill was finally passed that outlawed many tactics of what Governor Pete Wilson called the "stalkerazzi."

Civil liberties advocates joined the media in condemning these laws as overbroad, potentially criminalizing ordinary news photography. They also pointed out that existing laws against stalking and trespassing could be applied to overly intrusive media photographers.

Journalist Steven Brill developed two suggested guidelines for voluntary restraint by the media that would reduce the incentive for paparazzi-type behavior. The first guideline would *withhold publication of photographs or video images of children under age 14 without the permission of the children and one of their parents or a guardian and avoid posting reporters or photographers outside their homes without their permission. Children in show business or who accompany their politician-parents to campaign events are excepted.*

The second guideline would

withhold publication of current photographs or video images of family members who have lost a loved one within one week following the death and avoid posting reporters or photographers outside their homes, at the funeral, etc., without their permission. If a funeral or memorial service is deemed to be "newsworthy," the news organization may post photographers outside the location (or inside if given permission) unless explicitly asked not to do so by the family, in which case they "should place great weight on that request."[33]

Brill sent the proposal to 130 prominent media people. Fifty-three said they did not agree with these voluntary restrictions, 18 agreed, three offered mixed responses, and 56 took no position on them. Some cited opposition to the idea of applying general rules rather than treating things on a case-by-case basis. However, when Brill had a polling firm sample a representative group of the public, they agreed by a margin of nearly 80 percent.

According to a 1998 Scripps Howard News Service survey, 56 percent of the poll respondents said journalists should "be subject to criminal prosecution and even prison if they violate a citizen's privacy." A third said they believe such privacy invasions occur "often" and 45 percent believe they occur "sometimes." But the poll found that few Americans have personal reasons to be angry. Only 26 percent of respondents said they have been the subject of a newspaper or television story, and of that group 85 percent said the story was accurate.

Another type of injury occurs when false information in a news story reflects badly on a person's reputation or creates a misleading impression of the person. (Legally, a distinction is made between damage caused by written material (libel) and through speech (slander), although broadcast material is considered to be libel even though it is spoken. The general term *defamation* can be applied to either type of material.) A well-known case is the story of Richard Jewell. Jewell, a security guard at Atlanta's Centennial Olympic Park during the 1996 Summer Olympic Games, was at first hailed as a hero for discovering an unattended knapsack that proved to contain a bomb, raising the alarm, and evacuating most people from the crowded area. As a result, only one person was killed directly by the explosion (another died of a heart attack, and 111 were injured). The FBI, however, became suspicious about Jewell and tried to trick him by having him "pretend" for a "training film" that he was waiving his right to an attorney during interrogation about the bombing. The *Atlanta Journal-Constitution* learned of these events and featured Jewell on its front page as "the focus of the federal investigation." The TV networks and most major newspapers soon took up the story.

Swarms of reporters began to converge on Jewell's apartment, which was being searched by federal investigators. Most media outlets did mention in their stories that Jewell had not been charged with anything and was not officially a suspect. Meanwhile, however, stories reported on Jewell's supposed "overzealousness," his failed career in law enforcement, the hints that he fit the profile of a "wannabe" who might have staged the bombing in order to be able to play the hero. Months later the investigation wound down, and Jewell was never charged. In a court hearing, U.S. District Judge J. Owen Forrester decried what he called "the worst example of media coverage I've ever seen since watching *La Dolce Vita*." (Federico Fellini's 1960 film in which journalists are depicted as vultures.) The judge also cited evidence that suggested the details of the investigation had been leaked to the media.

Jewell threatened to sue for libel, and as of 2003 he has received some settlements, including $600,000 to settle a claim based on some comments made by NBC news anchor Tom Brokaw. An ABC News poll later revealed that 69 percent of respondents felt that Jewell had been unfairly treated, and 82 percent said it was not acceptable for the media to identify a suspect before he is charged.

The U.S. Supreme Court, starting with *New York Times v. Sullivan* (1964), has ruled that public officials and public figures must meet a high standard in order to claim damages in a libel action. Not only must they show that the news story contains false statements of fact—they must also show that the journalist either knew the facts were false ("actual malice") or had a reckless disregard for whether or not the story was true. This means that the media eventually prevails in most libel suits—but the key word is "eventually." As Richard M. Schmidt, general counsel for the American Society of Newspaper Editors, has observed:

> *It is not difficult to understand that defamation actions can themselves be a form of censorship. Libel suits can be and generally are tremendously expensive. . . . It is an established fact that plaintiffs in libel suits have an excellent chance of victory before a jury but the odds are overwhelming that either the trial judge or an appellate court will quite likely reverse such a finding because the case failed to meet the standards required by First Amendment rules.*[34]

As a result of the potential expense, media organizations must carry expensive liability insurance. Claims are often settled out of court even if they lack legal merit. But perhaps the biggest cost of a lack of regard for privacy by some aggressive journalists is the severing of the bond of trust between journalists and their audience. Bruce Sanford, an attorney who defends the media in court, suggests that

> *The consequences of the growing canyon of distrust between the public and the media are already discernible and should worry us even more than the knowledge that we understand the situation poorly. For the result of the public's misplaced fury has been a palpable willingness to silence the media—and to curtail its ability to gather and report the news, and to make us more dependent than ever on the government for our understanding of human events. There is no more certain road to the loss of freedom.*[35]

ACCURACY AND QUALITY CONTROL

The zeal to practice exciting investigative journalism can lead to journalists becoming careless with facts or taking dangerous shortcuts. An example of such dubious techniques was the use of incendiary devices by *Dateline* in 1992 to simulate a gas tank explosion in a defective vehicle. In this case journalistic integrity seems to have been a victim of intense competition with other network newsmagazines and the desire for dramatic footage.

The most serious problems arise when journalists deliberately falsify or fabricate information or even entire stories. Although this is likely a rare offense, there have been a number of prominent instances in recent years. James Fallows, former Washington editor and now national correspondent of the *Atlantic Monthly*, considers it to be the one unforgivable sin for a journalist: "This is something you never, never do. If you're a soldier, you don't desert. If you're a writer, you don't steal anyone's prose. It should be the one automatic firing." However, in practice, he also notes that "punishment is uneven, ranging from severe to virtually nothing even for major offenses. The sin itself carries neither public humiliation nor the mark of Cain. Some editors will keep a plagiarist on staff or will knowingly hire one if talent outweighs the infraction."[36]

The *Columbia Journalism Review* found that between 1988 and 1995 in 20 cases of plagiarism, in only eight cases was the reporter fired—and two of those reporters were rehired after arbitration. Many others received brief suspensions or other minor sanctions; five were completely unpunished. Some of the more prominent cases have included *Washington Post* reporter Janet Cooke, who in 1981 fabricated a story about an eight-year-old heroin addict, and the *Boston Globe's* Mike Barnicle, who was found to have plagiarized jokes and other material for use in his columns.

Plagiarism tends to be a compulsive, repeated behavior. It seems often to be driven more by psychological response to pressure than by lack of ability (or time) to do original work. Newspapers tend to be reticent about minor cases, citing them as internal personnel matters.

The most shocking story of journalistic fabrication occurred in 2003 when it was revealed that *New York Times* reporter Jayson Blair, considered for a time to be one of the paper's most promising young reporters, had fabricated large portions of numerous articles, often concealing the fact that he had not personally been present at the scenes of his stories. The fallout from this scandal at what is widely considered the premier U.S. newspaper soon resulted in the resignation of two senior *New York Times* editors, Howell Raines and Gerald Boyd.

Blair himself admitted his offense but suggested that he may have slipped into spinning stories out of whole cloth:

> *What I did was not entirely deliberate and conscious. Some people have made an argument that it was a cancer spreading and I was the first person to die from it. . . . It was obviously wrong . . . [but] I didn't invent the wheel. Somewhere in my head I knew people were getting away with this.*[37]

Because Blair (and earlier, Cooke) are black, critics of affirmative action argued that the overriding desire for a more diverse newsroom had led supervising editors to overlook warning signs and to give more second and third chances than might otherwise have been the case. Whether or not race played a part in these particular cases, there are certainly many pressures in the modern journalistic environment that emphasize getting the product over ensuring the quality of the process. The ultimate issue is whether journalists can create a strong enough ethic that, combined with more rigorous procedures for verifying sources, could minimize fabrication and plagiarism or at least catch it in its early stages.

One remarkably simple and effective procedure has been suggested by journalist, editor, and media critic Steven Brill, who began to send follow-up letters to people mentioned in stories in the *American Lawyer:* "In each case I sent a letter saying that the letter was simply a routine quality control check ... I then asked if the person had been treated courteously and quoted accurately and how the person would rate the overall quality of the article." Brill found that 99.5 percent of the time he got positive reports, with the occasional minor factual complaint or expression of discomfort with the article as a whole. However, Brill also learned that "[it] was the laziest, most dishonest reporters are often those who write things that won't offend, because they know those won't get complaints."[38]

A SEARCH FOR STANDARDS AND ETHICS

There are a number of ways in which journalists can try to ensure better accuracy, fairness, and accountability in their work. By and large, journalists take their professional obligations seriously. Organizations such as the Society of Professional Journalists, founded in 1909, and the American Society of Newspaper Editors, founded in 1922. Such organizations as well as many nonprofit foundations research problems in journalism and develop guidelines and recommendations.

In 1999 the Scripps Howard Foundation sponsored a roundtable in which 11 prominent journalists discussed journalism's "growing credibility crisis with the American people." Some of the suggested solutions to this crisis included:

The media should pay attention to the basics, respecting what the reader wants and avoiding doing harm in any way.

When reporters "fall in love" with their big stories, editors should take a step back before printing them.

The media should be more independent and avoid the so-called herd mentality.

Reporters, producers, and writers should be taught a "higher consciousness of ethics." When reporters cover a story the first filter should be "Is it right and is it ethical?"

The media should ask advice from customers more frequently than it does now.[39]

Journalists often confront difficult choices, such as whether to write about a minor criminal offense committed by a prominent person who has done many good things for the community. The journalist may have to decide whether the story has some value that outweighs the pain its revelation will cause to that person, his or her family, and indeed, the community.

Ethicist Sissela Bok suggests a process by which a journalist can come to a conclusion about whether to run a story:

First, consult your own conscience about the "rightness" of an action. *How do you feel about the action?*

Second, seek expert advice for alternatives to the act creating the ethical problem. Experts, by the way, can be those both living and dead—a producer or copywriter you trust or a philosopher you

admire. *Is there another way to achieve the same goal that will not raise ethical issues?*
Third, if possible, conduct a public discussion with the parties involved in the dispute. These include those who are directly involved, i.e. the reporter or the source, and those indirectly involved, i.e. a reader or a source. If they cannot be gathered, conduct the conversation hypothetically. The goal of this conversation is to discover *How will my action affect others?*[40]

There is not always an easy answer, but one can at least clarify the competing values in a situation (such as truth versus privacy) and decide where one's responsibility lies.

In the "old media" a consumer could cultivate a handful of trusted, reliable sources—the *New York Times*, Walter Cronkite, or a local newspaper run by people who also live in the community. In the new media, with its megacorporations and its bewildering variety of cable channels and web sites, the implicit partnership between journalist and audience must also change. The consumer of news media will have to take greater responsibility in evaluating the information being served up from various sources. The consumer will have to evaluate the quality of sources, perhaps with the aid of web sites set up for that very purpose. Comparing, winnowing and synthesizing, then sharing information—the news consumer will have to also become, at least on a small, personal scale, a journalist.

---

[1] Survey conducted by Gallup Organization, July 6–July 9, 2000, and based on telephone interviews with a national adult sample of 1,001 persons. Data provided by the Roper Center for Public Opinion Research, University of Connecticut.

[2] 1997 Roper Center Survey cited in "Do You Believe What Newspeople Tell You?" *Washington Post Parade Magazine* (March 2, 1997), p. 4.

[3] G. Ray Funkhouser and Eugene F. Shaw, "How Synthetic Experience Shapes Social Reality." *Journal of Communication.* Reprinted in Doris A. Graber, ed., *Media Power in Politics*, p. 59.

[4] G. Ray Funkhouser and Eugene F. Shaw, "How Synthetic Experience Shapes Social Reality," pp. 61–63.

[5] Bernard Cohen, *Foreign Policy in American Government.* Boston: Little, Brown, 1965, p. 196.

[6] Bernard Cohen, *The Press and Foreign Policy.* Princeton, N.J.: Princeton University Press, 1963, p. 13.

[7] Quoted in Phillip Patterson and Lee Wilkins, *Media Ethics: Issues & Cases.* Boston: McGraw-Hill, 2002, p. 181.

[8] Walter Lippmann, *Public Opinion.* Reprinted in Doris A. Graber, *Media Power in Politics*, Washington, D.C.: CQ Press, 2000, p. 41.

[9] Ben Bagdikian, *The Media Monopoly.* 5th ed. Boston: Beacon Press, 1997, p. ix.

[10] Quoted in Tom Goldstein, "Does Big Mean Bad?" *Columbia Journalism Review*, vol. 37, Sept.–Oct. 1998, p. 52ff.

[11] Ken Auletta, "Synergy City." *American Journalism Review*, vol. 20, May 1998, p. 18ff.

[12] Neil Hickey, "Money Lust: How Pressure for Profit Is Perverting Journalism." *Columbia Journalism Review*, vol. 37, July–August 1998, p. 28ff.

[13] Neil Hickey, "Money Lust: How Pressure for Profit Is Perverting Journalism," p. 28.

[14] David Croteau. "Examining the 'Liberal Media' Claim." Fairness and Accuracy in Media. Available online. URL: http://www.fair.org/reports/journalist-survey. html. Posted in June 1998.

[15] Philip Patterson and Lee Wilkins, *Media Ethics: Issues and Cases*. 4th ed. Boston: McGraw-Hill, 2002, p. 149.

[16] James Fallows, "Why Americans Hate the Media," *Atlantic Monthly*, February 1996, p. 45ff.

[17] Jay Rosen, *What are Journalists For?* New Haven: Yale University Press, 1999, p. 22.

[18] Carl Sessions Stepp, "Reader Friendly," *American Journalism Review*, July/August 2000, pp. 23–31.

[19] Both quotes from Carl Sessions Stepp, "Reader Friendly," pp. 23–31.

[20] Terence Smith, "Journalism and Patriotism." *PBS Online NewsHour*. Available online. URL: http://www.pbs.org/newshour/bb/media/july-dec01/patriotism_11-6.html. Posted on November 6, 2001.

[21] Eben Shapiro. "Fear of Terrorism is Curbing Travel." *New York Times*, January 28, 1991, p. A1.

[22] Jason DeParle, "17 News Executives Criticize U.S. for 'Censorship' of Gulf Coverage," *New York Times*, July 3, 1991, p. A4.

[23] Quoted in Justin Ewers, "Is the New News Good News?" *U.S. News & World Report*, vol. 134, April 7, 2003, p. 48.

[24] Quoted in *The CIA and the Media, Hearings of the Subcommittee on Oversight of the Permanent Select Committee on Intelligence, U.S. House of Representatives, 95th Congress, 1st and 2nd Sess., December 27–29, 1977, January 4–5 and April 20, 1979.* Washington, D.C.: Government Printing Office, 1996, p. 24.

[25] Quoted in Alicia C. Shepard, "The Web That Gary Spun." *American Journalism Review*, January/February 1997, p. 36.

[26] Neil Hickey, "Ten Mistakes that Led to the Great CNN/Time Fiasco." *Columbia Journalism Review*, vol. 37, September–October 1998, p. 26ff.

[27] Philip Patterson and Lee Wilkins, eds., *Media Ethics: Issues & Cases*, p. 179.

[28] David Welch, "News into the Next Century." *Historical Journal of Film, Radio, and Television*, vol. 20, March 2000, p. 5.

[29] Susan R. Trento, *The Power House: Robert Keith Gray and the Selling of Access and Influence in Washington*. New York: St. Martin's Press, 1992, p. 23.

[30] Promotional material from *TJFR Environmental News Reporter*, quoted in Stauber and Rampton, *Toxic Sludge Is Good for You*, Monroe, Maine: Common Courage Press, 1995, p. 186.

[31] Terence Smith, "Free Press vs. Fair Trial." *PBS Online NewsHour.* Available online. URL: http://www.pbs.org/newshour/bb/media/july-dec99/cbs_11-12a. html. Posted on November 12, 1999.

[32] Sherrie L. Wilson, William A. Babcock, and John Pribek. "Newspaper Ombudsmen's Reactions to Use of Anonymous Sources," *Newspaper Research Journal,* vol. 18, Summer/Fall 1997, p. 145.

[33] Quoted in Steven Brill, "Curiosity vs. Privacy." *Brill's Content,* vol. 2, October 1999, p. 98.

[34] Quoted in Robert J. Wagman, *The First Amendment Book.* New York: World Almanac, 1991, pp. 148–149.

[35] Bruce Sanford, *Don't Shoot the Messenger: How Our Growing Hatred of the Media Threatens Free Speech for All of Us.* New York: Free Press, 1999, p. 10.

[36] James Fallows, quoted in Trudy Lieberman, "Plagiarize, Plagiarize, Plagiarize . . . Only Be Sure to Call It Research." *Columbia Journalism Review,* July/August 1995, pp. 1–2.

[37] Quoted in Julian E. Barnes, "A Certain Kind of Rage." *U.S. News & World Report,* vol. 134, June 16, 2003, p. 28.

[38] Steven Brill, quoted in Jon Caroll, "Steven Brill Weighs In." *San Francisco Chronicle,* June 13, 2003, p. 122.

[39] Jon Jaben, "Credibility Crisis in the Newsroom." *Editor & Publisher,* February 27, 1999, p. 12.

[40] Patterson and Wilkins. *Media Ethics: Issues and Cases,* p. 3.

CHAPTER 3

THE LAW AND
THE NEWS MEDIA

The key to understanding the legal aspects of the news media and its interaction with society lies first in constitutional law, then in statutory or common law, and finally in regulation. This chapter therefore begins with the gradually expanding understanding of the First Amendment and the possible conflicts between the right of freedom of the press and other legal and societal interests such as privacy and the right to a fair trial. The next topic is the regulatory regime that was developed for the broadcast (radio and television) industry starting in the mid-20th century, the still-tentative attempts to regulate content on the Internet, and the constitutional limitations on regulating the print media. The chapter concludes with a survey of legal cases (mainly in the U.S. Supreme Court) dealing with various aspects of the rights and responsibilities of journalists and the regulation of the media.

THE FIRST AMENDMENT

The First Amendment is the primary constitutional provision relied upon by the media to allow it to work without interference. Like most of the Constitution, it is relatively clear and succinct:

> *Congress shall make no law respecting an establishment of religion, or prohibiting the free exercise thereof; or abridging the freedom of speech, or of the press, or the right of the people peaceably to assemble, and to petition the Government for redress of grievances.*

Evidence of the precise intentions of the framers of the First Amendment has not survived. We do know that in general the first 10 amendments, the Bill of Rights, were the result of the insistence of many of those who had fought for liberal ideals in the Revolution that the proposed strong new central government be explicitly checked by a written guarantee of fundamental rights. In the debate over the Constitution, James Madison introduced language about freedom of speech and the press that was very similar to what would be included in the final version passed in December 1791.

The combining of such matters as speech, the press, assembly and petition, and even religion may seem to be arbitrary or perhaps the result of editing for compactness. In the late 18th century, however, the victorious Americans were only a generation or two removed from a state that established (mandated) one religious denomination while often suppressing others. The government also "established" the press, in the sense that printing books or other publications in Great Britain and most other European countries (as well as colonial America) required a license from the local authorities that could be taken away if anything offensive to the government was printed.

The First Amendment essentially bundles into one package those things that make up political discourse: believing, speaking, writing, petitioning, and demonstrating. One of the enduring themes of First Amendment interpretation is acknowledging how vital free expression is if the people are to be able to sort through their democratic choices.

However, protection of the right to print words critical of the government would be affirmed only gradually. The Alien and Sedition Acts were passed in 1798 in the wake of hysteria about the intentions of revolutionary France, making it illegal to utter or publish "any false, scandalous, or malicious writing or writings against the Government of the United States, with the intent to defame . . . or to bring them into contempt or disrepute."

The Alien and Sedition Acts lapsed after the electoral victories of Jeffersonian liberals at the beginning of the 19th century. With the exception of measures enacted during the Civil War and during the "red scare" during and after World War I and restrictions on the mailing of certain items (such as lottery tickets or Mormon tracts advocating polygamy) there would be little further federal legislation threatening freedom of speech. Most of the legal restraints and pitfalls faced by journalists would come from the common law (defamation or libel) from state and local laws, or from the dictates of local judges—and for a long time the First Amendment would provide no real protection in such cases.

Until well into the 20th century, the First Amendment, like the rest of the Bill of Rights, was interpreted as restraining only the legislative power of Congress ("Congress shall make no law . . ."). However, in the otherwise rather obscure case of *Gitlow v. New York* (1925), the Supreme Court noted that because the Fourteenth Amendment required that all states provide their residents with "due process" and "equal protection of the laws," the freedom of speech and of the press guaranteed by the First Amendment would also have to be guaranteed by the states. (This concept of "incorporating" the rights in the first 10 amendments into the rights of citizens that must be respected by states and localities would soon grow to encompass many other parts of the Bill of Rights as well.)

As the 20th century progressed and rights came increasingly into conflict in an ever more complex and diverse society, the courts were called upon to determine under what circumstances freedom of the press or the actions of journalists could be restricted or punished. On the other hand, the implications of the First Amendment could also be used to protect the sources and work of reporters and editors or to require that the media be given access to hearings, trials, and other public acts of government.

There have generally been two competing theories of how to apply the First Amendment in media-related cases. The first is the balancing test: it seeks to balance the First Amendment right of the free press against some competing consideration. For example, suppose a reporter has information that might help a defendant prove his or her innocence, but that information was received under a promise of confidentiality. The defense attorney wants that source's name so this potentially valuable witness can be called into court to testify.

The balancing approach puts on one side of the scales the value of a reporter being able to promise confidentiality in order to get information that would otherwise be unobtainable. On the other side is the right of the defendant to have a fair trial and the ability to compel witnesses to testify on his or her behalf—rights guaranteed by the Sixth Amendment. With the balancing test in mind, a judge asks such questions as:

- How serious is the harm to the reporter and to the operation of the press if this information is disclosed?

- Is there some way to protect the defendant's interests without compromising the protection of the process of journalism as embodied in the First Amendment?

- Is the confidential information truly necessary for presenting an effective defense?

The alternative absolutist approach to the First Amendment does not attempt to balance competing considerations. Rather, it is based upon equal, independent claims. It suggests that the constitutional language be taken at face value: the freedom of the press should never be abridged. From that point of view, if the operation of a free press is truly as vital to ensuring a free society as the operation of law enforcement, the judicial system, national defense, or any other institution, then none of those other considerations have a claim to information gathered by the reporter. If the confidentiality of information means that a prosecutor or defendant will not have access to it, that is unfortunate, but it must be accepted, just as the possibility of "freeing a guilty person on a technicality" must be accepted by a fair judicial system.

In practice the balancing approach has generally prevailed over the absolutist stance in First Amendment interpretation but with the absolutists often contributing powerful dissents. Although balancing is usually done to some extent, how far the balance tips toward or away from the First Amendment rights of journalists varies with the particular issue. Key cases and bodies of law have developed along different lines in several important areas involving the news media.

RESTRICTIONS ON THE PRESS

It was clearly understood that the right to "free printing" did not imply the right to print anything with impunity. When they wrote the First Amendment, the framers had at hand Sir William Blackstone's *Commentaries of the Laws of England* as a standard reference to centuries of common law. There they found this explanation of the freedom of the press:

> *The liberty of the press is indeed essential to the nature of a free state; but this consists of laying no previous restraints on publications, and not in freedom from censure for criminal matters when published. Every freeman has an undoubted right to lay what sentiments he pleases before the public; to forbid this is to destroy the freedom of the press; but if he publishes what is improper, mischievous, or illegal, he must take the consequences of his own temerity.*

This implied that there are limits to freedom of the press. It does not include defamation—unfairly damaging a person's reputation through falsehood—or interfering with certain government functions, such as national security and the conduct of foreign policy.

SEDITION

Sedition is defined as an act that threatens the operation of government or the public order. The 1798 Alien and Sedition Acts were not the last attempt to outlaw speech or writing deemed threatening to the functioning of government. Particularly in times of labor or social unrest or during wartime, there is likely to be a rash of laws criminalizing expression. Thus, in the late 19th and early 20th century, courts frequently issued injunctions banning union meetings or strikes. The wartime Espionage Act of 1917 responded to fears of agitation by socialists, communists, or peace advocates. The ban on distributing literature also made the act potentially a threat to news media, particularly small, independent, politically radical publications.

In *Schenck v. United States* (1919) the Supreme Court upheld the conviction of a person who distributed antidraft leaflets. The Court did recognize that such writing is ordinarily protected by the First Amendment but asserted that in wartime Congress had the right (under its war powers) to prevent interference with the draft. Justice Oliver Wendell Holmes said that expression reached its limits if it created a "clear and present danger." He then used the famous analogy: "The most stringent protection of free speech would not protect a man in falsely shouting fire in a theater and causing a panic."

The Court, though, almost immediately began to move toward examining more strictly whether there truly was a clear and present danger. In *Abrams v. United States* (1919), for example, Justice Holmes stressed that the danger must be immediate and imminent. Although the Court then backed away from the "clear and present danger" test for several decades, it returned to it in such cases as *Terminiello v. City of Chicago* (1949) and *Brandenburg v. Ohio* (1969).

Generally, sedition is not a daily concern for journalists, but the seesaw history of the post–World War I and McCarthy periods serves as a reminder that standards can shift under pressure. For many civil liberties advocates, the period following the terrorist attacks of September 11, 2001, is such a period of potentially deforming pressure.

PRIOR RESTRAINT

As the phrase suggests, *prior restraint* refers to legal action before an article is published, forbidding its publication. It is thus different from action for libel, defamation, or contempt of court that is brought only after the article has been published. Although Blackstone denied that there was a power to "lay previous restraints on publication," the power to do precisely that has been exercised in certain types of circumstances—more so in the past than today. The general principle established by the U.S. Supreme Court in *Near v. Minnesota* (1931) was that prior restraint is not permitted by the First Amendment as a means for furthering the general interests of the government or to protect individuals from being defamed. However, there are two areas in which a case for prior restraint might still be made: matters affecting national security and judicial proceedings.

Power of the News Media

National Security

In general the courts have been very reluctant to allow the government to exercise prior restraint, even when the material in question has been classified as secret because its disclosure might harm national security. The classic case in this area is *New York Times v. United States* (1971), often called the Pentagon Papers case. Officials in the Nixon administration sought to prevent the publication of a classified report that included much embarrassing material about deceptions used to justify U.S. involvement in Vietnam. After the first installment of the Pentagon Papers was published by the *New York Times* and the *Washington Post*, the government sought to halt any further publication of the material.

The U.S. Supreme Court unanimously denied the government's request. The majority of the justices did not completely close the door to prior restraint but insisted that the government would have to prove that the information would "surely" cause "direct, immediate, and irreparable harm" to national security. The mere fact that the material had a secret classification would not suffice. Two justices, William O. Douglas and Hugo Black, went still further, denying that the First Amendment could ever allow prior restraint.

In the case of *United States v. Progressive* (1979) the question arose of whether a magazine could be prevented from publishing detailed plans for construction of an H-bomb. The case became moot when someone else published the information. Today, the existence of the Internet makes it likely that legal action to prevent the publication of most any kind of information would be ineffective.

Free Press versus Fair Trial

The Sixth Amendment to the Constitution guarantees the right of a defendant to a trial "by an impartial jury" and the right "to have compulsory process for obtaining witnesses in his favor." An important consideration in ensuring an impartial jury is to avoid too great an exposure to information that might be prejudicial. At the same time, many trials are of great interest to the public, and thus to the media—witness the popularity of *Court TV.* Sometimes judges issue "gag orders" to prevent parties (such as the prosecutor and defense attorney, or the police) from talking about the case. When a gag order is extended to the media, a conflict with the right of freedom of the press is created.

The modern standard for resolving this conflict was established in *Nebraska Press Association v. Stuart* (1976). Here the Supreme Court set aside the gag order of a state court against publishing information that might prejudice the trial of a criminal defendant. For a gag order to be allowed, there must first be a "clear and present danger" that the information being suppressed will prevent the defendant from receiving a fair trial. Further, the court must look at the overall nature and extent of pretrial news coverage, determine whether there are means other than a gag order that the trial court could use to minimize the harm, and finally, determine whether a gag order would actually prevent the threatened harm. Thus, for example, if proper jury instructions are sufficient to mitigate the effects of pretrial information, the court cannot use a gag order instead.

OBSCENITY

Like sedition, obscenity is a concept that generally has little direct effect on the news media, although it can be important for the arts and entertainment media. In the 19th century numerous state laws as well as federal law were inspired by the antivice crusade of Anthony Comstock. The "Comstock laws" prohibited the distribution or possession of material found to be "lewd," "indecent," "filthy," or "obscene." Up to the mid-20th century most obscenity cases involved literature, including such famous works as James Joyce's novel *Ulysses* and Allen Ginsberg's poem *Howl*. By setting the bounds of acceptable discourse, obscenity law could virtually keep entire topics out of the news, including, for example, discussion of birth control or the sexual transmission of disease.

In *Miller v. California* (1973) the Supreme Court created the modern test for whether a work is obscene. A work is obscene if it:

- appeals to the average person's prurient interest in sex,
- depicts sexual conduct in a "patently offensive" way as defined by contemporary community standards, or
- taken as a whole, lacks serious literary, artistic, political or scientific value.

Practically speaking, the print news media is unlikely to fall afoul of obscenity laws. However, the courts have shown greater willingness to be restrictive with other forms of media. For example, in *FCC v. Pacifica Foundation* (1978) the Supreme Court upheld FCC regulations against broadcasting seven sexual and scatological terms traditionally considered obscenities because of the pervasiveness and accessibility of radio and the ease with which children might listen in. The Court also considered the nature of the "broadcast" medium in deciding, in *ACLU v. Reno* (1996), that forcing web site providers to block indecent material was unworkable without compromising the First Amendment rights of adults. This last case is also a reminder of the distinction between obscene material (per the *Miller* definition) which can be banned, and merely "indecent" material, which adults have a First Amendment right to view.

LIBEL

A libel is a printed or broadcast communication that is false and that injures someone's reputation—for example, a false statement that someone has been convicted of a crime. (Spoken defamation that is not broadcast is called slander, and is not relevant to the news media.) Although the English and early American law of libel could also punish factually true statements that caused injury, modern American law requires that the statement contain one or more false facts.

As First Amendment interpretation expanded toward a greater appreciation of the importance of the news media, the question arose whether incidental or unintentional mistakes in news reports should leave reporters and their publications open to damages for libel. To continue to do so would cast a "chilling effect" that would make the journalistic investigation of powerful individuals and institutions less likely and make the timely production of news reports much more difficult.

In *New York Times v. Sullivan* (1964) the Supreme Court therefore ruled that when the person making the accusation of libel was a public official, he or she would have to prove not only that the defendant made false statements but did so with "actual malice"—that is, while knowing the statements were false, or with reckless disregard of whether the statements were false.

This decision in effect said that when someone is functioning as part of the government, the public interest in robust media coverage of his or her activities required a higher standard for proving libel. In *Gertz v. Welch* (1974) this special status was extended to "public figures" in general, including business leaders, entertainers, and other celebrities. Other cases tried to clarify under what circumstances someone who merely works for the government is a public official, and whether an otherwise private person could be treated as a sort of temporary "public figure" for purposes of a particular news event.

The practical effect for the media is that there is strong constitutional protection for reporters pursuing stories involving public officials or figures and being of public interest. However, that protection requires deep pockets, because angry people often sue even if they are unlikely to prevail on appeal, and media companies have to be able to foot the bills.

PRIVACY

Aside from the question of libel, the media often comes into conflict with individuals who are seeking to preserve their privacy. The aggressive pursuit of celebrities such as the late Princess Diana by camera-wielding paparazzi and reality police shows such as *Cops* (where faces are electronically blurred) are familiar examples.

In 1976, a Jacksonville, Florida, newspaper printed a photograph showing the charred silhouette of a 17-year-old girl who had burned to death in a fire. The girl's mother sued the newspaper, but in *Florida Publishing Co. v. Fletcher* (1976, *cert. denied* 1977) the Florida Supreme Court dismissed the suit, noting that "It is not questioned that this tragic fire and death were being investigated by the fire department and the sheriff's office and that arson was suspected. The fire was a disaster of great public interest and it is clear that the photographer and other members of the news media entered the burned home at the invitation of the investigating officers." The judge noted that such accompaniment was customary and that the presence of the media often helped officials develop leads for their investigations. (Indeed, in this case the fire investigator had asked the press photographer for help in making a sufficiently clear photograph of the silhouette.)

In other cases, claims of trespass on private property in the course of media coverage of some public investigation were rejected. Generally, the decisions observed that the media representatives did not damage property, had received the approval of the investigating authorities, and were covering a matter of public interest.

In recent years, though, some cases have gone the other way. For example, in *Ayeni v. Mottola* (1994) a federal judge in the Eastern District of New York ruled that CBS had to turn over a tape made during a fruitless Secret Service search of an apartment. In a subsequent civil case, the same judge found CBS liable for damages. In a related case brought against one of the Secret Service agents, a federal appeals judge declared that "a private home is not a soundstage for law enforcement theatricals." And in two 1998 cases (*Hanlon v. Berger* and *Wilson v. Layne*) the Supreme Court ruled that "ride-alongs," in which reporters accompany police, violated suspects' privacy rights.

In general, journalists can be prosecuted for committing acts that are illegal for any ordinary person, including trespass, breaking and entering, assault, and fraud. In the 1999 case of *Food Lion v. ABC* a U.S. appeals court ruled that reporters who became Food Lion employees in order to conduct a hidden-camera investigation of the company's food-handling practices were guilty of misrepresentation and breach of duty to the employer, although they were not liable for major damages without defamation being proven.

LEGAL PROTECTION FOR THE MEDIA

The law does not just limit the activities of the media; it can also facilitate them in various ways by protecting their ability to gather information and by requiring that the government provide a wide variety of information to the public.

PROTECTION OF SOURCES

To obtain information that powerful people and institutions want to hide, journalists rely greatly on confidential and anonymous sources. These people are willing to supply information—such as about corruption in a government office—but only on condition that they are not identified. As the example at the beginning of this chapter indicates, use of such sources can cause a conflict with prosecutors who want information about a crime or defense attorneys who want information that might prove their client's innocence.

The Supreme Court in *Branzburg v. Hayes* (1972) narrowly ruled that the First Amendment does not require a "journalist's privilege" giving a reporter the right to withhold the names of sources or other information when needed for a court proceeding. (Reporters may not be forced to actively aid a police investigation, however.) In his concurring opinion, Justice Potter Stewart suggested a standard that has been followed by some lower courts since. He said that a confidential source should be revealed only if:

- the information sought was shown to be clearly relevant to the proceeding,
- there were no alternative sources that could be used that would cause less damage to the First Amendment interest, and
- there was a "compelling need" for disclosure that outweighed the First Amendment interest.

In response to the lack of a firm constitutional guarantee, most states (but not the federal government) now have "shield laws" that provide varying degrees of protection of confidential sources and, in some states, the reporter's notes, tapes, and so on.

ACCESS TO TRIALS

The flip side of the case in which courts seek information from the media is when the media seeks information about trials, government hearings, or other proceedings. In a number of cases the Supreme Court has made rulings that give reporters the right to be present at a number of phases in the judicial process. In *Richmond Newspapers v. Virginia* (1976) the Court affirmed a First Amendment right for the media to attend criminal trials. In *Globe Newspaper Co. v. Superior Court* (1982) the Court said that testimony of minors in sex crime trials could not be automatically closed to the press: an individualized showing of harm to the witness would have to be made. In *Press-Enterprise v. Riverside County Superior Court* (1984) the court required that voir dire (the jury selection process) be open to the press. In a 1986 case of the same name, press access was extended to preliminary hearings. Although these cases set the "default" to press access, the proceedings could be closed if a compelling or overriding interest could be shown and no less drastic measure than closing the proceeding could be used. In cases where the issue was the defendant's right to a fair trial, the judge had to find that there was a "substantial probability" that an open proceeding would create prejudice and that closing the proceeding would prevent the prejudice.

The visual media initially had a harder time getting into the courtroom. In *Estes v. Texas* (1965) the Supreme Court reversed Estes's conviction because of the distracting effect of the television camera and the possibility it would cause attorneys and witnesses to "play to the camera." The following year the Supreme Court reversed the conviction of accused murderer Sam Sheppard for much the same reason. By the 1980s, with television firmly entrenched as a primary source of news, the Court relented in *Chandler v. Florida* (1981), saying that states were free to allow the cameras into the courtroom and set appropriate guidelines for their use. As of 2003, 47 states allow cameras in the courtroom under varying circumstances. New York, Mississippi, and South Dakota still ban them entirely from trial courts.

FREEDOM OF INFORMATION

The Freedom of Information Act (FOIA) of 1966 provided a comprehensive scheme for making many kinds of government-generated information available to the public, and thus to the media. The act applies to actual physical records controlled by a given agency (in 1987 this was extended to electronic equivalents to paper records). However, there are nine categories of information that are exempt from the FOIA: information affecting national security, agency rules and practices, material exempted by statute, confidential business information, agency memoranda, personal information such as personnel or medical records, material relating to law enforcement investigations, banking reports, and information about oil wells.

In general, courts have given considerable weight to personal privacy in not requiring the release of records relating to individuals. For law enforcement records, there generally has to be a showing that releasing the record would invade someone's privacy, disclose the identity of a confidential source, or endanger someone's life.

The FOIA can be a useful tool for journalists, but it is limited by the lengthy time often involved in resolving government objections to release of information. Nevertheless, some major stories such as the revelation of Federal Bureau of Investigation (FBI) harassment of civil rights and antiwar leaders in the 1960s were made possible mainly by use of the FOIA.

All states have also passed some form of "sunshine laws" (also called open meeting laws) that provide similarly for open access to information from government offices and proceedings. Generally, sunshine laws require that most meetings of legislatures or city councils be open to the public and the media except when they are discussing certain personnel matters or ongoing contract negotiations. Most police reports and official financial records must be publicly accessible. The details of what is covered vary from state to state.

REGULATING THE MEDIA

As a business, the various forms of media are also subject to federal, state, and local regulation. However, First Amendment interests limit regulation involving the content of the media or the ability of the media to distribute information.

REGULATING THE PRINT MEDIA

A series of Supreme Court cases established the boundaries for permissible regulation of newspapers and magazines. In *Grosjean v. American Press Company* (1936) the Court overturned a local fee or tax on advertising revenue from newspapers above a certain size. In *Minneapolis Star and Tribune v. Minnesota Commissioner of Revenue* (1983) the Court ruled that a tax cannot be applied to the press and not to other businesses. In *Arkansas Writers' Project, Inc. v. Ragland* (1987) the Court overturned a city tax that was imposed on some types of magazines but not on other types of publications. Earlier, though, in *Giragi v. Moore* (1937) the Court established the principle that taxes that applied to businesses in general could also be applied to the press.

Like other types of businesses, newspapers have been the recipient of subsidies or other benefits, including special low postage rates. The Newspaper Publicity Act (1913) requires that newspapers wanting this subsidy identify their owners, disclose their circulation figures, and label advertising that might be mistaken for news stories. The Supreme Court in *Lewis Publishing v. Morgan* (1913) upheld the regulations because they needed to be followed only by publications wishing the special treatment.

The Newspaper Preservation Act (1970) was a response to the Supreme Court's ruling in 1969 that cooperative arrangements between competing newspapers violated the Sherman Antitrust Act of 1890. When one of two major papers in a given city is in danger of failing, it can join with a more successful newspaper and set prices, market allocation, and distribution of profits between the two publications, which are supposed to remain editorially independent. The law has been a mixed success, with papers in a number of cities failing despite the help of a strong partner.

BROADCASTING REGULATION

The regulation of broadcasting is fundamentally different from regulation of print media. The courts have justified giving broadcast stations less First Amendment protection because the broadcast spectrum physically allows for only a limited number of stations.

The Radio Act of 1927 created the Federal Radio Commission. The most urgent mission of this body was to assign stations to specific frequencies and prevent interference. As radio growth exploded and the medium became commercially successful, a more comprehensive system of regulation was needed. Congress passed the Communications Act of 1934, which created the Federal Communications Commission (FCC). This body would regulate not only radio but the telegraph, telephone, and soon, television. Other major principles of broadcast regulation include:

- The government will not censor broadcast content, but it can ban "obscene, indecent, or profane" language.

- If a station provides access to a political candidate, it must provide equal access to opponents.

- The requirement to support public debate was extended in 1949 to require that stations provide an adequate amount of time to discussions of important issues, and in doing so, to provide coverage of opposing views (this is called the Fairness Doctrine).

- In deciding whether to grant a station a license to broadcast, the FCC is to be guided by the "public interest, convenience, and necessity." Stations that do not adequately serve public needs may be challenged when licenses come up for renewal.

In the 1980s a number of these regulations were weakened or abandoned. The expansion of radio (into FM) and television (into UHF, then satellite and cable) weakened the argument that scarcity of stations required holding them to high standards of content. In 1987 the Fairness Doctrine, which was hard to enforce due to the problem of determining what views about an issue had to be covered, was abandoned by the FCC. This movement was also influenced by a general tendency toward deregulation in the Reagan administration, with the belief that a sufficiently competitive market could provide for consumers' interests.

Concern about children's programming and the prevalence of objectionable material in programming led to several laws in the 1990s that have had only limited effect. The Children's Television Act (1990) requires that stations show how they are serving the educational and informational needs of children and limits the number of commercials that may be shown on children's programs. The Television Violence Act of the same year provides a three-year exemption from antitrust regulation for television networks to allow them to jointly develop standards for reducing violence on television.

REGULATING BROADCAST OWNERSHIP

The limited number of broadcast stations also led to regulations intended to limit the number of broadcast stations that could be owned by any one company. In 1941 the FCC ruled that one company could own no more than eight stations in a market with 45 or more stations, with proportionally lower limits for smaller markets. Companies were also prohibited from owning television stations covering more than 35 percent of households having sets. Further, in 1946, with the major radio networks moving into television, mergers between such networks were also forbidden.

In 1964 a company was limited to owning no more than two television stations in the same market. If a company did own two stations, only one station could be in the top four ranked by audience, and there must be at least eight other independent stations.

Regulations of "cross-ownership" (one company owning two kinds of media) were also enacted. A 1970 rule prevented the same company from owning a radio station and a television station in the same market, and in 1975 it was decided that the same company cannot own both newspapers and broadcast stations (although some exceptions were "grandfathered in").

The Telecommunications Act of 1996 relaxed ownership regulations. Companies could now own as many as eight radio stations in the same city, depending on the size of the market.

Finally, in 2003 a number of restrictions were further eased:

- The same company can now own television stations reaching up to 45 percent of the nation's viewers.

- A company can now own two television stations in any market that has five or more stations. A company can own three stations if the market has 18 or more stations. Any company owning multiple stations cannot have more than one station ranked in the top four in audience. However, the FCC may grant a waiver allowing a merger between two top-four stations in markets with 11 or fewer stations.

- There are no longer any cross-ownership restrictions in markets with nine or more television stations. Cross-ownership is banned in markets with three or fewer stations. Markets with four to eight stations would retain some restrictions.

- Subject to that limit, the same company can own as many as three television stations, eight radio stations, and one major newspaper, as well as a local cable system.

In late 2003, however, a number of voices were raised in Congress and elsewhere decrying the new regulations as permitting a too-great concentration of media power in too few hands. It is possible that the regulations might be tightened again, although President Bush and the dominant Republicans in Congress seem likely to resist such a reversal.

Cable television was also subject to some special regulations starting in 1962, when cable systems began to compete with broadcast networks in some areas. Cable stations were required to carry local station programming but not to duplicate programs available on local stations. The Cable Communications Policy Act of 1984 eliminated regulation of cable rates (although in 1992 price regulation of basic cable service would be restored). It also banned cross-ownership of cable systems and networks by telephone companies in their local telephone service areas.

During the 1970s the courts generally upheld the FCC's right to regulate cable, without delving into distinctions between cable and broadcast TV. In 1977, however, a federal appeals court for the D.C. circuit ruled in *Home Box Office v. FCC* on First Amendment grounds that the FCC could not limit the types of programs a cable outlet could offer.

INTERNET: THE ELECTRONIC FRONTIER

The Internet, the newest information medium in widespread use, has proven to be a minefield for regulators. Content regulation has mainly centered around keeping harmful material and people from children. The Communications Decency Act of 1996 was overturned by the Supreme Court in *ACLU v. Reno* (1996) because the practical realities of the medium meant that requiring age verification of Internet users would also block many adults from many kinds of noncommercial sites.

In *United States v. American Library Association* (2003) the Court did uphold a requirement that public libraries receiving federal funds install blocking software to keep objectionable material from children. In this case the technical problems with such software (which often blocks unobjectionable information) were apparently not given as great a weight by the Court. Although the decision implied that adults would be able to request unfiltered access, this decision may complicate things for media sites that want to be accessible to both adults and children.

In a way, the courts seem to be treating the Internet as a sort of hybrid of print and broadcast media. Like print media, the Internet is not subject to physical scarcity, but like broadcasting, it is pervasive and increasingly accessible to children. The lack of scarcity should preclude limitations on ownership.

The latest concerns about the Internet involve issues such as identity theft and other abuse of private information, and the massive increase in the distribution of unsolicited e-mail (spam). Online media outlets will have to deal with these issues as well, and they may affect journalists who use online sources such as "information brokers" for their research.

COURT CASES

There are a considerable number of cases involving the news media, with important decisions determining the rights and responsibilities of reporters, the extent of media access to government information, and the recourse for persons subjected to media coverage perceived to be unfair and damaging. This general legal area is often referred to as media law or communications law.

Cases by Topic

Because of the great variety of issues covered by communications and media law, the following list may be helpful for researching cases that feature a particular topic. Cases summarized at the end of this chapter are given in chronological order.

Access to Government Proceedings and Information *Houchins v. KQED Inc. (1978), Richmond Newspapers, Inc. v. Virginia (1980), Globe Newspaper Co. v. Superior Court (1982), Press-Enterprise v. Superior Court (1984), Press-Enterprise v. Superior Court (1986), Center for National Security Studies v. Department of Justice (2003)*
Cameras in the Courtroom *Chandler v. Florida (1981), Estes v. Texas (1965)*
Contempt and Interference with Court Proceedings *Bridges v. California (1941), Times-Mirror Co. v. Superior Court (1941).*
Fairness Doctrine, Right of Reply *Red Lion Broadcasting Co., Inc. v. Federal Communications Commission (1969), CBS v. Democratic National Committee (1973), Miami Herald Publishing Co. v. Tornillo (1974), Arkansas Educational Television v. Forbes (1998)*

70

The Law and the News Media

Investigative Reporting Techniques   *Food Lion v. ABC (1999)*
Libel   *Case of John Peter Zenger (1735), Near v. Minnesota (1931), New York Times v. Sullivan (1964), Curtis Publishing Co. v. Butts (1967), Associated Press v. Walker (1967), Rosenblum v. Metromedia (1971), Gertz v. Robert Welch (1974), Dun & Bradstreet v. Greenmoss Builders (1985), Herbert v. Lando (1979), Hutchinson v. Proxmire (1979),* Hustler *Magazine v. Falwell (1988), Milcovich v. Lorain Journal Co. et al. (1990)*
Media and Political Campaigns   *Miami Herald Publishing Co. v. Tornillo (1974), Buckley v. Valeo (1976), Arkansas Educational Television v. Forbes (1998)*
Minors and the First Amendment   *Hazelwood School District v. Kuhlmeier (1988)*
National Security, Sedition, etc.   *Schenck v. United States (1919), Yates v. United States, Gitlow v. New York, Whitney v. California, New York Times v. United States (1971), United States v. Progressive (1979), Center for National Security Studies v. Department of Justice (2003)*
Obscenity   *Miller v. California, Federal Communications Commission v. Pacifica Foundation (1978), Reno v. American Civil Liberties Union (1997), United States v. American Library Association (2003)*
Prior Restraint and Gag Orders   *Near v. Minnesota (1931), New York Times v. United States (1971), Nebraska Press Association v. Stuart (1976), United States v. Progressive (1979)*
Privacy   *Hanlon v. Berger (1998), Wilson v. Layne (1998), Bartnicki v. Vopper (2001)*
Protection of News Sources   *Branzburg v. Hayes (1972), Garland v. Torre (1958), Herbert v. Lando (1979), Cohen v. Cowles Media Co. (1991)*
Regulation and Taxing of Newspapers   *Grosjean v. American Press Co. (1936), Minneapolis Star and Tribune. v. Minnesota Commissioner of Revenue (1983), Giragi v. Moore (1937), Arkansas Writers' Project, Inc. v. Ragland (1987), Lovell v. City of Griffin, Georgia (1938), Miami Herald Publishing Co. v. Tornillo (1974)*
Regulation of Broadcasting   *National Broadcasting Co. v. United States (1943), Red Lion Broadcasting Co., Inc. v. Federal Communications Commission (1969), CBS v. Democratic National Committee (1973), Federal Communications Commission v. Pacifica Foundation (1978), Los Angeles v. Preferred Communications (1986), Turner Broadcasting v. Federal Communications Commission (1994)*
Regulation of the Internet   *Reno v. American Civil Liberties Union (1997), United States v. American Library Association (2003)*

Power of the News Media

CASE OF JOHN PETER ZENGER (1735)

Background

William Cosby arrived in New York to become its new royally appointed governor. Shortly after taking office, Cosby abruptly dismissed the colony's chief justice, Lewis Morris. James Alexander and other political allies of Morris started a newspaper called the *New-York Weekly* mainly as a vehicle for opposition to the governor. The paper published a satirical article ridiculing the governor. The governor demanded legal action, but the grand jury refused to indict John Peter Zenger, who had actually printed the paper. Nevertheless, Cosby had the sheriff arrest and jail Zenger to await trial for libel before the new chief justice, James DeLancey.

Legal Issues

At the time libel could be treated as either a criminal or a civil offense. The law allowed for conviction for defamatory statements whether they were true or not. Nevertheless Zenger's lawyer, Andrew Hamilton, while admitting that Zenger had printed the article in question, demanded that he be allowed to prove that the allegations about Cosby were true—and that if they were true, Zenger should be acquitted. Speaking more to the jury than to the judge, Hamilton made what was more a political and philosophical argument than a legal one:

> *Every man who prefers freedom to a life of slavery will bless and honor you as men who have baffled the attempt at tyranny; and by an impartial and uncorrupt verdict, have laid a noble foundation for securing to ourselves, our posterity, and our neighbors that to which nature and the laws of our country have given us a right—the liberty—both of exposing and opposing arbitrary power . . . by speaking and writing truth.*

Decision

Despite the judge's attempts to coerce the jury to convict Zenger, he was acquitted to the cheers of the courtroom audience.

Impact

The Zenger case did not at once rewrite the law of libel and defamation. It did express the growing sentiment in the British colonies in America that there were inherent rights, such as freedom of the press, that could be asserted even in the face of the existing legal and political apparatus. Further, the Zenger case is cited as one of the earliest examples of the controversial principle of jury nullification—that juries were not only the judge of fact, but also the ultimate judge of whether the legally required result was in keeping with the conscience of the community.

SCHENCK V. UNITED STATES, 249 U.S. 47 (1919)

Background

The Socialist Party, of which Charles Schenck was secretary, printed and mailed to prospective draftees a pamphlet declaring that government officials were violating the Constitution by not allowing opposition to the military draft, which the pamphlet asserted violated the Thirteenth Amendment prohibition against slavery. The pamphlet's readers were also urged to make their opposition to the draft known. Schenck was arrested under the 1917 Espionage Act, which made it illegal to interfere with or obstruct the operation of the draft.

Legal Issues

The basic question was whether national security and Congress's right to implement its war-making power could allow the prohibition of expression otherwise permitted by the First Amendment.

Decision

The unanimous court opinion by Justice Oliver Wendell Holmes upheld Schenck's conviction. It did so because Holmes believed that Schenck's pamphlet constituted a "clear and present danger" to national security in wartime, although the same writing might be protected by the Constitution "in ordinary times."

Impact

The real significance of the case is that it enshrined the "clear and present danger" test for government restraint of speech or writing. In coming decades the Court would become increasingly reluctant to find that this test had been met, particularly in peacetime. By *Yates v. United States*, 354 U.S. 298 (1957), the Court would insist that "clear and present danger" must mean actual or imminent physical danger, not advocacy or a mere threat, no matter how worrisome. On the other hand, the post-2001 "war on terror" would bring the distinction between wartime and peacetime back into question.

NEAR V. MINNESOTA,
283 U.S. 697 (1931)

Background

A pervasive issue in First Amendment jurisprudence is under what conditions the government can prevent publication of information deemed to endanger some overriding governmental interest. This is called "prior restraint." Jay M. Near copublished a newspaper called the *Saturday Press* that focused on what it saw as racketeering and corruption in city government. The paper was also virulently racist and xenophobic. For example, it accused the mayor of Minneapolis, the chief of police, and the grand jury of ignoring the criminal activities of "Jewish gangsters" in the city. The county attorney had the newspaper declared to be a "public nuisance" under a 1925 state law (commonly called the "Gag Law") prohibiting the publication of a "malicious, scandalous, and defamatory newspaper." The county court ordered the paper to cease publication until its publishers could demonstrate that they would avoid their offensive behavior in the future.

Legal Issues

The newspaper's attorney argued that the court's action violated the due process clause of the Fourteenth Amendment and that restraining further publication also violated the Constitution.

Decision

The Court's opinion, written by Chief Justice Charles Evans Hughes, agreed with the defense that by violating a fundamental constitutional right (freedom of the press), the lower court's action also violated the due process guaranteed by the Fourteenth Amendment. Further, Chief Justice Hughes noted that the Minnesota law had the effect of controlling whether a publication could publish, allowing what amounted to state censorship. This is incompatible with the right of freedom of the press in the First Amendment. Chief Justice Hughes noted that "the fact that the liberty of the press might be abused does not make any less necessary the immunity of the press from previous restraint in dealing with official misconduct."

Impact

This case firmly established the principle that prior restraint is not generally permitted by the First Amendment. A person can be held responsible after the fact for what is published (such as through libel law), but not prevented from publishing in the first place. Further, this case also signaled that the First Amendment's guarantees were to be included (incorporated) in the Fourteenth Amendment, thus making them applicable to state and local governments as well as to Congress. This incorporation doctrine would become a powerful force for expanding civil rights and liberties.

GROSJEAN V. AMERICAN PRESS CO., 297 U.S. 233 (1936)

Background

The State of Louisiana imposed a license fee of 2 percent on the receipts of newspapers that sold advertising and had a circulation of 20,000 copies per week or more. A group of nine publishers, including the American Press Company, sued to overturn the tax.

Legal Issues

The publisher argued that taxing the advertising revenue amounted to an infringement of freedom of the press as guaranteed by the First Amendment. Further, it violated equal protection under the Fourteenth Amendment by treating a relative few large newspapers differently from the numerous smaller newspapers that were not subject to the tax.

Decision

The Court reiterated that newspaper publishing was an activity fundamentally protected by the Constitution and pointed out that while corporations were not citizens, they were legal persons entitled to due process and equal protection under the Fourteenth Amendment. Further, by reducing revenue and by kicking in only when the newspaper reached a certain level of circulation, the fee served to limit or inhibit the activity of publishing information considered vital to the democratic process. This activity was analogous to the licensing used by the British crown to control the operation of the press in the American colonies. The framers of the First Amendment sought to ensure that this would never happen again.

Impact

The rule resulting from this case is that certain newspapers cannot be singled out for burdensome treatment by government. Similarly, in *Minneapolis Star and Tribune v. Minnesota Commissioner of Revenue* (1983) the Court ruled that a tax (on paper and ink supplies in this case) cannot be applied to the press and not to other businesses. In *Arkansas Writers' Project, Inc. v.*

Ragland (1987) the Court overturned a city tax that was imposed on "general interest" magazines but not newspapers or "religious, professional, trade, and sports journals." However, as shown in dismissing the claim in *Giragi v. Moore* (1937), nondiscriminatory taxes that applied to businesses in general could also be applied to the press.

The use of unduly burdensome licensing requirements for distributing literature has also been held to be unconstitutional, as in *Lovell v. City of Griffin, Georgia* (1938). Although that case was brought by a group of Jehovah's Witnesses, the principle also applies to cities regulating the distribution of newspapers. Thus some regulation on the placement of news racks may be permissible, but not if it substantially interferes with public access to the publication.

BRIDGES V. CALIFORNIA, 314 U.S. 252 (1941)

Background

Labor activist Harry Bridges sent a telegram to the U.S. Secretary of Commerce threatening a strike if a judge's "outrageous" decision in a labor dispute were enforced. A local newspaper published Bridge's comments while the court case was still pending. In a similar case (*Times-Mirror Co. v. Superior Court* [1941]) that the Supreme Court combined with this one, the *Los Angeles Times* published a series of editorials demanding tough sentencing of two union members convicted of assault, saying that the judge would be committing a "serious mistake" if he granted probation. Again, the comments were published while the court determination was pending.

Legal Issues

In both cases the courts used their contempt power to punish the newspaper for interfering with the "orderly administration of justice." The lower courts (and, in the Bridges case, the California Supreme Court) upheld the action against the newspapers, saying that writings had the "inherent" or at least "reasonable" tendency to interfere with the justice system. On appeal to the U.S. Supreme Court, the state argued that its interest in protecting its system of justice from disruption justified preventing the publication of threats designed to influence or obstruct the operation of that system.

Decision

The Supreme Court's opinion, written by Justice Hugo Black, noted that first of all, there was little reason to suppose that criticism from a newspaper would truly coerce the judge in making a sentencing decision. Besides, both sides agreed that the newspaper would certainly be allowed under the First Amendment to make similar comments after the court had made its ruling. Even in the case of Bridges, who the Court acknowledged was a powerful labor leader, the threat of a strike in the future (that might be expected to be violent or disruptive) was not sufficiently a "clear and present danger." "What finally emerges from the 'clear and present danger' cases," Justice Black noted, "is a working principle that the substantive evil must be extremely serious and the degree of imminence extremely high before utterances can be punished." Therefore the Court overturned the contempt citations in both cases.

Impact

Courts were generally not going to be allowed to use their contempt power to suppress or punish publications even when powerful interests sought to influence the outcome of a trial or sentencing. If judges felt such pressures (especially if they held an elective position), it was up to them to maintain the integrity of the system. They could not muzzle the free press just because its criticism made their job more difficult.

NATIONAL BROADCASTING CO. V. UNITED STATES, 319 U.S. 190 (1943)

Background

"Radio Chains" was a term used in the 1930s and 1940s for groups of radio stations linked together receiving programs from a central source—that is, networks such as the National Broadcasting Company (NBC) and its competitors American Broadcasting Company (ABC) and the Mutual Broadcasting System. After conducting a hearing in 1938 and responding to requests for amendment from various parties, the FCC enacted what became known as the Chain Broadcasting Regulations. These regulations used the government's power to control broadcasting licenses to prevent overconcentration of control of radio broadcasting in the hands of one or a few powerful networks. One provision, for example, said that no broadcasting license would be given to a station that signed an agreement to carry the programming of a particular network exclusively. Other regulations modified contractual arrangements that had given networks exclusive claims on certain broadcasting times. The FCC believed that since only individual stations, not networks, were licensed, it was the station that had the responsibility to seek the programming that best served the public interest.

According to the FCC, the general objective of the regulations was to preserve the positive features of networks (the ability to mobilize significant resources and to provide stability in programming) while minimizing features that reduced competition and choice for listeners.

NBC, the Mutual Broadcasting Service, and several other companies went to court to overturn the regulations. Their suit was denied by the district court, and the appeal went to the Supreme Court.

Legal Issues

The networks made two main arguments. The first was that the legislation establishing the FCC was not intended to allow the agency to interfere with the contractual relations between stations or networks, but simply to ensure orderly and adequate provision of broadcast services. The second was that even if the FCC had the powers it claimed, its implementation of them violated the free speech rights of the stations and networks under the First Amendment.

Decision

The Court ruled that the regulations were founded on proper legislative authority, properly delegated by Congress to the FCC. They also dismissed the First Amendment argument, noting that

> *Unlike other modes of expression, radio inherently is not available to all. That is its unique characteristic, and that is why, unlike other modes of expression, it is subject to governmental regulation. Because it cannot be used by all, some who wish to use it must be denied. But Congress did not authorize the Commission to choose among applicants upon the basis of their political, economic or social views, or upon any other capricious basis. . . . The question here is simply whether the Commission, by announcing that it will refuse licenses to persons who engage in specified network practices . . . is thereby denying such persons the constitutional right of free speech. The right of free speech does not include, however, the right to use the facilities of radio without a license.*

Impact

This decision accepted the basic rationale for regulation of broadcasting based on the medium's "scarcity"—the limited number of frequencies available. This is the key reason why limitations can be imposed on broadcasting that would not be acceptable for printed media under the First Amendment. However, technological developments later in the century, such as cable and satellite systems and the Internet, create areas in which the scarcity factor is diminished or no longer present.

NEW YORK TIMES V. SULLIVAN, 376 U.S. 254 (1964)

Background

The *New York Times* ran a full-page advertisement titled "Heed Their Rising Voices for the Committee to Defend Martin Luther King and the Struggle for Freedom in the South." It appealed for support for the ongoing antisegregation demonstrations in the South. The ad accused "Southern violators" of responding to peaceful demonstrations with violence and threats, including bombing Dr. Martin Luther King, Jr.'s home. Sullivan, an elected commissioner of the city of Montgomery, Alabama, who had oversight over police conduct, brought a libel suit, claiming that he had been defamed by the reference to "Southern violators."

Legal Issues

Both sides agreed that some minor items in the ad were factually incorrect. (For example, the "entire student body" of Alabama had not protested the expulsion of students demonstrating against segregation, although a majority had.)

Under the general law of libel, as instructed to the jury by the trial judge, that because of the false statements, the ad was "libel per se," and the jury could therefore assume that the ad was also malicious, thus entitling Sullivan to damages without proof that he had suffered a monetary loss. The jury accordingly returned an award of $500,000 against each of the defendants. The Alabama Supreme Court upheld the verdict.

Decision

In a unanimous opinion for the Supreme Court, Justice William J. Brennan overturned the libel verdicts. He said it was necessary to "consider this case against the background of a profound national commitment to the principle that debate on public issues should be uninhibited, robust, and wide-open, and that it may well include vehement, caustic, and sometimes unpleasantly sharp attacks on government and public officials." Americans, he said, had rejected the use of libel law (as in the Sedition Act of 1798) to punish criticism of government officials.

Allowing people who make statements about government officials only the traditional defense of truth is not sufficient because "erroneous statements are inevitable in free debate." Even false statements must "be protected if the freedoms of expression are to have the 'breathing space' that they 'need . . . to survive.'"

Because of the need to protect vital public debate, therefore, public officials cannot sue successfully for libel unless the statements in question are not just incidentally false, but involve actual malice, that is, "that the statement was made with . . . knowledge that it was false or with reckless disregard for whether it was false or not."

Impact

This decision essentially rewrote the rules for libel where government officials are concerned. It said that robust debate is so important to democracy that it cannot be inhibited by court wrangling over the accuracy of particular statements. Essentially, if someone is going to take on the responsibility of public office, he or she will have to accept vehement criticism, even some that might be actionable in a private context.

However, there are many other sorts of people who are the subject of news coverage because of public interest, including movie stars, athletes, and business tycoons. (Such people may not be public officials, but they are public figures.) In two 1967 cases, *Curtis Publishing Co. v. Butts* and *Associated Press v. Walker*, the Court went beyond the concern in *New York Times v. Sullivan* about preventing government officials from using libel laws to suppress political disagreement. Rather, it essentially said that public figures whose stock-in-trade is public activity must also allow criticism that falls short of actual malice.

CURTIS PUBLISHING CO. V. BUTTS, 388 U.S. 130 (1967)

Background

In *New York Times v. Sullivan,* the Supreme Court set a new, higher standard for a public official to prevail in a libel or defamation trial. Unlike ordinary private individuals, public officials would now have to show "actual malice" or knowing disregard for the truth. Three years later, two cases reached the Supreme Court in which the persons suing for libel were not public officials, but people who were in public life.

One of the plaintiffs, University of Georgia athletic director Wally Butts, sued the *Saturday Evening Post* for printing an article that alleged he had conspired to "fix" a football game. In the other case retired general Edwin Walker sued the Associated Press for stories in which he had been accused of participating in racial disturbances at the University of Mississippi. Both Butts and Walker prevailed in the lower courts, but the publications appealed and the Supreme Court took the cases, which would be combined under a single title.

Legal Issues

The key question is whether the "public official" category with its higher standard for proving libel should be extended to include "public figures"—people whose actions are under the scrutiny of the public (and of the media).

Decision

The Court ruled that public figures should also be required to meet the higher standard of proving actual malice. Applying that standard to the facts, the Court ruled that the *Saturday Evening Post* had shown reckless disregard by its lack of reasonable effort to check the factuality of the accusations before publishing them, and that verdict was upheld. In the Walker case, however, the Court ruled that the failure of the Associated Press to catch the factual errors was the result of deadline pressure and perhaps ordinary carelessness, but not actual malice, so the verdict was overturned.

Impact

The trend to give wider protection to the media from libel suits continued. In *Rosenblum v. Metromedia* (1971) the Court ruled that if a person's circumstances (such as being charged with the crime of obscenity) brings that person into the public spotlight, the actual malice standard should be applied, even if that person would not normally be considered a public figure. However, in *Gertz v. Robert Welch* (1974) the Court stepped back somewhat from that position, creating a more detailed set of criteria for determining whether someone was a public figure for libel purposes.

RED LION BROADCASTING CO., INC. V. FEDERAL COMMUNICATIONS COMMISSION, 395 U.S. 367 (1969)

Background

Under the FCC's Fairness Doctrine, individuals who are attacked in an editorial or other statement on a radio or television station must be provided the opportunity to air a reply. Fred Cook, the author of a book critical of

Arizona senator Barry Goldwater, was criticized in a broadcast statement by Rev. Billy James Hargis. The radio station WGCB refused to allow Cook to air a reply.

Legal Issues

With print media there is generally no "right of reply"—a Florida law requiring one would be declared unconstitutional in *Miami Herald Publishing Co. v. Tornillo* in 1974. The question was whether there was something in the nature of broadcasting itself that might require a different outcome here.

Decision

A unanimous Court did uphold the right of reply in the form of the FCC Fairness Doctrine. Observing that unlike the case with newspapers, only a relatively small number of radio stations were permitted to operate, due to interference considerations. Therefore, wrote Justice Byron White for the Court, it was "idle to posit an unbridgeable First Amendment right to broadcast comparable to the right of every individual to speak, write, or publish." Given the possibility that certain views may not be otherwise rebutted, it was the First Amendment rights of the listeners, not the broadcasters, that must prevail in this case.

Impact

The FCC's Fairness Doctrine was upheld, but the underlying rationale based on the scarcity of outlets has been steadily eroded by technological changes in the past 30 years. With hundreds of cable or satellite channels now accessible to viewers, not to mention Internet digital radio and satellite radio, it makes increasingly less sense to say that a right of reply must be offered because important views might otherwise not be heard. Indeed, as part of a deregulation trend during the Reagan administration, the FCC essentially abolished the Fairness Doctrine in 1987.

In *CBS v. Democratic National Committee* (1973) the Court ruled that broadcast stations could decide whether to carry advocacy or political ads. Having decided to carry them, however, the station must sell time to those having opposing views.

However, the possibility that the peculiar technological conditions of a medium might still dictate different application of First Amendment principles remains and comes into play with cable television and especially the Internet.

The Law and the News Media

NEW YORK TIMES V. UNITED STATES, 403 U.S. 713 (1971)

Background

On June 13, 1971, the *New York Times* published the first installment of the so-called Pentagon Papers, a voluminous classified report inquiring into the involvement of the United States in the Vietnam War. The report suggested numerous ways in which misleading information and other forms of deception were used to convince Congress and the American people to support the war. The documents had been leaked by Daniel Ellsberg, a Pentagon bureaucrat who had become a war dissenter. Other newspapers soon began to publish the material as well.

After a period of indecision, the Nixon administration decided that continued publication of the Pentagon Papers called its current policies into question and threatened its ability to keep information secret. On June 15 the administration received an order from a lower court restraining further publication, and a higher appeals court continued to block publication, pending an expedited appeal to the Supreme Court, which heard the case only a few days later.

Legal Issues

The basic issue was whether prior restraint of publication was justified by the need to protect classified information presumably vital to national security. The government further argued that releasing the information could endanger U.S. prisoners held by the North Vietnamese and disrupt delicate ongoing peace negotiations. This argument appealed to the considerable deference normally given by the Court both to national security and to the executive's need to carry out foreign policy. However, weighing on the other side were powerful precedents (such as *Near v. Minnesota*) that rejected prior restraint in most cases, unless an immediate and substantial danger to a government interest would result from publication.

Decision

The Court did not agree with the government's arguments, and by a 6-3 vote refused to make permanent the restraining order against publication of the Pentagon Papers. The Court, however, split several ways. Three justices, Hugo Black, William Brennan, and William O. Douglas, believed that the government had not met the extreme burden required for prior restraint, and the publication should not have been blocked in the first place. There was no immediate, credible danger in continuing to publish the

83

material. Absent that, the First Amendment simply did not allow the government to "halt the publication of current news of vital importance to the people of this country." Justice Potter Stewart also agreed that prior restraint was not justified in this case, but he did not want to say that it would never be. The remaining justices in the majority believed the government had not made a case for a permanent injunction.

In dissent, Chief Justice Warren Burger and Justices Harry Blackmun and John M. Harlan believed that the injunction might be justified and that the Court should have taken more time to consider it. In his opinion, Burger noted that even if prior restraint was not justified, publishers should be liable after the fact for printing classified information.

Impact

The decision further emphasized the extreme reluctance of the Court to indulge in prior restraint. The media could be fairly confident that if it obtained classified information it could publish it without being blocked ahead of time. However, such an act is not without consequences. Ellsberg was tried for his role in leaking the information, although he was acquitted when the government's own illegal activity (such as wiretapping the office of his psychiatrist) toward him came to light. Even for the media, the decision would generally be not to publish certain kinds of classified information (such as information that might endanger U.S. agents or informers abroad). Information like the Pentagon Papers that was classified but was mainly a political danger to the administration itself would be another matter.

BRANZBURG V. HAYES, 408 U.S. 665 (1972)

Background

Paul Branzburg, a reporter for the *Louisville Courier-Journal*, was subpoenaed by a Kentucky grand jury to provide more information about illegal-drug producers and users he had interviewed for an investigative report. He refused the summons because his testimony might compromise sources to whom he had promised confidentiality. In two other cases eventually combined with Branzburg's, television reporter Paul Pappas had refused a Massachusetts grand jury's summons to testify about his reports on the Black Panthers, and a *New York Times* reporter, Earl Caldwell, similarly refused to provide a grand jury with information about the Panthers. All three reporters were cited for contempt and appealed their cases.

The Law and the News Media

Legal Issues

There is a duty of all citizens to testify when summoned by a grand jury (unless they assert their Fifth Amendment privilege against self-incrimination). Most journalists believe that the ability to keep potentially identifying information about sources confidential is essential if they are to have access to the kinds of sources needed for reporting some of the most critical news stories in our society. Does the First Amendment trump the grand jury in such cases?

Decision

The Supreme Court, in an opinion written by Justice Byron White, ruled that the First Amendment did not confer on journalists a special privilege to withhold testimony from the grand jury. The interest of the grand jury was "compelling" and "paramount," and in these cases the state was neither exercising prior restraint against publication nor specifically demanding the identification of sources.

However, the opinion was sharply divided. Although concurring with the majority, Justice Lewis Powell noted that journalists should have some recourse against ill-founded "fishing expeditions":

> *if the newsman is called upon to give information bearing only a remote and tenuous relationship to the subject of the investigation, or if he has some other reason to believe that his testimony implicates confidential source relationships without a legitimate need of law enforcement, he will have access to the court on a motion to quash [the subpoena].*

Dissenting Justice Potter Stewart, apparently having had a change of heart since his earlier opinion in *Garland v. Torre* (1958), wrote an opinion, joined by Justices William Brennan and Thurgood Marshall, warning that the majority, by not protecting reporters' sources, would encourage government authorities to "annex the journalistic profession as an investigative arm of the government." Stewart insisted that protecting confidential sources was necessary to "a full and free flow of information to the public."

Justice William O. Douglas, in a separate dissent, went the farthest of all, insisting that the absolute language of the First Amendment required that the "journalist's privilege" to withhold sources should likewise be absolute: "It is my view that there is no 'compelling need' that can be shown which qualifies the reporter's immunity from appearing or testifying before a grand jury, unless the reporter himself is implicated in a crime."

Impact

Although the Court did not find that the Constitution required protecting reporters' sources from a judicial proceeding, the Court left open the possibility that Congress or state legislatures could pass a "shield law." Many (but not all) states now have such laws, but no federal shield law has been passed.

GERTZ V. ROBERT WELCH, 418 U.S. 323 (1974)

Background

Robert Welch, head of the anticommunist John Birch Society and editor of its magazine *American Opinion*, wrote an article about Elmer Gertz, an attorney who was suing a police officer who had killed his client's son. In the article Welch accused Gertz of having framed a person for murder. He also said that Gertz had a criminal record and that he was a "Leninist" and a "Communist-Fronter" as shown by his suing a law enforcement officer. Gertz sued Welch for defamation.

Legal Issues

While some of Welch's statements about Gertz might have been a matter of opinion, others, such as the one about Gertz's supposed criminal record, were definitely false. However, the Supreme Court had determined a number of circumstances in which simple falsity was not sufficient grounds for proving libel. In 1964 the Supreme Court had ruled in *New York Times v. Sullivan* that public officials could not successfully sue for libel or defamation simply because statements printed about them were false. Actual malice on the part of the writer would also have to be shown. This meant that the writer knows that the statements are false, but does not care. In *Curtis Publishing v. Butts* (1967) this higher hurdle for proving libel was extended to "public figures" whose actions would be presumed to be of public interest. Following these precedents, the lower court ruled in Welch's favor.

However, the question was whether Gertz was truly a "public figure." If so, Welch would not be guilty of defamation unless he had also shown actual malice.

Decision

The Court ruled that Gertz, although an attorney and thus involved with the justice system, was not a public official in the same way that an elected commissioner, for example, would be. He was also not a "public figure"—

such as a movie star who sought and relied on public attention. The mere fact that an attorney takes a case that is of public interest does not make the attorney automatically a public figure. Therefore, Gertz could apply the ordinary standards of defamation to Welch's accusations and thus could collect damages, which he did upon retrial.

Impact

This decision helped define what constituted a public official or figure for purposes of determining the standard for proving libel. Persons who voluntarily thrust themselves into the public spotlight could be considered "limited public figures" and held to the higher standard, but only with regard to such public activities.

The Court left it up to the individual states to set the standard for libel involving private persons. They could set it as low as showing negligence (as had been done traditionally) or they could raise it as high as the actual malice required with public officials or figures.

In terms of setting damages, the actual loss would have to be proven except where there is a showing of actual malice. Punitive damages can be awarded only if there is a showing of reckless disregard for the truth.

Another question that remained was whether there was a different standard when the defendant in a case of libel is a media outlet or some private information service. In *Dun & Bradstreet v. Greenmoss Builders* (1985) the business rating service was sued for falsely reporting that Greenmoss had filed for bankruptcy. In that case the Court did say that there was no distinction between media and private information services but went on to make a distinction between publications on "matters of public concern" and information privately provided, such as to Dun & Bradstreet's clients. In the latter case it was held that the First Amendment interests in promoting and protecting public discourse did not apply, so the lower standard applied to private plaintiffs could be used.

MIAMI HERALD PUBLISHING CO. V. TORNILLO, 418 U.S. 241 (1974)

Background

The *Miami Herald* printed editorials that criticized Pat Tornillo, a candidate for the Florida House of Representatives. Florida had a "right of reply" statute, so Tornillo demanded that the *Herald* print his rebuttal to the editorials. The newspaper refused, and Tornillo sued. A circuit court declared the statute unconstitutional, but the Florida Supreme Court reversed that decision, upholding the right to reply law as furthering "the broad societal appeal in the free flow of information to the public." Tornillo then appealed to the U.S. Supreme Court.

Legal Issues

This case pits two aspects of free expression against each other. On the one hand is the provision of more information (both editorials and rebuttals) to the public. On the other hand is a newspaper's right to decide what to print.

Decision

The Court declared that the Florida "right of reply" statute violated the First Amendment. Justice Warren Burger declared, "The choice of material to go into a newspaper, and the decisions made as to limitations on the size and content of the paper and treatment of pubic issues and public officials—whether fair or unfair—constitute the exercise of editorial control and judgment."

Impact

The Court apparently believes that the goal of assuring a robust public debate with diverse views is to be reached not by forcing newspapers to include opposing views but leaving papers free to exercise their judgment and compete to offer their views in the marketplace of ideas. Just as restraining content in newspapers is almost never justified, neither is forcing papers to print certain material. Note, however, that broadcast media are treated differently because of the physical scarcity of available outlets (see *Red Lion Broadcasting Co. v. Federal Communications Commission*).

NEBRASKA PRESS ASSOCIATION V. STUART, 427 U.S. 539 (1976)

Background

In a case involving the vicious murder of six members of a family, the trial court prohibited the press from publishing the defendant's confession to the crime as well as a note he had written on the night of the murders and evidence that had been raised in preliminary hearings. The court order was sustained in revised form by the Nebraska Supreme Court. The press association appealed to the U.S. Supreme Court.

Legal Issues

The trial court argued that with extensive pretrial publicity and given the horrible nature of the crime (including accusations of necrophilia), the defendant was in great danger of not being afforded his Sixth Amendment right to a fair trial. Restraining further publication of statements and rumors by the press or by broadcasters was the only way to ensure that the defendant could have a jury that was able to make a fair decision. The press association argued that freedom of the press must take precedence.

Decision

In an opinion delivered by Chief Justice Warren L. Burger, the Supreme Court noted that neither the trial court nor the Nebraska Supreme Court had considered actions short of prior restraint that might have protected the rights of the accused. Further, given the widespread publicity and the limited ability to stop the flow of information, it was far from clear that gagging the press would have significantly improved the situation. Further, the press always had the right to report on evidence presented in open court. Finally, the Court applied the "clear and present danger" test. It concluded that only in the most extraordinary cases might publication so directly interfere with a fair trial that it might be restrained.

Impact

This case is an important milestone in the ongoing conflict between two important rights: freedom of the press and the right to a fair trial. Generally, speculative or indirect considerations about the harmfulness of pretrial publicity will not be allowed to justify muzzling the press coverage.

FEDERAL COMMUNICATIONS COMMISSION V. PACIFICA FOUNDATION, 438 U.S. 726 (1978)

Background

One afternoon a New York station belonging to Pacifica, a left-wing radio network, broadcast comedian George Carlin's monologue "Filthy Words." Carlin's piece included seven words that have generally been forbidden to be aired in broadcasts. Pacifica did air a warning about sensitive language before the broadcast, but a man filed a complaint with the FCC, saying he had heard the monologue on his car radio while driving with his young son. The FCC decided that the language used in the broadcast was "patently offensive" if not necessarily obscene. It told the station that a notation would be made in its record (an action which might potentially affect the next renewal of its broadcasting license). An appeals court overruled the FCC with the three judges giving varying reasons, including that the rule was overbroad or amounted to censorship.

Legal Issues

The question is whether the First Amendment prevents the government from restricting the language that can be used in broadcasts—and whether the standards for broadcasts can be more restrictive than those for printed matter. The FCC argued that it should at least have the right to regulate the broadcast of objectionable language dealing with matters of sex or excrement during times when children are likely to be listening.

Decision

The Court reversed the appeals court and upheld the FCC. In his opinion, Justice John Paul Stevens noted that broadcasting was more "pervasive" than printed matter, since broadcasts permeate the air and can be received in various times and places, making it easy for children to be exposed to them. Therefore, while offensive (but not obscene) material could not be totally banned from the air, the government could place restrictions, such as requiring that it be broadcast late at night when children are unlikely to be listening.

Impact

This is another case that has been overtaken by technology. Most radio stations do not deliberately broadcast the seven "dirty words," except perhaps as embedded in certain genres of popular music. However, the presence of massive amounts of offensive or obscene material on the Internet, a medium available 24 hours a day almost anywhere, has led to reopening the question of how to protect children while allowing a full range of expression to be open to adults.

HOUCHINS V. KQED, INC., 438 U.S. 1 (1978)

Background

Following the suicide of a prisoner in the Alameda County, California, jail at Santa Rita, a public broadcasting service, KQED, sought access for its reporters and photographers to visit the jail as part of their investigation of the story. When their request was denied, KQED sued the authorities.

Legal Issues

Does the media, in the interests of a free press, have the right to demand access to government facilities beyond that given to the general public?

Decision

The Court, in a divided decision, ruled that while the public certainly has an important interest in reporting on jail conditions, the First Amendment does not require that the media be given special access to government facilities such as prisons or be allowed to take pictures there. In his opinion, Chief Justice Warren Burger also suggested that there were many cases in which the government was not obligated to provide access or information to the media. The dissenting justice Potter Stewart agreed that the press had no absolute right to access, but the press could be shown to warrant reasonable access beyond that given to the general public.

Impact

This decision suggests that the media must rely mainly on the Freedom of Information Act (and perhaps on public opinion) to pry loose information that the government does not want to reveal.

UNITED STATES V. PROGRESSIVE, 467 F. SUPP. 990 (1979)

Background

Federal officials discovered that *Progressive* magazine was about to publish an article that provided details about one of the most closely guarded national secrets—how to build a hydrogen bomb. At the time, only a handful of nations had this information. The government asked a federal district court to issue an injunction forbidding publication of the article.

Legal Issues

Since *Near v. Minnesota* (1931), the Supreme Court has generally rejected prior restraint—ordering that something not be published. Indeed, in 1971 the Court refused to prohibit continued publication of the Pentagon Papers even though the government argued that to do so would undermine national security and negotiations with North Vietnam. At that time the Court said that the mere fact that something was classified did not substitute for a showing of "immediate, direct, and irreparable harm." However, the possibility that information on building the world's most destructive weapon might become available to potentially unfriendly nations might constitute a compelling government interest warranting the extreme remedy of prior restraint.

Decision

The district judge, provided with extensive information (including testimony from distinguished nuclear scientists such as physicist Hans Bethe), concluded that publishing the bomb information would create a danger great enough to satisfy the Pentagon Papers standard—it "could pave the way for thermonuclear annihilation for us all." He issued an injunction barring publication of the article. However, as the *Progressive* and its supporters filed their appeal, the information was published by another periodical, making the matter moot.

Impact

Because the Supreme Court never decided this case, there is no answer to the question of how much danger might constitute a justification for prior restraint. It is possible that if a publication obtains information relating to terrorist devices or plans and the government moves to restrain its publication, the prior restraint might be sustained in the current atmosphere of heightened deference to national security.

RICHMOND NEWSPAPERS, INC. V. VIRGINIA, 448 U.S. 555 (1980)

Background

A defendant was undergoing his fourth trial for murder. The first trial had been overturned on technical grounds, while the next two had been declared mistrials. To try to avoid prejudicial pretrial publicity that might result in another mistrial, the trial judge granted the defendant's motion to exclude the press. The judge also relied on a Virginia statute that said he could remove anyone whose presence "would impair the conduct of a fair trial." The Richmond Newspapers group sued to force the judge to allow reporters to be present at the trial.

Legal Issues

This case squarely pits the interest in avoiding excessive and prejudicial publicity and providing a fair trial to the defendant (as required by the Sixth Amendment) with the First Amendment and public interest in access to judicial proceedings.

Decision

The Supreme Court, by a 7-1 vote, ruled that the trial should not have been closed. However, the majority was made up of a number of somewhat conflicting opinions. Writing for the Court, Chief Justice Warren Burger, said that there was a strong presumption in U.S. judicial history that trials should be open and accessible to the public, including the media. While there might be exceptional circumstances warranting the closure of a trial, the judge would have had to consider less drastic alternatives for protecting the defendant's interests, and would also have had to show that the risk of an unfair trial was so great as to justify setting aside the presumption of public access. Since the trial judge had done neither, the order closing the trial had to be overturned. Justices Byron White and John Paul Stevens concurred in the decision, but urged that the Court accept a broader constitutional principle requiring free access to judicial proceedings. Meanwhile, justices William Brennan and Thurgood Marshall developed a different constitutional theory. They looked to balance the rights of fair trial and public access, suggesting that the decision should be based on the purpose of a particular judicial proceeding and whether similar proceedings had been open in the past.

Impact

This decision left competing theories justifying upholding public access based on the First and Sixth Amendments, with the latter broadened to give consideration to public interest as well as that of the defendant. A number of questions were also left open. What kinds of proceedings must be open—were pretrial proceedings and civil trials included, or only criminal trials? Might quasi-judicial proceedings (such as regulatory hearings) also be included? Are there special circumstances in which proceedings might be closed?

In subsequent years the right of public access was extended to some types of proceedings and circumstances but not to others. In *Globe Newspaper Co. v. Superior Court* (1982) the Court declared unconstitutional a Massachusetts statute that required that trials be closed during testimony of minors who were victims of sexual abuse. The testimony could be closed only if there were a specific showing of likelihood of substantial harm to the witness. In *Press-Enterprise v. Superior Court* (1984) the Court ruled that voir dire (jury selection) proceedings must be open. In the unrelated case *Press-Enterprise v. Superior Court* (1986) the Court ruled that the public must have access to preliminary hearings unless the government can show a "substantial probability" that the defendant's right to a fair trial would be compromised, and that no less drastic action would be sufficient to safeguard that right.

While the question of whether civil trials can be closed to the public has not been specifically addressed by the Court, the general trend (with one exception) is to favor public and media access and to set a high threshold for courts to justify closing particular proceedings. The exception is secret proceedings called for under recent antiterrorism legislation, where the great deference courts give to the executive branch and to national security interests may make it less likely that the Court will insist on opening such proceedings or even providing basic information about detainees (as in the federal appeals case *Center for National Security Studies v. Department of Justice*, 2003).

CHANDLER V. FLORIDA, 449 U.S. 560 (1981)

Background

Florida had a pilot program allowing the media to use video cameras in the courtroom. Two police officers who had been charged with burglary objected to the broadcast of the video of their trial.

Legal Issues

The issue is whether the video camera and subsequent television coverage interfere with the defendants' right to a fair trial. Critics of bringing the television camera into the courtroom have argued that it may, particularly in sensational cases, change the way lawyers and witnesses behave and at any rate create a distraction.

In *Estes v. Texas* (1965) the Supreme Court had narrowly decided that the presence of television cameras had been distracting and had thus deprived Estes of a fair trial. However, one of the justices in the majority, John Marshall Harlan, had suggested that changes in technology or procedures might allow future televised trials to be fair. By the 1980s, with video cameras replacing bulky older camera equipment and glaring lights, many people were suggesting that television should be allowed into the courtroom. Given the central importance of this medium for conveying news in the modern world, an argument could be made that the public's First Amendment interest in judicial proceedings might allow courts to proceed at their own discretion.

Decision

Chief Justice Warren Burger took up the idea that with changing technology, allowing television cameras in the courtroom did not mean that trials would be unfair per se. Florida had imposed strict guidelines, including protecting the privacy of certain witnesses and giving the defendant the opportunity to argue against coverage in a particular case. The Court accepted these developments as reassuring and said that states were free to allow the cameras into the courtroom. By the end of the century 47 states (all but

New York, Mississippi and South Dakota) allowed courtroom video, with varying restrictions and guidelines.

Impact

Television has become so pervasive in modern culture that it is fair to say that the presumption today is that it should have access to all public proceedings. Thanks to C-SPAN, for example, the debates on the floor of Congress are available in all their dubious glory.

HAZELWOOD SCHOOL DISTRICT V. KUHLMEIER, 484 U.S. 260 (1988)

Background

Hazelwood East High School had a school-sponsored newspaper called *Spectrum* that was written and edited by students. Robert E. Reynolds, the school principal, reviewed the page proofs before publication. He found that two articles in a pending issue were objectionable. One article dealt with the experiences of pregnant students at the school; the other dealt with the impact of divorce on students at the school. Although the article on pregnant students did not reveal their names, he was concerned that the details might be sufficient for other students to identify them. He was also concerned that details about sexual activity and birth control were inappropriate for the younger students who read the paper. He therefore removed the articles from the proofs. Because there were only three days before the printing deadline, he simply had the paper printed without the pages containing the offending articles.

The student journalists sued in a federal district court, claiming that their First Amendment rights had been violated by the school's actions.

Legal Issues

If a school newspaper is equivalent to other newspapers, censorship (prior restraint of publication) would generally be presumed to violate the First Amendment. The question is whether the nature of the school setting and the newspaper's function within the school affects the application of the First Amendment. Is a school newspaper a public forum or part of the educational program?

The district court found against the students, declaring that the newspaper was part of the school's educational function and that the principal's actions had a "reasonable and substantial basis." The Eighth Circuit Court of Appeals, however, found for the students, saying that because the school newspaper was not only part of the school's curriculum but "was intended to be and operated as a conduit for student viewpoint," it was a public forum subject to First Amendment protection. There was no showing of a substantial danger (such as legal liability) that could justify censoring the articles.

Decision

The Supreme Court by a 5-3 ruling overturned the circuit court's ruling. It said that schools could censor newspapers published under school sponsorship and supervision. A school newspaper is not a forum open to the general public, but, rather, part of the school's educational program. Thus Justice Byron White wrote that:

> *First Amendment rights of students in the public schools are not automatically coextensive with the rights of adults in other settings, and must be applied in light of the special characteristics of the school environment. A school need not tolerate student speech that is inconsistent with its basic educational mission, even though the government could not censor similar speech outside the school.*

As long as the school's actions in exercising supervision over the school newspaper are "reasonably related to legitimate pedagogical concerns," there is no violation of the First Amendment.

Impact

As with most civil liberties issues, the status and needs of children create special problems. Note that the Court did not find that students were without First Amendment rights but rather that the nature of schools justifies limits on rights in some cases.

MILKOVICH V. LORAIN JOURNAL CO., ET AL., 497 U.S. 1 (1990)

Background

In order to determine whether someone is guilty of libel, it is first necessary to identify facts as false. The jury or judge can then apply the appropriate additional standards, such as actual malice in the case of libel actions by public officials or figures. Although the distinction between opinions and facts is commonly stressed starting in grammar school, it is not always easy to tell whether a statement involves provable facts.

Sportswriter J. Theodore Diadiun wrote a column in which Michael Milkovich, a wrestling coach, was accused of lying about his involvement in a fight that broke out at a state collegiate wrestling tournament.

The Law and the News Media

Legal Issues

This case had already undergone extensive litigation. At this point, however, the Supreme Court had to consider the columnist's (and newspaper company's) defense that calling Milkovich a liar was simply a matter of opinion—and that as such there were no provably false facts and thus no libel.

Decision

In his 7-2 majority opinion, Chief Justice William Rehnquist noted that "First Amendment protection of free speech does not create a wholesale defamation exemption for anything that might be labeled an opinion." For example:

> *If a speaker says, "In my opinion John Jones is a liar," he implies a knowledge of facts which lead to the conclusion that Jones told an untruth. Even if the speaker states the facts upon which he bases his opinion, if those facts are either incorrect or incomplete, or if his assessment of them is erroneous, the statement may still imply a false assertion of fact. Simply couching such statements in terms of opinion does not dispel these implications; and the statement, "In my opinion Jones is a liar," can cause as much damage to reputation as the statement, "Jones is a liar."*

Thus if a statement, even if phrased as an opinion, implies some sort of factual basis, it is not exempt from being considered libelous. The Court did note that, as in Hustler *Magazine v. Falwell* (1988), a statement is not libelous if its imaginative or satirical nature is so obvious that no reasonable person would consider it to be an assertion of fact.

Impact

This decision tried to put a small check on the general trend toward making it difficult to prove libel. The media cannot escape potential liability simply by characterizing a piece as opinion rather than as factual reporting.

TURNER BROADCASTING V. FEDERAL COMMUNICATIONS COMMISSION, 512 U.S. 622 (1994)

Background

The 1992 Cable Television Consumer Protection and Competition Act required that cable television systems set aside a percentage of their channels for carrying local broadcasters. Turner, which wanted to be able to market more channels with its own content, sued to overturn the requirement.

Legal Issues

Turner Broadcasting argued that the requirement was content-based. Laws that treat expression differently according to its content are generally overturned on First Amendment grounds.

Decision

The Supreme Court found that the requirement was content-neutral. This meant that, following the standard established in *United States v. O'Brien*, only an "intermediate scrutiny" need be applied, in which the law will be upheld if it serves important governmental interests that are not related to the content of the expression. The Court remanded the case to the lower court to determine whether that test was met here. In *Turner Broadcasting System et al. v. Federal Communications Commission et al.* (1997) the Court accepted the lower court's conclusion that the test had been met. Preserving access of local broadcasters to a market increasingly dominated by large cable systems was an important government interest, and thus the regulation was upheld.

Impact

These cases demonstrated that courts recognize justifications other than spectrum scarcity for federal regulation of broadcasting. With regard to cable, an ongoing problem is the fact that there is only one cable system in most communities (although satellite dishes offer competition). At any rate there are many regulations that will be upheld by the courts if they are content-neutral and not unduly burdensome.

RENO V. AMERICAN CIVIL LIBERTIES UNION, 521 U.S. 844 (1997)

Background

By the mid-1990s the Internet was becoming a pervasive medium for information and entertainment. Responding to public concern about the large amounts of pornographic and other objectionable material available on the Web (and potentially accessible to children), Congress passed the Communications Decency Act of 1996 (CDA), an amendment to the Telecommunications Act of the same year. Among other things, this law made it a criminal act to use an online computer service to display "indecent" or "patently offensive" material to minors, or to entice minors into illegal sexual activity.

98

The CDA aroused vigorous opposition from many people in the online community. Thousands of web site authors staged a cyberspace protest by displaying their pages with a black background. The American Civil Liberties Union promptly filed suit to overturn the CDA, and numerous other groups such as the Electronic Frontier Foundation (EFF) joined the legal assault.

Legal Issues

A major issue with the CDA, as with other laws using such terms, is just what makes material "indecent" or "patently offensive." Further, given the nature of the Internet itself, there is no practical way to control whether a web site is being viewed by an adult (who has a First Amendment right to view such material) or a child. (Although commercial sites require users to pay with credit cards, which were generally only available to adults, noncommercial, educational and advocacy sites generally have no way to verify ages.) Given these obstacles to applying and complying with the law, the ACLU and other civil liberties groups argued that it violated the First Amendment rights of Internet users.

Decision

The district court judges took pains to familiarize themselves with the Internet and how it is used—something that cannot always be said in other cases. The court agreed that there was no effective way to verify age over the Internet and that the language relating to indecent or patently offensive material was unconstitutionally vague. The district court therefore held the CDA's language relating to distribution of such material to be unconstitutional, but not the language relating to sexual enticement or harassment of children.

The Supreme Court's opinion affirmed that of the lower court. The CDA does not adequately define the material that it would make illegal for distribution to children. Without such a definition, people running web sites involved with legitimate activities such as sex education or AIDS awareness would have no way of knowing whether they were running afoul of the law. The government also does not address how the CDA could be enforced without infringing on the First Amendment right of adults to access such material.

Impact

The overturning of the CDA has preserved a full range of First Amendment rights for adults using the Internet. Filtering programs (of varying accuracy) are available for controlling children's access to problematic material. In *United States v. American Library Association* (2003) the Court upheld a federal law requiring public libraries to install Internet filters as a condition for receiving federal funds.

ARKANSAS EDUCATIONAL TELEVISION V. FORBES, 523 U.S. 666 (1998)

Background

Arkansas Educational Television (AETC), a state-owned public broadcasting service, sponsored a debate between candidates for the Third Congressional District. They decided to limit participation in the debates to major party candidates or other candidates "who had strong popular support." Forbes, an independent candidate who had qualified to appear on the ballot, was not invited. Forbes challenged his exclusion on First Amendment grounds.

Although the district court dismissed his suit for failure to state a cause of action, the court of appeals overruled the lower court and ordered it to try the case. At trial, AETC staff members testified that Forbes had been excluded because he lacked a campaign organization, had little evidence of voter support, and was not regarded as a serious candidate by the media. The district court entered a judgment in favor of AETC, but again, the Eighth Circuit Court of Appeals reversed and found for Forbes. AETC then appealed and the case was heard by the U.S. Supreme Court.

Legal Issues

AETC was a publicly owned television outlet. The question was whether its status meant that it had to include all ballot-qualified candidates in debates in order to avoid violating the First Amendment. First Amendment jurisprudence had concluded that in a "public forum" such as a city park, if some speakers were allowed to use the forum, other speakers could not be excluded on the basis of the content of their speech. That is, speech could be regulated as to "time, place, and manner" but the regulation must be "viewpoint neutral." Forbes argued that AETC should similarly be treated as a public forum. AETC disagreed, saying that it, like other journalists, was entitled to use its judgment to decide what candidates or viewpoints should be presented.

Decision

The Court's opinion, written by Justice William Kennedy, began by determining whether the AETC candidate debate constituted a public forum. It noted that:

Having first arisen in the context of streets and parks, the [public forum] doctrine should not be extended in a mechanical way to the different context of television broadcasting. Broad rights of access for outside speakers would be antithetical, as a general rule, to the editorial discretion that broadcasters must exercise to fulfill their journalistic purpose and statutory obligations.

The Court acknowledged that candidate debates are of exceptional significance in the electoral process. Deliberation on candidates' positions and qualifications is integral to the U.S. system of government, and electoral speech may have its most profound and widespread impact when it is disseminated through televised debates. Thus, the special characteristics of candidate debates support the conclusion that the AETC debate was a forum of some type.

The Court concluded that the debate was not a "traditional public forum"—a place such as a park that had long been used as a place of public meetings and discussion. It was not a "designated public forum" where the government opens a venue for general discussion to a particular class of speakers. Rather, the debate was an event to which the station was inviting speakers who met certain qualifications. It was a "nonpublic forum." AETC was free to exercise its journalistic judgment about who to include in that forum. The record showed that AETC did not discriminate against Forbes because of his views but because they had concluded that he was not a viable candidate. The Court further noted that if all public broadcasters were open to claims of viewpoint discrimination, they would not be able to function, and courts would be endlessly involved with suits by people who felt they were unfairly excluded.

Justice John Paul Stevens dissented, saying that he did not agree that all candidates had to be invited to the debate, but that AETC had been arbitrary and had not applied coherent standards to its decision to exclude Forbes, who had shown evidence of popular support in other races.

Impact

This decision affirmed that despite the special treatment of broadcasting (due to limited outlets) the exercise of journalistic or editorial discretion did not in itself violate the First Amendment, as long as the discretion was viewpoint-neutral. However, since the range of political discourse is often determined by the issues raised by "viable" candidates, excluding candidates outside the mainstream as nonviable is likely to reduce the diversity of viewpoints available in the media.

HANLON V. BERGER, 97-1927
AND *WILSON V. LAYNE* 98-83 (1998)

Background

A reporter and photographer from the *Washington Post* accompanied police officers to a Maryland residence. The residents sued the police, claiming that their Fourth Amendment privacy rights had been violated—in part, by allowing the media to accompany the police into the house.

Legal Issues

There were two main issues relating to the police and media's actions. First, did the police violate the Fourth Amendment by allowing the media to accompany them into a private residence? Second, were the police nonetheless entitled to "qualified immunity" from being sued?

Decision

The Court ruled unanimously that the police had violated the residents' Fourth Amendment rights. Although having the media closely observe law enforcement activities does serve an important public purpose, this does not mean that the media has the right to accompany an invasion of a private home—something allowed only for strictly investigatory purposes upon a proper warrant. However, the Court also ruled, 8-1, that the police were entitled to "qualified immunity" because their actions had not been definitively ruled unconstitutional at the time.

Impact

This ruling has curbed many police-media "ride-alongs." So-called reality-TV shows featuring police must be careful to obscure identifying characteristics of suspects or obtain their permission before airing footage.

FOOD LION V. ABC, U.S. COURT OF APPEALS, 4TH CIRCUIT (1999)

Background

Two ABC reporters applied for jobs at a Food Lion supermarket, using fake résumés. Their intention was to conduct an undercover investigation of the market's food-handling practices. They used a hidden camera, footage from which was shown on ABC's *Prime Time Live*. The footage showed disturbing activities, including the disguising of unwholesome food.

Food Lion sued ABC as well as the reporters and the show's producers. However, the basis of their suit was not defamation but rather allegations that ABC and the reporters used fraudulent means to obtain employment, violated their "duty of loyalty" to the employer by secretly spying on their workplace, committed trespass, and engaged in unfair trade practices. Food Lion won its original case in the lower court, but ABC appealed.

Legal Issues

This case ultimately asks whether the media can be held accountable for otherwise proscribed activities (such as fraud) or violations of contract undertaken in the course of developing a story. Food Lion apparently elected not to try to prove that the story was defamatory, probably because it would have had difficulty proving the story false and malicious. However, Food Lion and other businesses would like to deter investigative techniques that they feel are intrusive and unfair.

The district court found that the reporters had committed fraud, breached their duty of loyalty, and violated a state law against unfair trade practices. However, the court also ruled that Food Lion could not recover for its damage claims (such as for lost business due to the unfavorable publicity) because the fraud used in getting the reporters into the store was not closely enough connected to the story itself and the resulting publicity. ABC appealed the other findings to the circuit court.

Decision

The circuit court found that Food Lion had not proven all the elements of its fraud claim—such as that hiring the reporters who had misrepresented their backgrounds had, independently of the television story, caused the company substantial damages. The court did agree that the reporter-employees had breached their duty to their employer by secretly working for another organization whose interests conflicted with Food Lion's and that they had committed trespass by entering under false pretenses.

The court threw out all but the token $2 damages the jury had assigned for those offenses. It did not allow Food Lion to collect damages for its loss of reputation or resulting loss of sales. To collect damages for the story itself, Food Lion would have had to meet the same standards as for defamation of public figures.

Impact

This case reaffirmed that journalists and the media are not immune to being held accountable for breaking the ordinary criminal and civil laws that govern other activities. Certain deceptive investigative techniques such as misrepresenting one's background or intent or using hidden cameras may have to be modified. The attempt to get around the strict standards for libel or defamation (and thus around the First Amendment protection for news stories) was rejected by the court.

BARTNICKI V. VOPPER, 532 U.S. 514 (2001)

Background

Frederick Vopper, a Pennsylvania radio broadcaster, aired an intercepted cell phone conversation between labor leaders during heated negotiations between a teachers' union and a local school board. The conversation included a suggestion that union members go to the homes of school board members and "blow off their porches." Vopper was prosecuted under a recently enacted federal law making it a crime to intercept or disseminate such phone conversations.

Legal Issues

This case pits the privacy interest in protecting personal communications from interception and disclosure against the freedom of the media to report information that comes to them that bears on important public issues.

Decision

Voting 6-3, the Court ruled that the federal law could not be used against the media. The decision noted the principle in *New York Times Co. v. United States* (1971) affirming "the right of the press to publish information of great public importance obtained from documents stolen by a third party."

Impact

This decision made the media breathe a little easier because it would not have to undertake a detailed investigation of material to make sure it did not arise from an illegal activity such as wiretapping. However, the Court's decision also affirmed the importance of protecting privacy, and there might be cases where the public interest in disclosing the material falls short of overcoming privacy rights.

CENTER FOR NATIONAL SECURITY STUDIES ET AL. V. U.S. DEPARTMENT OF JUSTICE (COURT OF APPEALS, DISTRICT OF COLUMBIA CIRCUIT, 2003)

Background

Following the terrorist attacks of September 11, 2001, hundreds of persons were detained for investigation and questioning in connection with terrorist activities; many were eventually released or deported. The federal government refused to release any information about the detainees for many months. In response a number of public interest groups filed a Freedom of Information Act (FOIA) request for information, including the detainees' names, the names of their attorneys, dates of arrest or release, location of arrest and detention, and reason for detention. The government rejected the request.

Subsequently a district court ordered that the names of the detainees and their attorneys be released, but said that the rest of the information could be withheld under FOIA Exemption 7(A), which exempts "records or information compiled for law enforcement purposes . . . to the extent that the production" of them "could reasonably be expected to interfere with enforcement proceedings." The case was then appealed to the circuit court of appeals for the District of Columbia.

Legal Issues

The Freedom of Information Act is premised on the principle that the public is entitled to most information reflecting the official activities of government and the courts. However, the FOIA provides for a number of exceptions, including information relating to national security or to a criminal investigation. The issue was whether the names and other information about the post–September 11 detainees was covered by the latter exception. Further, the government argued that identifying the detainees and the circumstances of their detention might provide terrorist groups with valuable information about the progress of the investigation, enabling them to piece together a "mosaic" from the information. Releasing the names might also allow terrorists to intimidate detainees from cooperating with the investigation, perhaps by threatening their families.

The groups seeking the information argued that such speculative concerns did not override the fundamental right of the public to know basic information that is available for virtually any other case of arrest or detention. The government, they argued, was seeking a blanket exemption without the kind of individualized showing required by the FOIA. The District Court agreed with the latter argument so far as the names of the detainees were concerned.

Decision

The circuit court of appeals's three-judge panel ruled that the government had properly used FOIA Exemption 7(A) to withhold the requested information. The court ruled that the names had been "compiled for law enforcement purposes" and deferred to the government's national security concerns as showing a "reasonable likelihood of interfering with the terrorism investigation." The court reiterated the magnitude of the terrorist threat and the traditional deference given under the U.S. system of separation of powers to the prerogatives of the executive branch in protecting national security. The court agreed with the government that releasing any of the requested information (including the names of attorneys) might well enable terrorist groups to piece together the rest.

One judge, David Tatel, strongly dissented, looking to the intent behind the FOIA and the need to thoroughly justify the withholding of information that would otherwise be public. Tatel wrote that the majority decision "eviscerates both FOIA itself and the principles of openness in government that FOIA embodies." He further said that "the court's approach drastically diminishes, if not eliminates, the judiciary's role in FOIA cases that implicate national-security interests. Congress certainly could have written FOIA that way, but chose instead to require meaningful judicial review of all government exemption claims."

Impact

In the wake of the September 11, 2001, attacks and the subsequent war on terrorism, courts have generally shown great deference to federal agencies. If the terrorist threat diminishes and the war on terrorism becomes further attenuated, it is possible that the pendulum may start to swing back toward asserting a more robust interpretation of the FOIA and the underlying principles of the First Amendment. However, in January 2004 the U.S. Supreme Court declined to hear an appeal of this case.

UNITED STATES V. AMERICAN LIBRARY ASSOCIATION, 02-361 (2003)

Background

Since 1996 Congress has passed a number of laws attempting to keep objectionable material on the Internet from reaching children. At first the laws targeted web site operators directly, but by restraining material that would be acceptable in printed form, they ran afoul of the First Amendment. The latest law, the Children's Internet Protection Act, passed in 2000, took a different approach: It required that libraries that wanted to receive federal funds use filtering software on their Internet terminals to block objectionable material.

Legal Issues

The Supreme Court has upheld the right of adults to have access to a very wide range of material, including material that many people would consider indecent or offensive, but not legally obscene. The basic question is whether the new medium of the Internet should be treated like printed matter or like broadcasting, for which the courts have accepted greater restrictions, as in *FCC v. Pacifica Foundation* (1978).

Librarians have argued that the use of filtering software would put them in the position of being censors and would deny adults access to the range of material they are entitled to under the First Amendment. Further, the software can often inadvertently block legitimate sites (including news media) that happen to use words that have been put on a blocking list. For this reason, in 2002 a federal appeals court panel overturned the blocking law. The federal government then appealed to the Supreme Court.

Proponents of the law argue that pornography is pervasive on the Internet, and libraries no more have an obligation to offer it than they do to fill their shelves with X-rated magazines and videos.

Decision

By a 6-3 vote the Court, in an opinion written by Chief Justice William Rehnquist, upheld the Children's Internet Protection Act, requiring the use of blocking software. Four of the justices on the majority accepted the blocking unconditionally, while two justices concurred but said that adult library patrons should have the right to have the software turned off on request.

The dissent, written by Justice John Paul Stevens, complained that "a statutory blunderbuss that mandates this vast amount of overblocking abridges the freedom of speech protected by the First Amendment."

Impact

Because access to the Internet is so pervasive today and adults will apparently be able to request unblocked access at the library, it might seem that this decision will not have much direct impact. Librarians will likely view it as a dangerous precedent for overriding their traditional role as gatekeepers and mediators of knowledge. Filtering software that is defective or poorly configured could deprive library patrons of significant information and in effect block speech otherwise protected by the First Amendment. Since the filtering takes place silently, it will be difficult for people to determine how they are being affected. Finally, the decision is also a precedent for imposing more restrictive standards on the Internet than are applied to print media.

CHAPTER 4

CHRONOLOGY

1632

- The British government asserts control of the press by shutting down the *Coranto*, a weekly newspaper.

1643

- The British Parliament passes a Licensing Act. It requires government permission before anything can be printed.

1644

- In his essay *Areopagitica*, British poet John Milton urges freedom of expression: "liberty to know, to utter, and to argue freely according to conscience." He says that publishers can be held responsible for libel, but should not be censored beforehand.

1662

- The British Parliament passes a law restricting the number of licensed printers throughout the British Empire and limiting the types of materials they may print. These restrictions will inhibit the development of publishing and news media in America well into the 18th century.

1690

- *Publick Occurrences Both Forreign and Domestick*, published in Boston, becomes the first newspaper published in the British colonies in America. However, the Massachusetts governing council suppresses it after only one issue.

1702

- The *Daily Courant*, the first daily newspaper in English, is published in Britain.

1704

- The *Boston News-Letter* begins publication as a regular weekly newspaper. However, it is not an independent voice; it is operated by the postmaster under the authority of the colonial government of Massachusetts.

1721

- The first independent American newspaper, the *New England Courant*, is established by James Franklin, the older brother of Benjamin Franklin. The paper's criticism of the colonial government eventually leads to James Franklin serving time in jail.

1731

- In his "Apology for Printers" Benjamin Franklin writes that printers had a duty to print views from both sides in a controversy.

1735

- John Peter Zenger, editor of the *New-York Weekly Journal*, is charged with criminal libel for printing statements critical of colonial governor William Cosby. Although the law at this time does not recognize truth as a defense to libel, Zenger's attorney Andrew Hamilton (uncle of Alexander Hamilton) persuades the jury to acquit Zenger despite instructions from the court. The case will become a milestone in the development of freedom of the press.

1765

- In order to help pay the expenses of the French and Indian War, British Parliament passes the Stamp Act, which among other things requires that all printed matter bear tax stamps. Because the tax makes their newspapers more expensive, colonial newspaper editors bitterly oppose the law, joining activists who make a broader argument about "no taxation without representation" for Americans in Parliament.

Chronology

1772

- The Committees of Correspondence, organized by radical activist Samuel Adams and others, distribute news about British activities in what might be called one of the first "underground newspapers."

1787

- The *Pennsylvania Packet* begins publication. It is the first daily newspaper in the United States.

1791

- The first of 10 amendments to the Constitution, often called the Bill of Rights, are passed. The First Amendment affirms freedom of speech and of the press.

1792

- The U.S. Post Office begins to facilitate the development of newspapers by allowing editors to mail copies of their publications to one another postage-free. Newspapers can also be mailed to subscribers at special low rates.

1798

- With fears of war with revolutionary France in the air, Congress passes the Alien and Sedition Acts. The sedition provisions, which make it a crime to publish "any false, scandalous, or malicious writing or writings against the Government of the United States" challenge the wide-ranging freedom previously proclaimed in the First Amendment. Fourteen indictments are brought under the law, all resulting in convictions with fines and/or jail time. Most of the accused were involved with the Democratic-Republican Party, which opposed the ruling Federalists.

1799

- Congress passes a law requiring the secretary of state to select between one and three newspapers in each state to receive government contracts for printing official publications. Expanded over the years, the government contracts would help support many newspapers but also serve as a form of patronage by which an administration could reward newspapers that had supported it during the campaign.

1800

- Strongly opposed to the Alien and Sedition Acts, newly elected president Thomas Jefferson makes sure the law lapses.

1805

- Harry Croswell, editor of the *Hudson New York Wasp*, is charged in state court with criminal libel—ironically, for printing attacks on Thomas Jefferson. Alexander Hamilton, whose uncle Andrew Hamilton had defended John Peter Zenger, makes a similar argument in this case, but loses. Meanwhile, the legislatures of New York and many other states begin to pass laws making truth a defense to libel.

1819

- Elihu Embree of Jonesboro, Tennessee, founds the *Abolitionist Intelligencer.* Many other abolitionist publications will follow, many founded by Quakers.

1827

- Two African Americans, Samuel E. Cornish and John B. Russwurm, begin publishing *Freedom's Journal* in New York. Besides being the first black-owned abolitionist newspaper, *Freedom's Journal* also provides African Americans with a vehicle for news coverage and development of their community.

1828

- Andrew Jackson wins the presidency. His new style of populist campaigning included an effort to cultivate favorable treatment by the press.

1833

- The *New York Sun* under Ben Day brings newspapers to the masses by charging only a penny a copy rather than the usual five or six cents. To boost interest in this mass-market paper, Day focuses on daily crime reports and the courts, which continue to be popular media fodder today. Day also gains revenue by inventing the small "want ad," allowing small businesses and individual readers an inexpensive way to advertise their needs.

Chronology

1834

■ James Gordon Bennett offers a competitive penny paper, the *New York Herald*, that takes a greater interest in politics than the *Sun*. As more papers cover both national and local politics, the interest and participation of the electorate in political campaigns and issues will grow.

1835

■ The *New York Sun* publishes a series of illustrated articles about an astronomer's supposed discovery of living creatures on the Moon. It proves to be one of the most successful journalistic hoaxes in history.

1837

■ Reverend Elijah Parish Lovejoy, publisher of the abolitionist *St. Louis Observer*, is killed in an armed confrontation with a mob seeking to destroy his press for the third time.

1838

■ James Gordon Bennett decides to hire the first regular foreign correspondents for a U.S. newspaper. They cover the coronation of Queen Victoria.

1841

■ Horace Greeley founds the *New York Tribune*. Although he is a partisan Whig (and later helps found the Republican Party), Greeley begins the practice of separating news coverage from editorial opinion.

1846

■ Bennett and Greeley use a combination of telegraph and horseback to bring news of the U.S. war against Mexico. Meanwhile, Greeley sends journalist Margaret Fuller to report from Europe. Fuller is credited with being the first U.S. woman foreign correspondent.

1851

■ New York's preeminence in American journalism continues when Henry Raymond starts the *New York Times*, which adopts a high-minded journalistic tone.

1853

- Frank Leslie publishes his *Illustrated News*, the first U.S. newspaper to feature pictorial illustrations (drawn, not photographed). Several years later the magazine *Harper's Weekly* becomes Leslie's main competitor in pictorial journalism.

1860

- The Associated Press (AP) is founded. It brings together the many local press cooperatives that had been sharing news since the 1840s. Its nationwide telegraph links will help provide timely coverage of events during the Civil War.

1861

- The Civil War begins. General Winfield Scott begins censorship of reporters' telegraph dispatches.
- The government in the North takes heavy-handed measures against newspapers deemed to be disloyal. Many newspapers in the border areas of Maryland and Missouri are shut down and their editors arrested. Meanwhile, southern newspapers are hampered not by censorship but by lack of personnel and supplies (including paper).
- Throughout the war, pioneer photographer Mathew Brady documents the details and horrors of the conflict.

1866

- Sustained transatlantic telegraph cable service begins. It will greatly increase the timeliness and utility of foreign news reports.

1871

- The ability of journalists to expose corruption and stimulate reform is shown when the *New York Times* documents the $200 million raid on the treasury of the city of New York by "Boss" William M. Tweed and his Tammany Hall cronies. Thomas Nast's biting cartoons in *Harper's Weekly* add the power of graphics to the journalistic effort.

1880

- Stephen Horgan of the *New York Daily Graphic* develops a process for converting photographs to grids of dots using a halftone screen. Photographs can now be reproduced directly in newspapers and magazines.

Chronology

1883

■ Joseph Pulitzer buys the *New York World* and soon ratchets up the level of vivid sensationalism in the print media.

1892

■ The battle of the news agencies begins when the Associated Press and United Press stop their secret cooperation and start competing to provide news for U.S. newspapers. United Press is the loser and goes out of business in 1897. Although a new United Press will be founded in 1907, the Associated Press will dominate domestic news service through the 20th century.

1893

■ The University of Pennsylvania offers the first U.S. program in journalism. Courses in journalism and printing had been offered previously but within other departments, such as English.

1896

■ Maryland passes the first "shield law," giving journalists the right to refuse to disclose the identity of their confidential sources.

1898

■ Joseph Pulitzer and William Randolph Hearst (who had bought the *New York Journal* in 1895) seize upon the sinking of the U.S. battleship *Maine* in Havana Harbor to drum up support for war against Spain. This "yellow journalism" (named for a jingoistic comic strip character called the Yellow Kid) continues during the war, for which there is extensive and relatively "live" coverage.

1905

■ The *Chicago Defender* is founded by Robert Sengstacke Abbott. Pioneering the modern African-American newspaper, the *Defender,* true to its name, actively speaks out against racial prejudice, segregation, and lynching.

1909

■ President William Howard Taft begins the practice of holding scheduled news conferences, but he is dissatisfied with the results and soon discontinues the practice.

- The Society of Professional Journalists is founded. For some time it does not admit women to membership, so women journalism students start their own professional organization, Women in Communications, Inc.

1910

- The Kansas Editorial Association adopts a code of journalistic ethics. Many other state press associations will follow in the next two decades.

1911

- The first motion picture newsreels are shown in U.S. theaters. (Brief films of individual news events had been shown previously.)

1914

- World War I begins.

1917

- The United States enters World War I. Congress passes the Espionage Act, which makes it illegal to interfere with military conscription or the war effort.

1919

- The *New York Daily News* begins a new genre, the tabloid newspaper. Tabloids, of which the *Mirror* and *The Graphic* are later examples, use cheap printing and production methods to keep costs down, while featuring crimes and other sensational stories to maintain reader interest.
- In *Schenck v. United States* the Supreme Court upholds the conviction of socialists for distributing literature opposing the draft. The Court cites "clear and present danger" as a justification for suppressing a publication, and Justice Oliver Wendell Holmes makes his famous remark about freedom of speech not protecting "a man in falsely shouting 'fire' in a theater and causing a panic."

1920

- Commercial radio broadcasting begins in a few places. One pioneer is KDKA in Pittsburgh, which offers the first radio coverage of the returns of a presidential election.

Chronology

1923

- The American Society of Newspaper Editors adopts the Canons of Journalism, emphasizing responsibility, freedom, independence, honesty, accuracy, impartiality, fair play, and decency. The Society of Professional Journalists adopts these canons three years later.
- Edward L. Bernays's book *Crystallizing Public Opinion* helps define the profession of public relations.

1925

- The American Civil Liberties Union (ACLU) is founded. In coming years it will be in the forefront of litigation seeking to protect and expand freedom of expression and other civil rights.
- In response to sensational and often inaccurate stories in tabloids, Minnesota passes a "gag law," allowing the use of a court order to prevent publication of material deemed libelous.

1926

- National Broadcasting Company (NBC) becomes the first true radio network. It is owned by Radio Corporation of America (RCA). Its first program is carried by 25 stations. NBC eventually includes two networks, NBC Red and the smaller NBC Blue.

1927

- With more than 700 radio stations now broadcasting, interference is becoming a significant problem. In response, Congress passes the Radio Act of 1927 and the Federal Radio Commission (FRC) is established. Besides serving as a traffic cop of the airwaves, the commission establishes the federal role in regulating broadcasting.
- The Columbia Broadcasting System (CBS) provides a competing radio network service.

1928

- Inventor Philo T. Farnsworth completes the first successful all-electronic television system.
- The National Association of Broadcasters responds to the activity of the new Federal Radio Commission (FRC) by drafting the Radio Code, voluntary guidelines for conduct of radio stations. Over the years the code will gradually become more detailed and specific.

1931

■ The Supreme Court ruling in *Near v. Minnesota* overturns Minnesota's gag law. The Court rules that prior restraint of a publication, even by a convicted libeler, is unconstitutional under the First Amendment. This will become an important precedent in protecting publications or broadcasters against preemptive government censorship.

1932

■ The growing influence of radio news is beginning to alarm newspapers, so the American Newspaper Publishers Association urges press associations not to distribute news to radio stations.
■ Throughout the decade FBI chief J. Edgar Hoover mounts a campaign to enhance the image of the organization through carefully leaked details about the catching of famous criminals. Hoover also keeps tabs on whether reporters are "cooperative," as well as monitoring radical or dissident publications.

1933

■ President Franklin Delano Roosevelt (FDR) takes office in the midst of the Great Depression. FDR will use radio effectively not only for press conferences but for "fireside chats" addressed directly to the public.

1934

■ The Federal Communications Commission (FCC) replaces the Federal Radio Commission. The FCC has a broader mandate that also includes the telephone system and the nascent television industry.

1935

■ Newspapers effectively give up their attempt to keep radio stations from gaining access to news services. By now radio has developed its own news services and networks.

1938

■ The power of radio news is inadvertently demonstrated when Orson Welles's radio adaptation of H. G. Wells's *War of the Worlds*, about a Martian invasion of Earth, in the form of a realistic-sounding live newscast causes considerable panic. The FCC issues a statement condemning programs that "caused widespread excitement, terror and fright."

- The FCC holds hearings into "chain broadcasting," meaning the three large radio networks. Critics argue that the networks have virtually monopolistic control over their affiliate stations and the radio market in general.
- The modern mass market paperback book makes its debut when Robert de Graff founds Pocket Books. He will be joined by several other publishers during the 1940s, including Popular Library, Dell, Avon, and Bantam.
- The Supreme Court rules in *Lovell v. Griffin* that a city cannot require prior official approval before literature can be distributed.

1939

- RCA demonstrates television to thousands of visitors at the New York World's Fair. The company also builds the first mobile television news van to broadcast live events.

1940

- Beginning with the words "This is London. . ." Edward R. Murrow broadcasts live from the British capital as it is pounded by German bombers during the Blitz.
- In what becomes known as the Mayflower Decision, the FCC rules that radio stations cannot broadcast editorials expressing their own views on issues. This decision will be revoked in 1949 in favor of the Fairness Doctrine.

1941

- The United States abruptly enters World War II following the bombing of Pearl Harbor by Japan. Wartime conditions impose military censorship and some other restrictions on publishing and broadcasting.
- The ever-growing radio market and the nascent television industry prompt new FCC regulations. The number of radio stations a single company can own in a given market is restricted, and no company will be allowed to own television stations that would reach more than 35 percent of households with television.
- Commercial television begins on a limited scale with FCC approval. However, wartime needs essentially halt the expansion of the new medium: In 1945 there are only seven television stations with regular broadcast schedules, most broadcasting only a few hours per day.

- The first television news reports are delivered by Richard Hubbell on WCBW, New York. The reports consist of Hubbell sitting at a desk and reading wire service dispatches aloud before a single camera.

1942

- The Office of Censorship is established to control military information, while the Office of War Information serves as a public information or propaganda effort. Many media officials take government posts (Byron Price, the head of the Office of Censorship, is the former executive news editor of the Associated Press). There is little sense of an adversarial relationship between the media and the government or military.

1943

- In *NBC v. United States* the Supreme Court upholds the 1941 FCC ruling forcing NBC to sell off its smaller Blue network. However, the major networks still dominate radio broadcasting.

1945

- The radio program *Meet the Press* begins the important genre of topical news interview shows. It will later successfully migrate to television.

1946

- The FCC prohibits mergers between the major television networks (ABC, CBS, and NBC).

1948

- Newspapers that had endorsed Republican Thomas E. Dewey over President Harry S. Truman (more than four in five did) are embarrassed when their predictions of a Dewey landslide are proven wrong. The *Chicago Daily Tribune* had gone so far as to run headline "Dewey Defeats Truman" the morning following the election. During the campaign Truman had used media bias as one of his major issues.
- The FCC announces a temporary freeze on the issuance of television broadcast licenses. With hundreds of applications pending, the agency says it needs time to develop ground rules for allocating space on the television spectrum (such as for educational broadcasting) as well as

extending the spectrum through the use of the ultra-high-frequency (UHF) band.

- The Voice of America (VOA) is established as the main U.S. official broadcast information service, competing with Soviet propaganda broadcasts. VOA broadcasters will often face conflicts between journalistic standards and cold war political agendas.
- The United Nations, in its Universal Declaration of Human Rights, asserts that all people should be able to express themselves freely.

1949

- An FCC ruling results in the Fairness Doctrine. This will be interpreted to allow broadcasters to air editorial opinions as long as they also provide access for people with opposing viewpoints.
- The first cable television system begins operation. For the next two decades cable will mainly serve as a way to distribute broadcasts to remote areas where on-air reception is poor.

1950

- An anticommunist business group publishes a pamphlet titled *Red Channels*. It alleges widespread communist influence in U.S. radio and television, singling out 151 prominent individuals as having ties to "Communist causes."
- The public relations profession receives some guidance when the Public Relations Society of America adopts a code of professional standards.
- The monthly magazine *One* becomes the first widely distributed publication for gays and lesbians. Later in the decade it will be joined by the gay men's publication *Mattachine Review* and the lesbian journal *Ladder.*

1951

- Edward R. Murrow begins the pioneering television documentary series *See It Now.*

1952

- Richard Nixon uses television effectively in responding to charges of misuse of campaign funds. In a half-hour speech he uses his dog, Checkers, as an example of his humble background. The "Checkers" speech is credited with keeping Nixon as the vice presidential candidate in the upcoming election.

- This year's presidential election sees the first significant impact from television. The winner, Republican Dwight Eisenhower, proves to be an effective communicator. His Democratic opponent, Adlai Stevenson, echoes Truman's earlier charges that the press was biased against his party.

1954

- Edward R. Murrow confronts Senator Joseph McCarthy on the television program *See It Now*. Murrow criticizes McCarthy's wholesale smear campaign against alleged communists, and McCarthy is caught flatfooted and unable to make a coherent defense. Along with McCarthy's badgering of witnesses in the televised Army-McCarthy hearings, this broadcast creates unfavorable exposure that helps bring McCarthy down.

1955

- Eisenhower becomes the first president to allow his press conferences to be televised, although the broadcasts are delayed to allow for review.
- Television begins an important role in another arena: broadcasts of the confrontations in the Montgomery, Alabama bus boycott will bring the civil rights struggle into living rooms around the United States.

1956

- The team of Chet Huntley and David Brinkley on NBC bring a new level of sophistication to television commentary, covering what will be the first of many political conventions and other events.

1959

- The FCC briefly extends the "equal time" rule to news programs, requiring that all candidates in a race be given equal coverage. Congress later passes legislation exempting news and documentary programs (and later, presidential debates) from this requirement.

1960

- In a series of four televised presidential debates, Democratic candidate John F. Kennedy faces Republican candidate Richard M. Nixon. Nixon is never able to overcome the contrast between his strained, poorly made-up appearance and that of the youthful-looking Kennedy, who goes on to narrowly win the election.

Chronology

1961

- Kennedy continues his effective use of television by holding the first presidential news conferences to be televised live.
- Emilio Azcárraga founds Spanish International Network, starting with television stations in Los Angeles and San Antonio, Texas. By the late 1990s the network's successor, Univisión, will have more than 6,600 affiliates.

1962

- TV coverage of the Cuban Missile Crisis shows how television can convey the immediacy of events. Millions of Americans watch as Soviet ships reinforcing Cuba turn away at the last minute.

1963

- Nightly national television news on CBS and NBC is expanded from 15 minutes to half an hour.
- Station WJW in Cleveland, Ohio, adopts a news format with two anchors who engage in dialogue with each other while delivering the news. (Previous anchor teams such as Huntley and Brinkley simply took turns presenting items.)
- President Kennedy's assassination and funeral are covered by continuous live television. All showing of commercials is suspended for the duration.

1964

- In the landmark case of *New York Times v. Sullivan* the Supreme Court defines a stricter standard for libel in the case of public figures such as government officials. In order to collect damages, such persons must now prove actual malice or reckless disregard for the truth. As a result, the news media can be less restrained and more critical in their coverage of government actions such as the violent suppression of civil rights protesters in the South.
- The FCC restricts companies from owning more than two television stations in the same market. Only one of the stations can be ranked in the top four.

1966

- The Freedom of Information Act (FOIA) is passed by Congress. It will become a basic tool for the media and members of the public for accessing records that government agencies often want to restrict.

1967

- Racial unrest explodes in many major cities. The Kerner Commission, given the task of determining the causes and possible cures for the violence, blames the media both for exaggerating the extent of the violence and for not adequately covering the underlying issues and problems in African-American communities.
- Journalism scholar Ben Bagdikian suggests that newspapers appoint an ombudsman to address reader complaints and make publications more accountable to the public they serve.

1968

- Television covers perhaps the most tumultuous year in U.S. politics, including the assassinations of Martin Luther King, Jr., and Robert Kennedy, race riots in several major cities, bloody conflict on the streets of Chicago at the Democratic convention, and the growing number of protests against the war in Vietnam. The media is criticized by some liberals and African-American activists for its poor coverage of minorities and by some conservatives for giving too much coverage to protests and riots.
- The CBS program *60 Minutes* begins airing. Biweekly at first, the program's magazine-style format becomes very popular and the show goes weekly after three seasons.
- New local news formats begin to challenge the staid network tradition. They include an informal, chatty "happy talk" approach and "eyewitness news," featuring a regular team of local reporters.

1969

- The Nixon administration begins a preemptive attack against what it considers to be a hostile and biased media. Vice President Spiro Agnew characterizes the press as "nattering nabobs of negativism."
- The first manned Moon landing becomes one of the most watched events in television history.
- A network for transmitting data packets between computers is successfully demonstrated. It will eventually become the Internet.

1970

- With many weaker newspapers in large urban markets threatened with bankruptcy, Congress passes the Newspaper Preservation Act. This allows competing newspapers to share some facilities (such as printing plants).
- The FCC rules that the same company cannot own both a television and a radio station in the same market.

1971

- The Nixon administration gets an injunction to stop the *New York Times* from publishing a classified study of the decisions leading to U.S. involvement in Vietnam (the Pentagon Papers). When the *Times* appeals, the U.S. Supreme Court rules that publication of the document does not endanger U.S. security, and that prior restraint against its publication is not justified. The decision in the Pentagon Papers case suggests that the government will be able to block publication only in extreme cases.
- Computer users at universities start the first online newsgroups, allowing them to read and post messages on a variety of topics.

1972

- A burglary at Democratic National Committee headquarters in Washington, D.C., escalates into the full-blown scandal called Watergate. Two young investigative reporters, Carl Bernstein and Robert Woodward, will become famous for uncovering the web of illegal operations, resulting in Nixon's resignation in 1974.
- For the first time, the total number of color televisions installed in U.S. homes surpasses the number of black-and-white models.

1975

- The FCC rules that the same company cannot own both newspapers and broadcast stations. However, some existing ownership arrangements are "grandfathered in."
- Cable television companies begin to distribute television programs downloaded from satellites.
- Ted Turner turns WTBS in Atlanta, Georgia, into the first "superstation." It offers its programming to any cable system that wants it.
- Practical portable video recorders (VCRs) are introduced: Sony's Betamax this year, and Matsushita's VHS the following year. VHS will eventually predominate.

1976

- Following the 1960 election the major parties had been unable to agree on a framework for continuing presidential debates. However, the League of Women Voters now steps in, and the FCC agrees to allow debates with only the major candidates.

■ In *Buckley v. Valeo* the U.S. Supreme Court overturns restrictions in the Federal Election Campaign Act of 1971 on campaign spending. The need of candidates to spend growing amounts for access to the media is cited.

1979

■ The U.S. Justice Department rules that the Television Code (a set of ethics and practice guidelines similar to the older Radio Code) violates antitrust law by limiting the number of commercials broadcast.

1980

■ Ted Koppel's *Nightline* brings news and interviews to the previously little-used late-night television time slot.
■ CNN (Cable News Network) is founded.

1981

■ The newspaper *USA Today* begins publication. It emphasizes high-impact visual graphics and short articles, appealing to an audience used to getting its news from television.

1983

■ The Reagan administration refuses to allow journalists to cover the U.S. invasion of Grenada and removes any journalists found on the island. The resulting outcry from major journalistic and newspaper organizations leads to the creation of a new system of pooled reporting to allow controlled access to the battlefield.
■ By the mid-1980s computer bulletin board systems (BBS) start to provide forums for news and discussion for personal computer users using modems.

1984

■ Ben Bagdikian's book *The Media Monopoly* spurs debate over corporate control of the news media.

1987

■ The FCC suspends enforcement of the Fairness Doctrine. This rule had been acknowledged as unworkable because of the difficulty of defining points of view that deserved coverage and of determining who gets how much time. One effect of the FCC action will be to allow for an explosion in explicitly ideological talk radio programs.

- The Fox television network is started by Australian-American entrepreneur Rupert Murdoch.

1988

- The growing influence of TV political ads is highlighted by a controversial Republican campaign ad featuring Willie Horton, an African American who had committed murder after being furloughed from a Massachusetts prison. Its purpose was to attack the Democratic candidate, Michael Dukakis, who had been governor of Massachusetts at the time of the furlough. However, the ad is also criticized for blatantly exploiting racist stereotypes.

1989

- The military's system for pool coverage breaks down during the U.S. invasion of Panama that removes Manuel Noriega from power. Breakdowns in bureaucratic communication and transportation problems mean that reporters see little of the first two days of the operation.
- Film and music producer Warner Communications and publisher Time, Inc., join to form Time-Warner. It is the first of the late 20th-century media mega-mergers.

1991

- The Persian Gulf War becomes the first major war in history to be carried live on television, including broadcasts from Baghdad hosted by CNN's Peter Arnett as the city undergoes Coalition missile and bomb attacks. In the coverage of the desert war in Kuwait and Iraq, the U.S. military restricts coverage to pool reporting and maintains strict control over information being transmitted from the battlefield.

1992

- Congress passes legislation requiring cable TV networks to make their programming available to competing services such as satellite TV.

1993

- NBC admits and apologizes for having used "sparking devices" in staging film footage for *Dateline NBC* showing alleged hazards in General Motors pickup trucks.

1995

- Thanks to graphical web browsers such as Netscape, the World Wide Web is starting to become a ubiquitous medium for information and commerce. Newspapers start to put some of their features on web sites.
- CBS withdraws a *60 Minutes* segment before airing it. The report would have featured a former tobacco executive's revelations about industry practices, but CBS executives decided not to risk a legal onslaught from the tobacco industry. Mike Wallace and other reporters bitterly protest the action.
- Two new television networks are started: United Paramount Network (UPN) and Warner Brothers (WB). They have limited success.

1996

- Congress passes the Telecommunication Reform Bill, which includes the Communications Decency Act (CDA). This law provides for fines and/or imprisonment for those who distribute "indecent" or "patently offensive" materials on the Internet without blocking it from minors. Thousands of web site owners turn their pages black as a virtual protest.
- Veteran CBS producer Bernard Goldberg creates a furor by writing opinion pieces asserting that the national media is biased in favor of liberal views.
- *August:* San Jose Mercury News journalist Gary Webb's series alleging CIA involvement in contra drug-running in Nicaragua and the crack cocaine epidemic in the United States ignites a firestorm of controversy. Other reporters and a congressional committee find little corroboration, but the story becomes a staple of conspiracy theory.

1997

- The Supreme Court upholds a lower court ruling finding that the CDA is unconstitutionally vague.

1998

- President Bill Clinton's sexual relationship with White House intern Monica Lewinsky eventually leads to an unsuccessful attempt to impeach the president. Many observers consider the media coverage of the whole affair to be grossly excessive.

- Two *Boston Globe* columnists resign after accusations of journalistic malfeasance. Mike Barnicle is found to have plagiarized material from other writers, while Patricia Smith was found to have used made-up characters in her reports.
- *June 7:* CNN airs a blockbuster story about "Operation Tailwind," developed in conjunction with *Time* magazine. It alleges that the U.S. military used nerve gas to kill American defectors in Laos during the Vietnam War. A firestorm of criticism results.
- *July 2:* First Amendment expert Floyd Abrams, hired by CNN to investigate the Tailwind story, issues his conclusion that while the report included "no falsification of an intentional nature," it was "unsupportable." CNN and *Time* both retract the story.
- *August 31:* Princess Diana and Dodi al-Fayed die in a car crash in a Paris tunnel after being chased by paparazzi. Although the cause of the crash is unclear, many people blame it on the overly aggressive photographers.

1999

- More than 300 staffers and editors of the *Los Angeles Times* sign a letter protesting an advertising revenue arrangement between the paper and the new Staples Center sports and entertainment facility. They complain that the arrangement represents a conflict of interest and compromises the paper's editorial independence.
- The Internet becomes a growing force in journalism, typified by the controversial Matt Drudge, whose entirely Web-based news operation "scoops" mainstream media outlets on some issues. Drudge, however, is accused of not following journalistic standards such as verification of sources.

2000

- *September 26:* In a lengthy editorial note, the *New York Times* admits that its coverage of the case of accused Los Alamos physicist Wen Ho Lee was flawed. Although taking some blame for not investigating more thoroughly, the paper also blames politicians and other media for creating an overblown atmosphere.
- *November:* The national election debacle brings criticism that the media had prematurely "called" the results in some parts of Florida while the polls were still open.

2001

- *September 11:* The terrorist attacks on the World Trade Center and Pentagon bring a spate of media coverage comparable to that of the

Kennedy assassination a generation earlier. Some experts believe that children and others may be adversely affected by the seemingly endless repetition of airplane crashes, flames, and collapsing buildings.

2002

- The coverage of the ongoing war on terrorism (first in Afghanistan, and 2003 in Iraq) tests the new concept of "embedding," where journalists travel with military units and report live from the field. Although the coverage brings some sense of the immediacy and chaos of war, critics suggest that it lacks the ability to show the overall picture with its strategic and political considerations.
- *February 21:* The death of *Wall Street Journal* reporter Daniel Pearl, an American foreign correspondent in Pakistan, is confirmed. Pearl had been kidnapped the previous month, apparently after being lured by a promise of a meeting with a militant leader. Pearl's gruesome murder (a videotaped beheading) highlights the dangers faced by journalists who seek to cover war and terrorism firsthand.
- *December 20:* Senator Trent Lott (Republican-Mississippi) resigns his position as Senate majority leader. He had made comments favorable to Senator Strom Thurmond's pro-segregationist 1948 presidential campaign. Largely ignored by the media at first, Lott's remarks were taken up by web logs (blogs), an emerging new force in journalism.

2003

- *April:* The *New York Times* discovers that Jayson Blair, considered one of the paper's most promising young reporters, had plagiarized or fabricated large portions of numerous articles, often concealing the fact that he had not personally been on the scene of his stories. Another reporter, Rick Bragg, is also revealed to have used interviews conducted by a freelance "stringer" without attribution. Blair will resign on May 1. The *Times* undertakes and publishes a detailed investigation of these failures in quality control.
- *June 2:* The Republican majority on the FCC votes to relax restrictions on ownership of media outlets. Under the new rules, one company will be able to own a number of television stations accounting for 45 percent of the national rather than the previous 35 percent. The same company will be able to own up to three television stations in the same area, depending on the size of the market. Restrictions against cross-ownership of television and radio stations are removed in large markets and eased in medium-sized ones. The same company will now also be able to own both

a newspaper and a broadcast station in the same market. Critics argue that this will lead to greater concentration of media ownership in a few large companies. Some opposition is heard in Congress.

■ *June 5:* Two *New York Times* senior editors, Howell Raines and Gerald Boyd, resign in the wake of the Jayson Blair and Rick Bragg reporting scandals. The editors had long cultivated Blair's and Bragg's careers and were accused by some critics within the paper of having showed favoritism and poor judgment.

■ *June 18:* Defense Department spokesperson Victoria Clarke announces that the program of "embedding" about 700 journalists with U.S. military units during the recent war in Iraq was so successful that the military plans to expand the program in future conflicts. Clarke cites the ability to give journalists and the public a better view of the conflict while countering enemy propaganda. Some critics, however, warn that embedding can lead to "tunnel vision" and lack of objectivity.

■ *October:* An anonymous source tells columnist Robert Novak that former ambassador Joseph C. Wilson's wife is an undercover CIA agent. Novak publishes this information in his column, leading to a Justice Department investigation. Some administration critics believe the leak may have been in retaliation for Wilson's having criticized the administration's claim that Iraq had tried to buy uranium from Niger. The incident also leads to public discussion of the ethical obligations of journalists who are given such information.

■ *December 10:* The U.S. Supreme Court upholds the Bipartisan Campaign Reform Act of 2002, including the provision banning so-called issue ads produced by advocacy groups around election time to target certain candidates. The ultimate effect on the relationship between the media and political campaigns remains uncertain.

2004

■ *January 12:* The U.S. Supreme Court declines to hear an appeal in the case of *Center for National Security Studies v. U.S. Department of Justice.* This leaves standing the decision of the Washington, D.C., appeals court that the federal government does not have to disclose identities and other basic information about the hundreds of people detained following the September 11, 2001, terrorist attacks.

■ *January 20:* Once anointed as front runner in the Democratic presidential primary race, former Vermont governor Howard Dean turns in a disappointing performance in the Iowa caucuses. Dean's forceful speech vowing to carry on the fight to other states is portrayed as "the Dean scream" by the media, which in turn is criticized for an overblown characterization.

- *January 28:* Speaking at a congressional hearing, several prominent House members from both parties indicate their support for legislation that would greatly increase the fines for broadcasters who allow indecent language to be used on the air. Meanwhile, the FCC testifies that it has already stepped up enforcement of existing decency regulations.
- *January 28:* A special British commission concludes that the British Broadcasting Corporation (BBC) published erroneous reports accusing the British government of having "sexed up" (embellished) the threat of Iraq's weapons of mass destruction. The BBC had identified weapons expert David Kelly as the source for its story; Kelly committed suicide shortly thereafter. The BBC's chairman and chief executive both resign, and the network issues an apology to British prime minister Tony Blair.

CHAPTER 5

BIOGRAPHICAL LISTING

This chapter provides brief biographical sketches of some of the more significant figures in the development and study of the news media.

Robert Sengstacke Abbott, pioneering African-American newspaper publisher. Inspired by the words of famed African-American leader Booker T. Washington, Abbott attended the Kent College of Law in Chicago, graduating in 1899 with a law degree. In 1905 Abbot started the *Chicago Defender* as a four-page weekly newspaper dedicated to the advancement of the black community: The motto on its masthead read "American race prejudice must be destroyed!" The always forceful *Defender* soon lived up to its name as an advocate for black civil rights and economic development, serving the hundreds of thousands of blacks who had begun to migrate from the South to industrialized northern cities during World War I. By the 1920s Abbott had become one of the nation's first African-American millionaires, and the *Defender* survived the Great Depression to become an enduring institution.

Bess Furman Armstrong, pioneering woman correspondent who covered Eleanor Roosevelt, the first first lady to have her own press corps. She learned the newspaper business from her father, who ran a small weekly newspaper in Nebraska. She then worked at the *Omaha Bee-News* through the 1920s until she became an Associated Press reporter in Washington in 1929. After Armstrong began covering Eleanor Roosevelt, she encouraged her to begin holding press conferences, which Roosevelt permitted only women to attend. From 1938 to 1942 Armstrong also became a pioneering woman entrepreneur in the news business. Together with her sister Lucile Furman, she ran a successful publicity and news features writing firm, producing campaign material for Franklin Roosevelt's re-election campaign in 1940.

Peter Arnett, controversial television war correspondent best known for live reporting during the Gulf War of 1991. Arnett was born in New

Zealand and worked there on newspapers during the 1950s. He then went to Thailand and Laos, working on newspapers and becoming a war correspondent as the conflict in Vietnam heated up. He received a Pulitzer Prize in 1966, having gained a reputation for fearlessness and enterprise. He continued his reporting on a variety of foreign and domestic issues through the 1970s and 1980s. However, he became best known in 1991 when he became the last Western correspondent in Baghdad and was allowed to broadcast live on CNN as U.S. missiles and bombs pounded the city. Critics charged that Arnett had lost all claim to objectivity by interviewing Saddam Hussein and reporting under conditions tightly controlled by Hussein's regime. Arnett defended his actions, saying that his cooperation with Iraq was the only way to bring viewers an essential viewpoint on the conflict. During the renewed U.S.-Iraq conflict in 2003 Arnett was fired as an NBC correspondent for conducting interviews and making analyses on Iraqi state-controlled television.

Ben Haig Bagdikian, influential critic of the corporate media. Bagdikian had a successful career as a newspaper reporter and editor from the 1940s to the early 1970s, becoming assistant managing editor of the *Washington Post*. He is best known for his subsequent emergence as a media scholar and critic. His book *The Media Monopoly*, published in 1984 and regularly revised, analyzes the concentration of the media into a handful of huge conglomerates such as AOL-Time Warner. By detailing the impact of corporate policy and the changing marketplace on journalistic standards and practices, Bagdikian helped ignite an ongoing debate on the health of contemporary American journalism.

James Gordon Bennett, founder of the *New York Herald* in 1835 and pioneer of the popular journalistic vehicle called the "penny press." By the end of the 1820s Bennett had become a nationally known political reporter, going to Washington to cover contentious congressional debates on issues such as slavery and tariffs, as well as a partisan political advocate (which was not considered to be incompatible with journalism at the time). Inspired by Benjamin H. Day's success with the *New York Sun* in 1833, Bennett founded the *Herald* two years later. His paper became known for wide-ranging, bold, contentious journalism. His was the first major city newspaper to extensively cover crime and the courts, the stock market, and sports. He also was the first publisher to establish regular Washington and foreign correspondents. He went on to offer some of the best coverage of the American Civil War.

Edward L. Bernays, pioneer in public relations and "media management." During World War I, Bernays worked with the Committee on Public Information, which was developing new ways of using public information (and propaganda) to form public opinion. This ability to systematically influence public perceptions became Bernays's new career, in which he began to systematically apply psychological and communication principles to helping corporations manage and improve their public image. Bernays coined the term "counsel on public relations" for this profession. One of his more dubious achievements was linking cigarettes (or "torches of freedom") with the ideal of the liberated woman in the 1920s. Bernays's 1923 book *Crystallizing Public Opinion* focused on the more socially useful goals of the profession and is considered a classic in the field.

Carl Bernstein, together with Bob Woodward, would become part of a famous duo of investigative reporters who broke the Watergate scandal while becoming a role model for aspiring journalists. As a young reporter for the *Washington Post,* Bernstein had covered a variety of local stories, but was not shy about maneuvering himself onto more promising beats. Originally working independently, Bernstein and Woodward eventually joined forces as they began to connect the dots of the Watergate mystery, tracing the links between the burglars and the unfortunately named CREEP (Committee to Re-Elect the President) and top members of the White House staff. They told the story of their investigation in a popular and engaging book, *All the President's Men* (1974). Its sequel, *The Final Days* (1976), which chronicled the events leading to Nixon's resignation, received criticism for its reliance on hard-to-verify interviews "on background." Nevertheless, Bernstein and Woodward's work would become a model for a new generation of aggressive investigative reporters.

Jayson Blair became the center of a firestorm at the *New York Times* in April 2003 when he was revealed to have fabricated part or all of numerous stories. Blair earned a considerable reputation for his energy and brilliance as a student at the Philip Merrill College of Journalism in Maryland. As a young intern for the *Times* starting in 1998, Blair was soon looked upon with favor and enthusiasm—in part because of his genuine talent and in part because, as an African American, Blair was seen as a valuable addition to the paper's much-sought-after diversity. However, there was also a growing suspicion among editors that Blair was too often slipshod with facts and prone to fabrication. More disturbingly, there were indications that Blair may not have been physically present while supposedly covering certain important stories. Blair's resignation in April 2003 eventually led to the resignation of the paper's executive and managing editors, Howell Raines and Gerald Boyd, as well as spurring a raging debate about the lack of a system of accountability that could hold such deceptive journalism in check.

Nellie Bly, the pen name of Elizabeth Cochrane Seaman, a pioneering reporter who refused to be limited to society affairs and other assignments traditionally given to women. After she wrote a letter in 1885 to the editor of the *Pittsburgh Dispatch*, demanding that the paper support women's suffrage, she was hired to work there as a journalist. The next year she was sent to Mexico, where her reports on grinding poverty and rampant government corruption got her expelled by the government. Going to New York, Bly impressed Joseph Pulitzer, who hired her for the staff of the *New York World*. In a daring coup of what would later be called investigative reporting, Bly disguised herself as a mentally ill person in order to report firsthand on the terrible conditions in New York's mental hospitals. Perhaps her most famous exploit was her challenge of the 80-day world-circling trip of Jules Verne's fictional character Phineas Fogg. Bly made the trip in only 72 days, filing reports from many places along the way. During World War I, Bly covered the eastern front, becoming one of the first woman war correspondents.

Mathew B. Brady, Civil War photographer who demonstrated the power of the camera to convey the stark realities of war and helped create modern photojournalism. A self-taught art student, Brady learned around 1840 about the development of the daguerreotype, an early form of photography. Sometime around 1843 Brady established his own photographic portrait studio in New York. His work was greatly praised and he received several awards during the next 10 years. When the Civil War began, Brady was able to convince President Abraham Lincoln and other officials to support his effort to photograph camp and battle scenes. Brady and his assistants accompanied the Union army under hazardous conditions while wrestling with primitive and bulky photographic equipment. All together, Brady and his team made more than 3,500 photographs, some showing actual fighting and many showing the carnage following the battles. Besides creating an unprecedented picture of war and military life, Brady's work made it clear to newspapers and magazines that the photographer's eye was an invaluable tool of the new popular journalism.

David Brinkley, a pioneer television news commentator and anchor. In the subtitle of his 1985 memoir, Brinkley referred to having covered during his career "11 Presidents, 4 Wars, 22 Political Conventions, One Moon Landing, 3 Assassinations [and] 2,000 Weeks of News and Other Stuff on Television." Unlike some modern news anchors, Brinkley had a newspaper background and carefully crafted his on-air commentary. He started in 1942 as a reporter for United Press in Atlanta, but in 1943 he was hired to write copy for NBC radio. Brinkley's superiors at NBC soon came to appreciate his ability to write clear, succinct prose. They also decided that Brinkley had a good radio voice and began to assign him 10-minute newscasts. In the early 1950s Brinkley, unlike many radio newscasters, adapted easily to television, seeming to have an instinctive understanding of pacing and the weaving together of pictures and commentary. Brinkley was then teamed with Chet Huntley, creating the most famous duo in television news history, whose broadcasts would always end with "Good night, David. Good night, Chet." Starting in 1956 the Huntley-Brinkley anchor team covered several political conventions and other key events, including the Kennedy assassination in 1963 and the Apollo moon landing in 1969. In 1981 Brinkley left NBC for ABC and his own program, *This Week with David Brinkley*. Brinkley was one of the most honored members of his profession, having won three Peabody Awards and 10 Emmy Awards.

Walter Cronkite, often considered to be the dean of television anchors and a distinguished correspondent. In 1976 *U.S. News and World Report* called Cronkite "the most trusted man in America." Born in Kansas City, Missouri, Cronkite gained broadcasting experience working for a Kansas City radio station for a year, then became a United Press (UP) correspondent during World War II, parachuting into the Netherlands with the 101st Airborne and also covering the Battle of the Bulge. After the war, Cronkite was the head UP reporter for the Nuremberg war crimes trials and then bureau chief in Moscow. In 1950 he entered the television field as a correspondent for CBS. He began covering political conventions in 1952 as well as hosting documentaries. In 1962 Cronkite became the anchor for *CBS Evening News*, covering the Kennedy assassination the following year. Concern about ratings led CBS to replace Cronkite for the 1964 convention coverage with the team of Robert Trout and Roger Mudd, but Cronkite was soon back literally by popular demand. By 1967 Cronkite's evening news had surged ahead of NBC's Huntley-Brinkley report as the leading network news broadcast. In 1968, following the Tet Offensive by the North Vietnamese, Cronkite said that he believed that "the bloody experience of Vietnam is a stalemate." Whether he provoked or crystallized public opinion, many historians believe that these words from the trusted anchor pushed President Lyndon Johnson to decide to negotiate with North Vietnam as well as to decide not to run for reelection. A generation also remembers Cronkite's enthusiastic coverage of the Apollo moon landing in 1969. Cronkite retired from CBS in 1981 but continued hosting documentaries for PBS and, in the 1990s, the Learning Channel and the Discovery Channel.

Matt Drudge, pioneering but controversial Internet journalist who short-circuited the traditional "news cycle." Drudge's background was as far from that of a typical journalist as his online site is from a typical newspaper. Drudge grew up in Takoma Park, Maryland, where he listened to a steady diet of talk radio, itself a maverick medium at the time. Discovering the Internet around 1995, Drudge began to experiment with online writing, seeing himself as a new kind of journalist in the old muckraking tradition, digging up facts from an eclectic mix of sources and getting them straight to the people. At first mainly via Usenet newsgroups and e-mail, Drudge compiled whatever news he could gather from his growing network of informants and served it up as the Drudge Report. By 1997, however, he shifted his focus to his web site. He became famous (and infamous to some) for breaking the Clinton-Lewinsky affair while the mainstream media outlets were still trying to decide how to handle the story. However, Drudge's lack of attention to traditional standards involving independent sources and fact-checking has brought considerable criticism from mainstream journalists and journalism experts. In his book *Drudge Manifesto* (2000), Drudge makes no apologies for his approach to journalism in the Internet era. Ironically, Drudge's fame brought him an invitation to enter the traditional media world and do his own radio version of the Drudge Report. However, ABC Radio canceled his show in November 2000, saying that it was not profitable enough—although he later returned to the air.

Stephen Tyree Early managed press relations for President Franklin Roosevelt and helped establish the press secretary as an important post in presidential administrations. After graduating from high school, Early worked for the United Press and Associated Press, covering the State, War, and Navy Departments until 1917. When the United States entered the war, Early enlisted in the army and eventually took charge of the new army newspaper *Stars and Stripes*. During the 1920s Early became increasingly close to Franklin Delano Roosevelt, working on his unsuccessful campaign for the vice presidency. Meanwhile he rejoined Associated Press and also worked with two new media technologies, the film newsreel and radio. When Roosevelt became president in 1933, he appointed Early as assistant secretary in charge of press relations, a post later upgraded to full secretary. Early used radio and newsreels effectively to familiarize the public with Roosevelt's New Deal programs and to counter opposition from business interests. Early's personal knowledge of the needs and instincts of reporters helped him maintain good relations with the press and shape favorable coverage, although World War II and the now ailing Roosevelt's estrangement from the press complicated matters. Early's legacy was the White House's recognition of the need for active, full-time management of the media.

Pauline Frederick, the first woman network radio news correspondent. Born in Gallitzin, Pennsylvania, Frederick began her journalism career while still a teenager, covering society news for the *Harrisburg Telegraph*. Offered a full-time position after high school, she turned it down in favor of studying political science at American University, in Washington, D.C. She also studied international law and diplomacy, as well as interviewing diplomats' wives as part of her research. This experience led her to an offer of employment by NBC's director of women's programs, Margaret

Cuthbert. During World War II she worked both in-house at NBC and abroad with other journalists covering Africa and Asia and, after the war, the trials at Nuremberg. The prevailing bias against admitting women to "serious" journalism limited her opportunities. However, when a male reporter was not available to cover a foreign ministers' conference for ABC, Frederick filled in successfully. Eventually she held a regular post covering the United Nations and foreign relations for ABC and later NBC. From 1974 to her death in 1990 she was a foreign correspondent for National Public Radio.

Fred W. Friendly, pioneering CBS news producer and media scholar. He was born Ferdinand Friendly Wachenheimer in New York City. He entered the infant radio industry during the depths of the depression, at a tiny radio station in Providence, Rhode Island. Starting in 1937 he began to produce radio documentaries and served as an army information officer during World War II. In the late 1940s Friendly began to work with famed correspondent Edwin R. Murrow in the new medium of television, producing his award-winning documentaries, including the *See It Now* series. Together with Murrow, Friendly produced a documentary denouncing Senator Joseph McCarthy's anticommunist tactics when the hysteria was at its height. During the 1960s Friendly helped develop other pioneering programs, including *CBS Reports* and a political discussion program that would become *Meet the Press*. However, as the decade wore on, Friendly became increasingly concerned with the effects of corporate profit motives on the integrity and autonomy of news operations. In 1966 Friendly resigned in protest when CBS decided to air reruns of *I Love Lucy* rather than a Senate hearing investigating the growing U.S. involvement in Vietnam.

William Lloyd Garrison, leading abolitionist and influential journalist. Born in Newburyport, Massachusetts, Garrison was apprenticed as a teenager to the local newspaper editor. He became a skilled compositor and was also allowed to write anonymously for the paper. After completing his seven-year apprenticeship, Garrison became editor of another local paper, the *Free Press*. After he lost his job in that paper's failure, Garrison went to Boston and became coeditor of the *National Philanthropist*, a newspaper crusading for temperance and against lottery gaming. When he met Benjamin Lundy, a Quaker abolitionist, Garrison became increasingly interested in writing against slavery. Soon Garrison and Lundy were editing a weekly paper called *The Genius of Universal Abolition*, as well as speaking out against slavery at public gatherings. Garrison was sued for criminal libel for an accusation involving the domestic slave trade and had to serve seven weeks in prison before being bailed out by a philanthropist. Shortly thereafter, undaunted, Garrison started the *Liberator*, with the motto "Our country is the world—Our countrymen are mankind," and a manifesto ending with the ringing words: "I am in earnest—I will not equivocate—I will not excuse—I will not retreat a single inch—and *I will be heard.*" Garrison became increasingly radical, even advocating that the North secede from the Union rather than continue to accommodate the evils of slavery. In his later years Garrison continued his reform efforts, mixing civil rights for women and Native Americans with temperance-type movements against alcohol and prostitution. Garrison's long career is a reminder of the intertwining of journalism and reform advocacy in the 19th century.

Doris A. Graber, communications scholar who has done pioneering work on how audiences process media information. Born in St. Louis, Missouri, Graber worked as a feature writer for various newspapers while earning a doctorate in international law and relations at Columbia University in 1947. She edited legal periodicals and taught political science, but she is best known as a professor and researcher in communications theory. Her specialty is the connection between the media and political behavior, as well as the study of how people process the information they receive based on their preconceptions and existing structure of belief. She has written a number of important books, including *Media Power in Politics* (1984), *Processing the News* (1984, revised in 1993), and *Mass Media in American Politics* (6th edition, 2001).

Horace Greeley, influential editor of the *New York Tribune*. Struggling as a young adult to make a living as a printer, Greeley arrived in New York in 1831. He was eventually able to establish a small printing firm. However, Greeley also wanted to write, and in 1834 he started the *New Yorker,* a journal not related to the modern magazine of the same name. It was literarily but not financially successful. Greeley then took part in the intense partisan political journalism of the era, supporting Whig leaders. Inspired (or perhaps provoked) by the New York "penny paper," the *New York Herald* of James Gordon Bennett, Greeley borrowed enough money to launch the *New York Tribune*. Unlike the *Herald*, the *Tribune* under Greeley avoided police reports and sensational scandal journalism. Besides high intellectual standards, Greeley also promoted social reform and activism, particularly against the evils of exploitive corporations, and was a staunch abolitionist. After the Civil War Greeley became disillusioned with what he saw as corruption in the Republican Party and ran as a Democrat against President Ulysses Grant, being decisively defeated. He is perhaps best remembered for his advice to those seeking better opportunities: "Go west, young man."

William Randolph Hearst, powerful and influential media tycoon of the late 19th and early 20th century. His family's wealth ensured young

Hearst a first-class education and opportunity to travel in Europe. At Harvard he was something of a troublemaker, although he did useful work for the campus humor paper, the *Harvard Lampoon*. Hearst's interest in journalism led him to an apprenticeship at Joseph Pulitzer's *New York World;* in 1887 Hearst's father, who had been elected to the U.S. Senate, somewhat reluctantly turned his *San Francisco Examiner* over to young Hearst to run. Hearst reorganized the paper and changed its journalistic and marketing style to focus on public interest. Despite the danger of angering his father's political connections, Hearst took on a crusade against the powerful Southern Pacific Railroad and hired the sharp-penned satirist Ambrose Bierce. After Hearst's father died and he inherited the family copper fortune, Hearst entered the New York journalism market and revitalized the small and failing *New York Journal*. Applying similar techniques to those he had used at the *Examiner,* Hearst took on Joseph Pulitzer and his *Evening World.* His approach, soon termed "yellow journalism," has been praised for its populist concern with immigrants and the working class and criticized for its lack of objectivity and cheapening of journalistic standards. Hearst's most famous "crusade" followed the explosion and sinking of the U.S. battleship *Maine* in Havana Harbor in 1898, featuring lurid coverage of alleged Spanish atrocities and, later, glorious American military actions. Historians are divided as to how much responsibility Hearst had for pushing the United States into war with Spain. Hearst later embarked on his own not terribly successful political career. His legacy was a powerful chain of newspapers and San Simeon, an elaborate castle in the California coastal hills.

Chet Robert Huntley (Chester Huntley), together with David Brinkley, one of the most successful news broadcasters of the "Golden Age of Television." Huntley was born in Cardwell, Montana. He grew up on a ranch and then graduated from the University of Seattle in 1934. His broadcasting career began while he was still in college, at a small Seattle radio station, where he later recalled he did everything, including sweeping the floor. Eventually he became program director. He would serve as an announcer, newscaster, or program director for a variety of other radio stations and major networks over the next 20 years. During World War II Huntley produced programs that sought to counter discrimination against Hispanic Americans (following the so-called Zoot Suit Riots) and against the internment of Japanese Americans. After the war he began to gain some experience with the new medium of television while fighting off McCarthy-inspired attacks on his liberal politics. In 1956 Huntley joined David Brinkley to anchor the NBC coverage of the year's political conventions. For the next 15 years, Huntley-Brinkley would be the most recognized television news broadcast in America.

Kathleen Hall Jamieson, expert on politics and the media (particularly campaign advertising) and dean of the Annenberg School for Communication at the University of Pennsylvania. Throughout her career as a scholar of political communications, Jamieson has focused on political advertising and the techniques campaigns have used to "sell" presidential candidates. In 1988 she published (with David S. Birdsell) *Presidential Debates: The Challenge of Creating an Informed Electorate* and *Eloquence in an Electronic Age: The Transformation of Political Speechmaking.* She continued in the 1990s with works including *Dirty Politics: Deception, Distraction, and Democracy* (1992) and *Everything You Think You Know About Politics—and Why You're Wrong* (2000), which uses the results of research studies to dispel common preconceptions about campaigns and political advertising. Her latest book (with Paul Waldman) is *The Press Effect: Politicians, Journalists, and the Stories That Shape the Political World* (2003), which argues that the media has abdicated its responsibility to make politicians respond to substantive issues.

Thomas Jefferson, third president of the United States and proponent of freedom of the press. Jefferson attended the College of William and Mary, studying philosophy, science, and law, and was exposed to the ferment of political debate surrounding issues such as the Stamp Act of 1765, leading to debates over the proper rights and representation for the colonists. In 1774 Jefferson wrote the influential *A Summary Review of the Rights of British America,* and in 1776 he drafted the Declaration of Independence, which was accepted by the Continental Congress with only a few changes. As a Virginia legislator and governor, Jefferson worked during the Revolutionary War to improve the state's educational system as well as promoting guarantees of religious tolerance. As secretary of state in George Washington's administration, Jefferson and his followers clashed with Alexander Hamilton and his nascent Federalist Party, which promoted a stronger central government and the furtherance of large business interests. In the late 1790s, with the Federalists in ascendancy, President John Adams signed the Alien and Sedition Acts, which included provisions criminalizing criticism of government officials. Jefferson strongly opposed the law, authoring resolutions in the Kentucky and Virginia legislatures that asserted the rights of states to "nullify" such federal laws as they believed compromised their essential liberties. Jefferson asserted a robust support for freedom of speech, remarking that if he had to choose between having a government and having newspapers, he would opt for the latter. However, Jefferson was also the target of stinging attacks by the opposition press.

Rush H. Limbaugh, conservative radio talk show host who became a powerful mobilizer of right-wing sentiment. Limbaugh fell in love with radio from an early age. As a bored high school student of 16, he pestered his father into helping him get a job at a local radio station. Although Limbaugh did attend college for a year, he gravitated to the life of a roving disk jockey, mixing music with satirical commentary that sometimes got him in trouble. In the early 1980s Limbaugh attempted a more stable career as a marketing executive for the Kansas City Royals Baseball Club. However, by 1983 he was back in Kansas City as a radio news announcer, only to lose his job for being too controversial. When he took a radio job at KFBK in Sacramento, California, his blend of humor and barbed comments caught on with the audience. In 1988 Ed McLaughlin, an independent radio producer-distributor, decided to give Limbaugh a shot at a national syndicated audience. Somewhat surprisingly, Limbaugh's program caught on rapidly, even though many stations preferred to use the daytime slot for their own programming and local advertising. Limbaugh's unabashed conservatism appealed to many people who identified themselves as "ordinary Americans" whose concerns and fears were being ignored by a "media elite" that they perceived to be too liberal and out of touch. By the mid-1990s Limbaugh's influence seemed to be peaking; many political pundits gave him considerable credit for mobilizing his legions of "ditto-heads" to go to the polls in 1994 and vote the Republicans into control of Congress. In the late 1990s Limbaugh's overt criticism of President Bill Clinton and first lady Hillary Clinton may have helped fuel the ultimately unsuccessful impeachment effort. In October 2003 Limbaugh's own reputation was rocked by his admission of addiction to prescription pain medicines. He entered a treatment center while authorities continued their investigation of possible drug links.

Walter Lippmann, influential columnist, editor, and early writer on public opinion. While at Harvard, Lippmann took advantage of the opportunity to consult with such notable intellectuals as philosopher George Santayana and psychologist William James. After graduation he entered journalism, in particular working as an assistant to the pioneering investigative journalist Lincoln Steffens, who was investigating corruption in financial institutions. Lippmann, who had presided over the Socialist Club at Harvard, also engaged in socialist politics and political writing, including a book, *A Preface to Politics* (1913). Lippmann's writing called him to the attention of Herbert Croly, editor of the *New Republic*, who in 1914 invited him to join his staff. During World War I Lippmann served in a variety of positions in the Wilson administration. After the war Lippmann joined those opposing the Versailles peace treaty's harsh treatment of the defeated Germans. Besides the *New Republic*, Lippmann wrote for other publications, including *Vanity Fair*. He also became interested in understanding how public opinion was formed by the media, advertising, and other inputs. His 1922 book, *Public Opinion*, issued a challenge still relevant today: How can people make the decisions required of them in a complex modern democracy when they seem unable to obtain or grasp the required information? Lippmann was a nationally syndicated political columnist in the 1930s through the 1960s, winning Pulitzer Prizes in 1958 and 1962. A supporter of President John F. Kennedy, Lippmann eventually broke with President Lyndon Johnson over the Vietnam War, which he considered to be an unnecessary waste of lives and resources.

Robert C. Maynard, a pioneer African-American journalist and editor, who became the first black editor-publisher of a major metropolitan newspaper, the *Oakland Tribune*. Born in New York City to immigrants from the island of Barbados, Maynard was fascinated by writing and newspapers from an early age, but opportunities in the virtually all-white world of journalism seemed slim. However, there were black newspapers, and young Maynard went to work for the New York *Age-Defender* while still trying to get a reporting job in a mainstream paper. He finally received a post as a police reporter at the *York Gazette and Daily* in York, Pennsylvania. His hard work overcame racial prejudices, and he won a prestigious Niemann Fellowship to Harvard University. At Harvard, Maynard met influential editors such as Ben Bradlee of the *Washington Post*, who hired him to work for that elite newspaper. Covering such events as the Watergate scandal, Maynard rose in the *Post* ranks while trying to promote hiring opportunities for minorities. He also taught journalism and helped establish the Institute for Journalism Education. Moving to the West Coast, Maynard found his career taking a different turn when he was asked by the Gannett Corporation to become editor-in-chief of the *Oakland Tribune*. Maynard reoriented the formerly conservative *Tribune* so it could address the growing black, Asian, and Hispanic communities.

Rupert K. Murdoch, Australian (later American) media mogul. Murdoch was born in Melbourne. His father was a newspaper editor who also ran newspapers in Adelaide and Brisbane. After graduating from Oxford University in England, Murdoch returned to Australia and took over his deceased father's *Adelaide News and Sunday Mail*. He soon added newspapers in other cities, including Perth and Sydney. More an entrepreneur than a journalist, Murdoch was able to turn unprofitable newspapers into moneymaking enterprises whose revenue could then be used to fuel further acquisitions. In the 1960s Murdoch bought two British tabloids, the *News of the World* and the *Sun*, reinforcing his reputation for journalistic sensationalism. (In 1981 he also bought the London *Times*, but did not tinker much with its conservative character.) In the 1970s Murdoch began to buy media properties in the United States, including the tabloid *Star*. In

144

the mid-1980s Murdoch burst into the broadcast arena, buying the Metromedia group of independent television stations and the Twentieth Century-Fox Studio, meanwhile becoming a U.S. citizen in order to meet FCC requirements. The rich resources he had gained in content creation and distribution facilities in turn enabled him to create the Fox TV network, the first broadcast network to successfully compete with the "big three" of CBS, NBC, and ABC. Murdoch has been criticized by liberals for his union-unfriendly labor practices and for the conservative slant of his Fox News network, which in the mid-1990s adopted the slogans "fair and balanced" and "we report, you decide."

Edward R. Murrow, legendary radio and television news correspondent. After graduating from Washington State University, Murrow worked with the Institute of International Education. In 1935 he joined CBS as director in charge of arranging broadcast speeches and concerts, going to London in 1937. When World War II broke out, Murrow remained in London as a news correspondent. His "This is London" radio broadcasts live from the Blitz in 1940 brought the reality of the war into American homes. Later wartime broadcasts covered a bombing raid against Berlin and the liberation of the Buchenwald concentration camp. In 1951 Murrow inaugurated his television career with the program *See It Now*, which brought a new level of political discussion to the medium. In 1954 the program challenged anticommunist demagogue Senator Joseph McCarthy, helping turn the tide against him. By the end of the 1950s, however, Murrow had largely left commercial broadcasting, disillusioned with what he viewed as its lack of commitment to serious journalism.

Thomas Nast brought the political cartoon to a new level of effectiveness. He was born in Ludwig, Bavaria, but his family immigrated to New York six years later. He showed early talent as an artist, and when he was only 15 he showed some drawings to *Leslie's Weekly* and was hired as an illustrator. During the Civil War he worked with *Harper's Weekly*, creating patriotic drawings to boost the morale of the North. By the Reconstruction period Nast had turned his art from illustration to barbed caricatures with explicitly political messages, attacking those who wanted to abandon Reconstruction (and southern blacks). In the early 1870s Nast took on New York City corruption and, in particular, Boss Tweed and his Tammany Hall henchmen. Nast was offered a $200,000 bribe to stop his attacks, but to no avail: his drawing pen proved mightier than the machine. Nast was also responsible for those enduring party icons, the Democratic donkey and the Republican elephant.

Arthur Charles Nielsen, market researcher who invented a system of broadcast ratings. Born in Chicago, Nielsen graduated from the University of Chicago as valedictorian and with the highest grades ever awarded to an engineering student. After serving a year in the Naval Reserve during World War I, Nielsen began a career as an engineer. His specialty was monitoring the quality and performance of manufacturing equipment, and in 1923 he founded the A. C. Nielsen company to market his services. When the manufacturing slump of the Great Depression threatened his company's survival, Nielsen expanded his services to include monitoring the sales of groceries and drugstore products. These businesses eagerly welcomed information that they could use for targeting their advertising and distribution efforts. In 1938 radio station owners began to ask Nielsen if he could develop a similar service to monitor the distribution of their ultimate "product"—that is, their listeners; whom they marketed to advertisers. He invented the Nielsen Audimeter, a recording device that kept track of what station a radio set was tuned to. His Nielsen Radio Index soon became an essential subscription for radio marketing managers. In 1950 Nielsen adapted his Audimeter and monitoring procedures to the burgeoning television industry, adding the use of a viewer diary. Although very successful, the Nielsen ratings were criticized for alleged tampering, lack of accuracy, and for not using a sufficiently representative sampling of the population. On a more philosophical level, critics complained that the Nielsen ratings gave broadcasters too much incentive to chase short-term gains instead of enduring journalistic quality. Despite these criticisms, Nielsen ratings are still used today and largely influence advertising expenditure on broadcasted programs.

Richard Milhous Nixon, 37th president of the United States, had a stormy relationship with the news media throughout his career. Born in Yorba Linda, California, in modest circumstances, Nixon was a successful debater and student politician at Whittier College, and then became a lawyer. He served during World War II as a federal regulator and then as a naval officer. In 1946 he successfully ran for Congress, attacking his Democratic opponent as liberal and too pro-union. In 1950 he won election to the Senate but not without angering many people by accusing his opponent of being "soft on communism." Nixon also served on the House Un-American Activities Committee (HUAC), playing a major role in the conviction of Alger Hiss. As he campaigned for vice president with Dwight Eisenhower, Nixon's abrasive personality and polemic brought him into frequent conflicts with reporters plus a scandal, in which he was accused of misusing campaign funds. He took the offensive on television, giving a speech in which he said he had not taken anything from his supporters except for a puppy named Checkers. Although Nixon had used the medium to successfully deflect criticism, his televised debate against Democratic candidate John F. Kennedy during the 1960 presidential campaign was much less successful. The youthful-looking, energetic, articulate Kennedy appeared in startling contrast to Nixon, who was ill and poorly made-up. After losing that election and a subsequent one for governor of California, Nixon told reporters that they "won't have Nixon to kick around anymore." Returning to the campaign trail in 1968, Nixon decided to strictly control media access, refusing to debate Hubert H. Humphrey and relying instead on carefully scripted appearances. When Nixon became president, his administration often attacked the press, his point man being Vice President Spiro Agnew, who criticized the media for perceived elitism and liberal bias. Nixon's strategy of media restriction and management seemed to work well in 1972, when he easily won re-election over Senator George McGovern. However, a "second-rate burglary" at the Watergate Hotel began a painful unraveling that would end with Nixon's resignation in August 1974. The scandal made the careers of two young *Washington Post* investigative reporters, Carl Bernstein and Bob Woodward, and as a legacy put relations between politicians and the press on a more adversarial level.

Joseph Pulitzer, influential 19th-century journalist and practitioner of "yellow journalism." Pulitzer was a Hungarian immigrant who settled in St. Louis, where he became a reporter for a German-language newspaper. His aggressive journalistic and business instincts enabled him to acquire several newspapers, eventually forming the *St. Louis Post-Dispatch.* He also became involved in the rambunctious politics of the time, serving as a state legislator (although legally he was too young) and shooting and wounding a prominent lobbyist. After other contentious and sometimes violent encounters, Pulitzer left the St. Louis newspaper scene and went to New York City, where he bought the nearly defunct *New York World.* In the next two decades he turned that paper into a formidable competitor, gaining much support from his forthright endorsement of workers' rights. Pulitzer competed with William Randolph Hearst, editor of the *New York Journal,* to be more populist and sensational, practicing what became known as "yellow journalism," named for the political comic strip character the "yellow kid." This era reached its height with U.S. agitation over the sinking of the battleship *Maine* and the Spanish-American War. Ironically, this rough-and-tumble journalistic entrepreneur would leave a more genteel legacy: the funding of the Columbia School of Journalism and the prestigious Pulitzer Prizes for various areas of journalism.

Jacob August Riis, documentary photographer who showed the power of the image for covering social problems. A Danish immigrant and carpenter, Riis experienced firsthand life in New York City's slums. He began to train himself as a journalist, became a reporter with the *South Brooklyn News* in 1874, then worked on the police beat at the *New York Tribune* starting in 1877. This work in turn brought him back into daily contact with the effects of poverty, and his journalism sought to arouse public concern with slum conditions. In photography Riis saw a powerful new tool for conveying these realities, and his best pictures and his book *How the Other Half Lives* (1890) remain haunting today. Riis's photographic portrayal of the wretched lives of child laborers also played an important role in the passage of child labor laws. Along with the Civil War photography of Mathew Brady, the work of Riis established the modern discipline of photojournalism.

James Romenesko, Internet journalist and "blogger" who became a purveyor of "insider" media stories in the wake of the *New York Times*–Jayson Blair scandal of 2003. Originally an online reporter for the *St. Paul Pioneer Press*, Romenesko started his own web site, MediaGossip.com, in his spare time in 1999. He quickly learned that media people had an appetite for gossip and scandal as insatiable as their readers'. The prestigious Poynter Institute soon agreed to pay him to maintain the site. Another reason for the site's popularity is that it took up the "blog," or weblog format, a kind of online diary/opinion column that was becoming increasingly popular. The ability of the Internet to turn a local story into a national one in a matter of hours, plus the instant feedback available in this interactive medium, also made Romenesko's efforts compelling and effective. However, his site was not well known outside the journalistic and Internet communities until April 2003, when reports of journalistic falsification by reporter Jayson Blair ignited an uproar at (and around) the *New York Times*. Journalists covering the story gravitated to the Romenesko site, both to learn the latest "dish" and to dish out tidbits of their own. This in turn led to more of the general public learning about Romenesko and the burgeoning phenomenon of weblogs.

Franklin D. Roosevelt, 32nd president of the United States and one of the first politicians to use the broadcast media effectively. Roosevelt himself had some journalistic experience, writing for the *Harvard Crimson* as a student as well as for various magazines during the 1920s. When Roosevelt assumed the presidency in 1933, the country was in a deepening economic depression and there was a considerable atmosphere of panic and despair. Roosevelt cultivated good relationships with the print and broadcast media, holding regular, in-depth press conferences to explain his New Deal programs. He also directly mustered support for his programs by speaking directly to the American people in his famous radio "fireside chats." However, for all his seeming openness, Roosevelt tightly controlled the release of information when it suited his purposes. He also had an implicit understanding with the media that photos and newsreels would not show him in his wheelchair, the result of his bout of polio.

Roosevelt's efforts to manage the media were greatly aided by his press secretary, Stephen Tyree Early.

Ida Tarbell, one of the foremost reforming journalists, or "muckrakers," of the early 20th century. She began her career as a teacher and an editor for the Chautauqua Literary and Scientific Circle (an influential adult educational and cultural movement). In the 1890s she moved to Paris and supported herself by writing articles for American magazines until she was hired full time by *McClure's*. For that publication she wrote her most famous work, *History of the Standard Oil Corporation*, which described the rise of John D. Rockefeller's monopoly and its unfair business practices.

Ted Turner (Robert Edward Turner), entrepreneur who founded Turner Broadcasting and CNN and revolutionized cable television. Turner, kicked out of Brown University for excessive partying, became a manager in his father's advertising company, although he had a contentious relationship with the elder Turner. After his father's death Turner reorganized the company, calling it Turner Communications (it would later become Turner Broadcasting). He began to buy television stations, grabbing market share from competitors by relentlessly offering the most popular kinds of programs, including sports and movies. He also became interested in the slowly growing area of cable television. Cable had originally been an alternative means of broadcast distributions for areas without good access to signals. Turner, however, turned his flagship station, WTBS, into an all-cable station. He also developed the "superstation" concept, wherein the station distributed programming to other cable stations, in effect functioning as a new kind of network. In 1986 Turner created CNN, the Cable News Network, the first national 24-hour all-news television network. CNN defied industry expectations in 1988 by actually showing a profit from news. Turner also created another service, TNT (Turner Network Television), showing movies and wrestling. In 1995, Turner sold his Turner Broadcasting to Time-Warner for $7.5 billion, becoming Time-Warner's vice chairman and largest shareholder. In January 2001 America Online (AOL) merged with Time-Warner and Turner became vice chairman of the new media giant. Turner was soon frustrated by what he saw as his marginal role in AOL/Time-Warner, and the company suffered a downturn as the result of the collapse of the "dot-com" boom. Turner's other broadcast operations include Turner Network Television (TNT), the Cartoon Network, and Turner Classic Movies. A pioneer in media organization and formatting, Turner and his success leave critics with many questions about the effects of the corporate media.

Robert Woodward, together with Carl Bernstein, unraveled the Watergate scandal, creating a model for investigative journalism. Woodward started his career in the U.S. Navy and then took up journalism. As a police beat reporter for the *Washington Post*, Woodward attended the arraignment of what seemed to be ordinary burglars—except their target had been the Democratic National Committee headquarters at the Watergate Hotel, and their connections seemed mysterious. Working at first independently and then joined by Carl Bernstein, Woodward traced the links that led from the Watergate burglars to the highest officials in the White House, creating a scandal that ultimately led to the resignation of President Richard Nixon. Woodward and Bernstein chronicled their investigative efforts in their book *All The President's Men*, and then explored the unraveling of the Nixon administration in *The Final Days*. Woodward undertook many later investigations and books, some controversial, as a senior editor and investigative journalist at the *Washington Post*.

John Peter Zenger, printer whose libel trial turned into an assertion of freedom of the press. Zenger was a printer who worked for James Alexander, editor of the *New-York Weekly Journal*. Alexander launched barbed attacks at many political officials, including the governor of New York, William Cosby, whom he called a "rogue." Cosby ordered his police to destroy the newspaper and jailed Zenger for criminal libel. There was no right to an attorney in those days, so Zenger faced trial alone until a member of the audience, Andrew Hamilton, stood up and agreed to defend him. Hamilton's defense was that Zenger had printed facts that justified his conclusion about Cosby. However, truth was not recognized as a defense to libel, and the judge ordered the jury to convict Zenger. Hamilton nevertheless appealed to the jury's love of freedom and hatred of tyranny, and the jury returned a verdict of not guilty. While law and precedent would not change immediately, the Zenger case would be cited in arguing that the press must be free to print the truth without being punished.

CHAPTER 6

GLOSSARY

The following journalistic, legal, and other terms and names are often found in discussion of the news media and related issues.

actual malice   The finding in libel or defamation cases that the defendant writer knew that certain factual statements about the plaintiff were false and recklessly proceeded anyway. This threshold is required when the subject of the writing is a public official or public figure (as in the Supreme Court case *New York Times v. Sullivan*).

agenda setting   The theory, supported by many studies, that the raising of issues in the media plays an important role in determining what issues or policy agenda will be in the public mind, and thus in play in political campaigns.

Alien and Sedition Acts   Federal laws enacted in 1798 that made it a crime to publish "false, scandalous, or malicious" writings about government officials. The laws lapsed in 1801.

anonymous source   A person who provides information to a journalist on the condition that his or her name not be revealed.

Associated Press (AP)   A major source for news stories for newspapers and broadcasters, founded as a newspaper news cooperative in 1860.

audience research   The effort to determine the demographics, degree of involvement, and preferences of a broadcaster's or publication's audience.

background (on background)   Information that is provided by a journalist but attributed only to a generic source such as "a high Defense Department official."

blowback   The taking up by the domestic media of a false story that had been planted in the foreign media by an intelligence agency.

Blue Book   A set of guidelines issued by the Federal Communications Commission (FCC) in 1946. It attempted to promote the idea that a station using the public airwaves had a responsibility to serve the public interest. Stations were expected to carry programming that met diverse needs, provide substantial news coverage (including local news), discuss public issues in depth, and restrain excessive carrying of commercials. The deregulation efforts of the 1980s made most of these considerations moot.

broadside   A statement, often referring to current issues or events, printed on a poster-sized sheet of paper. Broadsides were a common way to spread news and public communications in the 17th and 18th centuries.

Cable News Network (CNN)   Television network founded by entrepreneur Ted Turner in 1980. It features a 24-hour television news format. The growth in cable television subscribers and CNN's aggressive reporting and ability to cover breaking news such as the 1991 Gulf War made it a formidable challenger to the broadcast networks.

civic journalism   Also called public journalism, this is a recent movement in which journalists, rather than simply reporting on events in the community, become directly involved, often becoming advocates for social reform. This raises questions of objectivity.

clear and present danger   A danger so immediate that it might justify the prior restraint of a publication by the court.

CNN effect   This term was coined during the Gulf War of 1991 to describe how millions of people spent most of their waking hours watching the war, particularly on CNN. It now applies to any event, such as the terrorist attacks of September 11, 2001, or the Iraq War of 2003, in which, the urge to stay home and watch television leads to a considerable drop in tourism, restaurant, and movie revenue, and so on.

Columbia Broadcasting System (CBS)   An organization founded in 1927 as a radio network. In the television era it became one of three dominant broadcast television networks.

Committee on Public Information   This organization was started by the U.S. government during World War I. It combined the distribution of official information and propaganda with managing a voluntary censorship program.

confidentiality   In journalism, a commitment to a source that the source's identity will not be revealed.

contempt   A finding that a person has violated rules set by the court. Contempt has sometimes been used as a means of enforcing restrictions on the press, such as by gag orders.

Corporation for Public Broadcasting (CPB)   Established by Congress in 1967 to help develop programming for noncommercial television and radio stations.

cross-ownership   The ownership by the same company of different types of media companies (such as newspapers, radio or television stations) in the same market. This has been restricted by the FCC but many of the restrictions were eased in 2003.

defamation Injuring a person's reputation unfairly. It encompasses libel (written material) or slander (spoken material).

docudrama A hybrid of "documentary" and "drama," a docudrama is a dramatization of real-life persons (biography) or events. The accuracy of the portrayal is often open to question.

documentary A radio or television feature that explores an issue or topic in depth.

editorial A statement expressing the official views of a publication or broadcaster. Broadcasters were not allowed to have editorials until the FCC allowed them, subject to the Fairness Doctrine, in 1949.

"equal time" rule Originally part of the Radio Act of 1927, this regulation requires that if a broadcast station offers access to the airwaves to any candidate for public office, all other legally qualified candidates for that office must be given the same opportunity.

fabrication In journalism, the creation of fictional characters or events that are reported as actual news. An example was Janet Cooke's 1981 *Washington Post* story about an eight-year-old heroin addict.

Fairness Doctrine A 1949 FCC ruling that allowed broadcasters to have editorial opinions provided they allowed opposing viewpoints to be aired. The Fairness Doctrine was dropped in 1987 as the FCC began to promote deregulation of broadcasting.

Federal Communications Commission (FCC) The federal agency responsible for regulating electronic communications and broadcasting. It was established by the Communications Act of 1934.

Federal Radio Commission (FRC) Established by the Radio Act of 1927, the FRC was the first attempt at federal regulation of the rapidly growing industry of electronic broadcasting. The commission established the fundamental criteria of "public interest, convenience, and/or necessity" for licensing broadcast stations. The FRC also established rules for preventing interference between stations. It was replaced in 1934 by the Federal Communications Commission.

Federal Trade Commission (FTC) A federal agency that has had an impact on the media in two ways. First, it regulates against misleading practices in commercial advertising. Second, it enforces antitrust or anticoncentration laws to restrain certain mergers between media companies.

First Amendment The first article in the Bill of Rights, it (among other things) guarantees freedom of speech and of the press.

Fourteenth Amendment This amendment, passed following the Civil War, guarantees all citizens due process and equal protection of the laws. During the 20th century courts began to hold that the Fourteenth Amendment also implied a guarantee of many of the rights specified in the first 10 amendments, and that state and local governments were also bound by them.

Fox Network   A relatively new television network formed in 1985 by Australia-born entrepreneur Rupert Murdoch. During the 1990s Fox was quite successful in luring broadcast TV stations away from the three traditional networks. In recent years Fox has promoted itself as a "fair and balanced" (although many critics say "conservative") alternative to the mainstream media's perceived liberal bias.

Freedom of Information Act (FOIA)   A law, enacted in 1966, that provides for public access to federal government records upon request. Although there are some exceptions (such as classified information and personnel matters), the FOIA has become a basic tool for investigative reporters.

gag order   A court order prohibiting parties in a case from talking to the media, usually in the interest of minimizing prejudicial pretrial publicity. Attempts to gag the media directly usually run afoul of the First Amendment.

gatekeeping   The role editors and other professionals play in the selection and coverage of news material. Much of the allegations of ideological or corporate bias in the media are concerned with forces shaping the decisions made by gatekeepers.

global village   The idea, popularized by Marshall McLuhan, that modern means of communication have given people a sense of living in an interconnected community, with distant events such as wars being brought into the living room by television.

interpretive (or interpretative) reporting   Reporting that, while striving to be accurate, also tries to provide analysis and perspective rather than just recounting facts and opinion.

investigative reporting   Reporting that involves active digging into the story "beneath" some phenomenon or issue, often confronting established interests that resist disclosure of key information.

joint operating agreement (JOA)   Allows a newspaper to share some of the resources of a competitor without violating antitrust regulations. The Newspaper Preservation Act of 1970 allowed this agreement in order to preserve competition in markets that might end up with only a single daily newspaper.

libel   Defamation, or injury to a person's reputation, carried out through writing or pictures, or broadcast.

market   For purposes of media ownership regulation, a market is a local area in which media outlets compete for an audience. Markets range from isolated rural areas to huge metropolitan areas such as New York City and Los Angeles.

Glossary

Mayflower Decision   The 1940 FCC ruling that prohibited radio stations from broadcasting editorials. The ruling was replaced by the Fairness Doctrine in 1949.

muckraking   Writings by crusading journalists in the first decades of the 20th century that exposed horrendous social conditions, corporate depredations, and corruption in government. Modern investigative reporters often find inspiration in the muckraking tradition.

National Broadcasting Company (NBC)   Started as the first national radio network in 1926, the following year NBC consisted of two networks called NBC-Red and NBC-Blue. After World War II NBC became one of the three major television broadcast networks.

National Public Radio (NPR)   A cooperative production and distribution network providing programming for public (noncommercial) radio stations.

New Journalism   A new style of newspaper journalism promoted especially by Joseph Pulitzer during the 1880s. It featured inexpensive but attractive newspapers, a vigorous writing style, and a commitment to exposing and reforming social problems. In the 1960s and 1970s the term was also applied to alternative or "underground" journalism and new styles of writing.

news councils   Local groups consisting of representatives from the media and diverse groups in the community. They attempt to resolve complaints about press coverage and improve service to the community.

news leak   The releasing or publication of information without an identified source, usually in an attempt to gain political or business advantage. Journalists are often torn between the lack of verifiability and accountability of such sources and the value of the information.

newsmagazine   In the print media, a weekly or less frequent publication devoted mainly or entirely to covering the news. Many prominent newsmagazines, including *Time* and *Newsweek*, were founded in the 1920s and 1930s. In television, a newsmagazine is a program format featuring in-depth investigative or feature stories, such as *60 Minutes* or *Dateline NBC*.

news management   The attempt by government or business officials to control (or sometimes strategically use) news affecting their organization.

Newspaper Association of America   A major trade organization formed in 1992 by combining seven major newspaper trade associations.

Nielsen ratings   Sometimes used as a generic term for television audience ratings, which have been dominated by the Nielsen Company.

Office of Censorship (OC)   An agency established in 1941 to oversee voluntary censorship by newspapers and broadcasters.

Office of War Information (OWI)   An agency established in 1942 that was responsible for information promoting the U.S. war effort at home and abroad.

ombudsman   A person hired by some newspapers to resolve public complaints about the fairness or accuracy of stories and to obtain general feedback from readers.

op-ed   The page in a newspaper, traditionally opposite the editorial page, containing syndicated opinion columns, opinions by staff writers, and sometimes articles submitted by members of the public. The *New York Times* introduced the op-ed page in 1970.

opinion magazines   Also called journals of opinion. A general term for magazines featuring essays on political or social topics. *The Nation,* founded in 1865, is generally credited with establishing this genre.

pack journalism   The tendency of journalists to move in groups when covering major events and to rely on other journalists (rather than primary sources) for cues on how to cover a story. The result can be unseemly (and occasionally dangerous) behavior as well as a lack of diversity of viewpoints in the news media.

paparazzi   From the Italian, meaning someone who rummages through papers; a freelance photographer who aggressively pursues celebrities. Paparazzi are often accused of trespassing or harassment and get into legal (and occasionally physical) confrontations.

participatory journalism   An approach to journalism in which a person has a role in creating the news that is being reported. For example, a reporter might enter a marathon or volunteer to help in a soup kitchen and then describe the experience. The practice is defended as bringing journalists into closer, more meaningful contact with the community, but critics are concerned about loss of objectivity.

plagiarism   Using the material of another writer as one's own or not giving proper credit to the author.

pool coverage   The designation of a group of journalists to cover an event such as a war to which independent access is impracticable or considered too dangerous. The resulting reports are then accessible to the media as a whole. Critics argue that restricting coverage to pool reporters gives the government too much control over the reporting.

precision journalism   This term, originated in the 1970s, refers to an approach to reporting that emphasizes the use of polls, survey research, and various statistical and research tools to analyze the causes of events or the significance of issues. Ideally, the resulting reporting would combine academic rigor with clear and compelling language.

press agent   A person whose job it is to get favorable press coverage for a client, often an entertainer. Press agents can also work in politics, although these days they generally have titles such as media relations specialist.

Glossary

press secretary   The official in the administration of a president or other executive who is charged with managing relations with the press, satisfying demands for information, and attempting to "spin" events so as to create a favorable impression. The first official press secretary served in the Hoover administration.

prior restraint   The prohibition by government or legal action of the publishing or distribution of certain information. The information may be considered prejudicial to a defendant's fair trial or harmful to national security. In the 1971 Pentagon Papers case, the Supreme Court said that the government had to demonstrate a significant threat to national security, not simply assert it. Prior restraint is seldom allowed by the courts.

public access television   Channels and studio facilities offered by cable television systems to local groups, enabling them to produce and distribute public service programming, forums on local issues, and so on.

public broadcasting   In referring to television or radio, this generally means noncommercial, nonprofit stations. These can include stations in major markets (affiliated with the Public Broadcast System) as well as local and university-related stations.

Public Broadcast Service (PBS)   A noncommercial network serving most of the nation's public television stations.

public figure (or public official)   In modern libel law, persons who, because of their presumptive newsworthiness, must prove actual malice rather than just falsehood when claiming they have been libeled. An ordinary person can become a "public figure" even if only temporarily involved in matters of public interest.

public interest, convenience, and necessity   This language, first included in the Radio Act of 1927, embodies the concept that a broadcaster using the public airwaves has obligations to serve the public in certain ways. In recent decades, however, deregulation and the growth of nonbroadcast television not subject to FCC regulation has reduced the applicability of this principle.

public journalism   *See* **civic journalism.**

public relations (PR)   The managements of the public's image or perception of a person, organization, or product through communications techniques and relationships with the media. The goal is to generate favorable media attention while minimizing negative coverage. The PR field became formalized in the 1920s and further professionalized after World War II.

Radio Act of 1927   The first attempt at federal regulation of broadcasting. It included the "equal time" rule.

slander   Defamation, or injury to a person's reputation, carried out through speech. Broadcast material is treated as libel rather than slander.

source   In journalism, a person providing information.

spin   Commentary intended to portray events in a way that is favorable to an individual or issue, or to minimize the impact of negative events. Experts at creating spin are known as "spin doctors."

sunshine law   A law (found in many states) that requires that public meetings, hearings, deliberations, and the like be open to the public and the media except for certain specified cases, such as discussion of personnel or legal matters, or certain contract or purchasing negotiations.

superstation   A television station that offers its programming to cable systems around the country, in effect having the reach of a network. Ted Turner created the first superstation in Atlanta, Georgia, in 1975.

syndication   The production of media content (such as newspaper columns, comics, or broadcast programs) for sale to outlets. Syndication makes high-quality material available to outlets that lack the resources to produce it themselves. Critics argue that radio syndication in particular has led to a loss of diversity in programming formats and content.

underground publishing   In the United States, this term refers to radical or countercultural publications, many of which flourished from the mid-1960s through the early 1970s. Analogous movements in other countries include the Russian *samizdat*, or "self-publishing" by dissidents.

United Press (UP)   A press cooperative founded in 1882 as an alternative to the Associated Press.

United Press International (UPI)   A news cooperative formed in 1958 by a merger of United Press and the International News Service.

PART II

GUIDE TO FURTHER RESEARCH

CHAPTER 7

———————◼———————

HOW TO RESEARCH
THE NEWS MEDIA

This chapter presents a guide to resources and techniques for students and others who are researching topics in journalism and media studies.

ONLINE RESOURCE SITES

Today, most researchers will turn first to the Web rather than to the local library. After all, the news media itself is vigorously (if not always enthusiastically) embracing the World Wide Web. The Web is now a primary source for news stories and feature articles (even those also available in print). It is also often the first place to look for resources about a subject, such as topic guides, bibliographies, and lists of additional Web links. A number of web sites offer extensive resources on many aspects of the media, ranging from business developments to journalistic ethics. Here are some suggested starting points. Of course, each site will point to many more!

MEDIA INDUSTRY RESOURCES

Each of the major sectors of the media (television, radio, and print) has sites that track the industry and provide relevant background material and resources:

- **Current Online** (http://www.current.org) is sponsored by *Current*, a journal devoted to public broadcasting. The site has stories, links, and background material on public broadcasting in the United States.
- **Cyber Atlas** (http://cyberatlas.internet.com) compiles a wide variety of statistics about Internet use, e-commerce, and related matters. Given the importance of the Internet to the modern news media, keeping up with trends in the online world is essential.

- **Data Directory** (http://www.washingtonpost.com/wp-srv/politics/polls/datadir.htm) provides links to many sources of polling and survey information on various topics that are available online. This is a useful resource for monitoring current public attitudes toward, and use of, the media.

- **The Future of News** (http://www.ojr.org/ojr/future) is a feature of the USC Annenberg Online Journalism Review. In addition to feature articles on the future of online news sites and their sometimes dubious business plans and on the future of newspapers, there are other topical sections and an archive.

- **I Want Media** (http://www.iwantmedia.com) is a site covering news affecting the media industry. It also provides links to media organizations, jobs, and other resources.

- **MediaChannel.org** (http://www.mediachannel.org) is a resource site on global media issues geared toward activists promoting media reform and providing "toolkits" and other issue links.

- **The Newspaper Industry** (http://www.newspaper-industry.org/index.cfm) is designed to provide newspaper executives with useful, timely information on the industry, but the current and archived links would also be very useful to students tracking developments in this sector of the media.

- **Television Advertising Bureau** (TVB, http://www.tvb.org/rcentral/mediatrendstrack/tvbasics/index.asp) provides information about television advertising volume, revenue, and television usage.

- **Television and Radio News Research** (http://www.missouri.edu/~jourvs/index.html) offers "a systematic look at the people and institutions that bring you television and radio news in the United States" based on ongoing surveys by Vernon Stone, professor emeritus of the Missouri School of Journalism. These surveys provide detailed information on the personal and educational background of broadcast professionals, job satisfaction and mobility, and other factors. Most information is from the mid-1990s, with some updates.

- **Television Week** (http://www.tvweek.com) is a web site (that incorporates Electronic Media) for the print magazine. It offers a variety of links to industry developments as well as to specific shows and networks.

JOURNALISM AND MEDIA RESEARCH

There are a number of organizations oriented toward doing research on journalism and the media. They tend to be associated with universities and/or foundations.

- **Center for Media Literacy** (http://www.medialit.org) provides a rich collection of resources, including lesson plans and handouts for teachers, as well as presentations of dozens of media-related topics and the complete archives of *Media Values* magazine.

- **First Amendment Center** (http://www.firstamendmentcenter.org) at Vanderbilt University offers news and resources on First Amendment issues, which often involve the power and responsibilities of the media. Follow the "press" link under First Amendment Topics. Resources include background papers on legal issues as well as cases.

- **Internet and American Life** (http://www.pewinternet.org) is a project of the Pew Research Center and Tides Center. It provides reports covering research on many aspects of Internet use, many of which are relevant to the online extension of the news media.

- **Medialiteracy.com** (http://www.medialiteracy.com/index.htm) is a resource site for media literacy education. Its links are divided into a number of sections including teaching and learning about the media; parents, kids, and media; media and health choices; media economics, social issues, and activism; and resources for journalists.

- **Pew Center for the People and the Press** (http://people-press.org) presents a wide variety of reports reflecting its ongoing surveys and other research. They cover not only domestic attitudes toward the media but also perceptions and attitudes toward world events.

THE PRACTICE OF JOURNALISM

Many of the following sites are geared for working journalists or journalism students but that does not mean that much of the material offered is not of great value to students of the media:

- **B-Roll Online** (http://www.b-roll.net) is a clearinghouse for news photography. Although it is focused on resources and job contacts for photographers, it also has interesting information and critiques useful to students of photojournalism.

- **Broadcast Media and Journalism Career Guide** (http://www.khake.com/page43.html) from the Vocational Information Center provides extensive links not only to dozens of media-related jobs but also to media and journalism organizations and resources.

- **CAR/CARR Links Page** (http://www.ryerson.ca/%7Edtudor/mega11.htm) is devoted to "computer-assisted reporting," a journalistic term for using computer techniques (such databases, as Web searching, spreadsheets, statistical programs) for researching stories. Many of these techniques are quite adaptable to students researching journalism and media issues as well.

- **CyberJournalist.net** (http://www.cyberjournalist.net), sponsored by the Media Center of the American Press Institute, serves as a resource center to help journalists (and all media-savvy people) keep up with the many changing facets of online journalism, including the apparent latest hot topic, blogs (weblogs), which are covered by "The Weblog Blog."

- **IRE Resource Center** (http://www.ire.org/resourcecenter) is sponsored by Investigative Reporters and Editors, Inc. It includes a large archive of news "tipsheets" (reporting guides) and an archive of more than 19,000 investigative news stories. Abstracts can be viewed free online; full materials are available to members or for purchase by journalists or journalism students.

- **Pew Center for Civic Journalism** (http://www.pewcenter.org) seeks to foster this movement, which brings journalists into closer relationship with the community and its concerns. The site includes links to publications, research, and an online newsletter.

- **Poynter Online** (http://poynter.org), from the Poynter Institute, is geared to working journalists but has many links that would also be useful to students and other investigating journalism issues. Featured sections include design/graphics, diversity, ethics, leadership, online journalism, photojournalism, writing/editing, and television/radio. There are also selected current and past stories from the *Poynter Report*. A "convergence chaser" tracks industry developments and legal issues relating to media ownership concentration.

- **Project for Excellence in Journalism** (http://www.journalism.org/default.asp) is a creation of the Committee of Concerned Journalists and the Nieman Foundation at Harvard. The project has sought to respond to widespread concerns about the independence and quality of journalism by clarifying and giving examples of good journalistic practice.

- **Romenesko** (http://poynter.org/column.asp?id=45), online journalist James Romenesko's web site, became famous as a source for hot inside media news in the wake of the Jayson Blair plagiarism scandal at the *New York Times*. It continues to be a popular site for both journalists and students of the media.

WATCHDOGS AND CRITICS

The following sites evaluate and criticize the performance of the media, usually from an ideological point of view.

- **Accuracy in Media** (http://www.aim.org) is a conservative media watchdog group. Its site offers current controversies and a variety of reports that are likely to be controversial (one suggests that coverage of Senator Joseph McCarthy was more reckless and inaccurate than anything McCarthy himself ever did; another attributes the Jayson Blair scandal at the *New York Times* to the corrupting effects of the effort to promote diversity).
- **Fairness and Accuracy in Reporting** (FAIR; http://www.fair.org), the liberal media watchdog and activist group, offers commentary on current media coverage, "counterspin," and other resources.
- **Media Whores Online** (http://www.mediawhoresonline.com) is a quite irreverent site that displays what it considers to be the craven or self-interested behavior of the media in the face of corporate or government power. On the other hand, it features links to left-liberals who are "in exile" from the establishment media.
- **Project Censored** (http://www.projectcensored.org) is a well-known effort to highlight stories that its activists believe should be covered by the media, but are not, for various reasons. The project issues yearbooks listing and explaining such stories (including sources); the first chapter of each yearbook (covering 25 stories) is available online. The top "censored" story of 2001–02 was "FCC Moves to Privatize Airwaves."

HISTORY OF MEDIA

A number of sites specialize in the history of media. Some have extensive archives of radio or television broadcasts or print news stories.

- **Encyclopedia of Television** (http://www.museum.tv/archives/etv/index.html) is provided by the Museum of Broadcast Communications. There is online access to more than 1,000 essays on broadcast pioneers, specific shows, broadcast formats, and topics such as violence and tabloid television. Entries include bibliographies.
- **Library of American Broadcasting** (http://www.lib.umd.edu/LAB) is part of the University of Maryland library system. It has extensive holdings relating to the history of broadcasting, including books, periodicals, pamphlets, and a photo archive of which samples can be viewed online. The library also offers bibliographies and other guides to various topics.
- **Television News Archive** (http://tvnews.vanderbilt.edu) at Vanderbilt University describes itself as the world's most extensive and complete archive of television news. It includes more than 30,000 news broadcasts and more than 9,000 hours of special news-related programming including

such programs as *ABC Nightline* since 1989. Videotape loans are available (for a fee) on request.

MEDIA WEB SITES

The major broadcast cable networks, news (wire) services, most newspapers, and many magazines have web sites that include news stories and links to additional information. For breaking news the following sites are also useful.

- Associated Press (AP) wire: http://customwire.ap.org/specials/bluepage.html
- Cable News Network (CNN): http://www.cnn.com
- *New York Times:* http://www.nytimes.com
- Reuters: http://www.reuters.com
- *Time* magazine: http://www.time.com
- *Wall Street Journal:* http://online.wsj.com/public/us
- *Washington Post:* http://www.washingtonpost.com

Yahoo! maintains a large set of links to many newspapers that have web sites or online editions: http://dir.yahoo.com/News_and_Media/Newspapers/Web_Directories.

Another site useful for tracking down recent news stories is Google News at http://news.google.com. The site describes itself as

> *highly unusual in that it offers a news service compiled solely by computer algorithms without human intervention. While the sources of the news stories vary in perspective and editorial approach, their selection for inclusion is done without regard to political viewpoint or ideology. While this may lead to some occasionally unusual and contradictory groupings, it is exactly this variety that makes Google News a valuable source of information on the important issues of the day.*

WEBLOGS (BLOGS)

The latest hot source for news and commentaries is the weblog, commonly shortened to "blog." An increasing number of respected journalists are "blogging" because they find that the format allows them the freedom to comment on a wide range of issues and the ability to easily interact with readers. Of course anyone with a minimum of money and skill can create a blog, so the credibility of the source for any factual assertions must be evaluated.

Some starting points for finding and sampling blogs include Blogwise (http://www.blogwise.com), a categorized directory of blogs at Blog Universe (http://www.bloguniverse.com/radlinks/index.php).

Two examples of popular political blogs are Daily Dish (http://www. andrewsullivan.com/index.php), a freewheeling, conservative-oriented blog by former *New Republic* editor-in-chief Andrew Sullivan, and InstaPundit. com (http://www.instapundit.com), which provides an independent, individualistic commentary on the news.

FINDING MORE ON THE WEB

Although the resource sites mentioned earlier provide a convenient way to view a wide variety of information, it will eventually be necessary for the researcher to look for information or views elsewhere. The two main approaches to Web research are the portal and the search engine.

WEB PORTALS

A Web guide or index is a site that offers what amounts to a structured, hierarchical outline of subject areas. This enables the researcher to zero in on a particular aspect of a subject and find links to web sites for further exploration. The links are constantly being compiled and updated by a staff of researchers.

The best known (and largest) Web index is Yahoo! (http://www.yahoo. com). The home page gives the top-level list of topics, and the researcher simply clicks to follow them down to more specific areas. Within Yahoo!, "News and Media" (http://dir.yahoo.com/News_and_Media) is the most general category, including links to categories and types of media and to topics or aspects of the media. There is also a subcategory for Industry Information at http://dir.yahoo.com/News_and_Media/Industry_Information/. Another important category is Media Ethics and Accountability at http:// dir.yahoo.com/News_and_Media/Industry_Information/Media_Ethics_ and_Accountability/. Finally, one can find Media Literacy (including Youth Media Awareness) at http://dir.yahoo.com/News_and_Media/Industry_ Information/Media_Literacy/. In addition to following Yahoo's outline-like structure, there is also a search box into which the researcher can type one or more keywords and receive a list of matching categories and sites.

Web indexes such as Yahoo! have two major advantages over undirected surfing. First, the structured hierarchy of topics makes it easy to find a particular topic or subtopic and then explore its links. Second, Yahoo! does not make an attempt to compile every possible link on the Internet (a task that is virtually impossible, given the size of the Web). Rather, sites are evaluated for usefulness and quality by Yahoo!'s indexers. This means that the researcher has a better chance of finding more substantial and accurate information. The disadvantage of Web indexes is the flip side of their selectivity: the researcher is dependent on the indexer's judgment for determining what sites are worth exploring.

SEARCH ENGINES

Search engines take a very different approach to finding materials on the Web. Instead of organizing topically in a "top down" fashion, search engines work their way "from the bottom up" scanning through Web documents and indexing them. There are hundreds of search engines, but some of the most widely used include:

- AltaVista: http://www.altavista.com
- Excite: http://www.excite.com
- Google: http://www.google.com
- Hotbot: http://www.hotbot.com
- Lycos: http://www.lycos.com
- Northern Light: http://www.northernlight.com/news.html
- WebCrawler: http://www.WebCrawler.com

Search engines are generally easy to use by employing the same sorts of keywords that work in library catalogs. There are a variety of Web search tutorials available online (try "Web search tutorial" in a search engine to find some). One good one is published by Bright Planet (http://www.brightplanet. com/deepcontent/tutorials/search/index.asp). Here are a few basic rules for using search engines:

- When looking for something specific, the researcher should use the most specific term or phrase. For example, when looking for information about libel, the researcher should use the specific term **libel,** since this is the standard term, but should be aware that he or she might need to check the more general term **defamation** as well.
- Phrases should be put in quotes if the researcher wants them to be matched as phrases rather than as individual words. A good example is **"civic journalism"** or **"media convergence."**
- When looking for a general topic that might be expressed using several different words or phrases, the researcher should use several descriptive

words (nouns are more reliable than verbs): for example, **television audience statistics.** (Most engines will automatically put pages that match all three terms first on the results list.)

- The researcher should use "wildcards" when a desired word may have more than one ending. For example, **journalis*** matches both "journalist" and "journalism."

- Most search engines support Boolean *(and, or, not)* operators that can be used to broaden or narrow a search. AND is used to narrow a search: for example, **media and poll** will match only pages that have both terms. OR is used to broaden a search: **blog or weblog** will match any page that has *either* term, and since these terms are often used interchangeably, this type of search is necessary to retrieve the widest range of results. NOT is used to exclude unwanted results: **television not cable** finds articles about television but (probably not) cable television.

Since each search engine indexes somewhat differently and offers somewhat different ways of searching, it is a good idea to use several different search engines, especially for a general query.

Several "metasearch" programs automate the process of submitting a query to multiple search engines. These include Metacrawler (http://www.metacrawler.com) and SurfWax (http://www.surfwax.com/). Note that metasearch engines tend to have two drawbacks: they may overwhelm you with results (and insufficiently prune duplicates), and they often do not use some of the more popular search engines (such as Google or Northern Light). There are also search utilities that can be run from the researcher's own computer rather than through a web site. A good example is Copernic (http://www.copernic.com).

FINDING ORGANIZATIONS AND PEOPLE

Chapter 9 of this book provides a list of organizations involved with journalism and the media, but new organizations emerge occasionally. Many of the resource sites listed earlier will have links to organizations, as will Yahoo! and the other general Web portals.

If such sites do not yield the name of a specific organization, the name can be given to a search engine. Generally, the best approach is to put the name of the organization in quotation marks such as "Reporters Committee for Freedom of the Press." This signifies to the search engine that you are looking for sites in which all these words appear in the exact order as you write them.

Another approach is to take a guess at the organization's likely Web address. For example, the American Civil Liberties Union is commonly known by the acronym ACLU, so it is not a surprise that the organization's web site is at www.aclu.org. (Note that noncommercial organization sites normally use the .org suffix, government agencies use .gov, educational institutions have .edu, and businesses use .com.) This technique can save time but does not always work. In particular, watch out for "spoof" sites that mimic or parody organizational sites. Such a site, for example, might have the same name as that of a government agency but end in .org instead of .gov. (Of course, such sites may be of interest in themselves as forms of criticism or dissent.) Also, there may be other organizations or companies that have the same acronym or initials.

There are several ways to find a person on the Internet:

- One can put the person's name (in quotation marks) in a search engine and possibly find that person's home page on the Internet.

- One can contact the person's employer (such as a university for an academic or a corporation for a technical professional). Most such organizations have webpages that include a searchable faculty or employee directory.

- One can utilize one of the people-finder services, such as Yahoo! People Search (http://people.yahoo.com) or BigFoot (http://www.bigfoot.com). This may yield contact information such as an e-mail address, regular address, and/or phone number.

PRINT SOURCES

As useful as the Web is for quickly finding information and the latest news, in-depth research still sometimes requires trips to the library or bookstore. Getting the most out of the library requires the use of bibliographic tools and resources. *Bibliographic resources* is a general term for catalogs, indexes, bibliographies, and other guides that identify the books, periodical articles, and other printed resources on a particular subject. They are essential tools for the researcher.

LIBRARY CATALOGS

Researchers are probably familiar with the basics of using a library catalog but may not know that many catalogs besides that of the local library can be searched online. Access to the largest library catalog, that of the Library of Congress, is available at http://catalog.loc.gov. This page includes a guide to using the catalog and both basic and advanced catalog searches. Yahoo! offers a categorized listing of libraries at http://dir.yahoo.com/Reference/Libraries. Of course, for materials available at one's local public or university library, that institution will be the most convenient source.

Most catalogs can be searched in at least the following ways:

- An author search is most useful if one knows or suspects a person has written a number of works of interest. However, it may fail if one does not know the person's exact name. Cross-references are intended to deal with this problem but cannot cover all possible variations.
- A title search is best if one knows the exact title of the book and just wants to know if the library has it. Generally one needs to use only the first few words of the title, excluding initial articles *(a, an, the)*. This search will fail if one does not have the exact title.
- A keyword search will match words found anywhere in the title. It is thus broader and more flexible than a title search, although it may still fail if all keywords are not present.
- A subject search will find all works that have been assigned that subject heading by the library. The big advantage is that it does not depend on certain words being in the title. However, using a subject search requires knowledge of the appropriate subject headings (see below).

Below are some often useful Library of Congress subjects relating to journalism and the media. If one browses the subject headings catalog, one can find many more:

Afro-American Newspapers
American Newspapers
Broadcast Journalism (can have many of the same subheadings as journalism)
Cable Television
Community Newspapers
Documentary Television Programs
Free Press and Fair Trial
Freedom of the Press
Freelance Journalism
Government and the Press
Internet (Computer Network)
Internet Industry
Internet Marketing
Internet Publishing
Internet Users
Interviewing in Journalism
Journalism (many subdivisions)
Journalism and Literature

Mass Media
Mass Media and Minorities
Mass Media and Public Opinion
Motion Picture Journalism
Newspapers
Press
Press Law
Public Radio
Public Television
Radio
Radio Audiences
Radio Broadcasting
Radio Broadcasting Policy
Radio in Politics
Radio in Propaganda
Radio Journalism
Radio Stations
Sensationalism in Journalism
Television (many subdivisions)
Television and Women
Television Broadcasting
Television Broadcasting of News
Television in Education
Television Programs
Television Stations
Television Viewers
Women in Journalism

Many of these headings can be further qualified by geographical location, as in "Journalism—Study and Teaching—United States" and by period (such as 20th century).

Once the record for a book or other item is found, it is a good idea to see what additional subject headings and name headings have been assigned. These in turn can be used for further searching.

AN ALTERNATIVE: BOOKSTORE CATALOGS

Many people have discovered that online bookstores such as Amazon.com (http://www.amazon.com) and Barnes & Noble (http://www.barnesandnoble.com) are convenient ways to shop for books. A less-known benefit of online bookstore catalogs is that they often include publisher information, book reviews, and readers' comments about a given title. They can thus serve as a form of annotated bibliography.

BIBLIOGRAPHIES, INDEXES, AND DATABASES

Bibliographies in various forms provide a convenient way to find books, periodical articles, and other materials. How far back to go in one's reading depends, of course, on one's research topic and goals. Obviously, material about the social significance or economics of the Internet is not likely to be found earlier than the mid-1990s, while references to various forms of "new media" go back considerably further.

Popular and scholarly articles can be accessed through periodical indexes that provide citations and abstracts. Abstracts are brief summaries of articles or papers. They are usually compiled and indexed—originally in bound volumes, but increasingly available online. Some examples of printed indexes where you might retrieve literature related to journalism or the media industry include:

- Business Periodicals Index: 1958–
- Communication Abstracts: 1978–
- Communication Serials: 1992–
- Humanities Index: 1974–
- Journalism and Mass Communication (dissertation abstracts): 1963–93
- Social Sciences Index: 1974–
- Television News Index and Abstracts: 1972–95

Some of these indexes are available online (at least for recent years). Generally, you can access them only through a library where you hold a card, and they cannot be accessed over the Internet (unless you are on a college campus). Consult with a university reference librarian for more help.

There is, however, a provider of unrestricted search access. UnCover Web (http://www.ingenta.com/) contains brief descriptions of about 13 million documents from about 26,000 journals in just about every subject area. Copies of complete documents can be ordered with a credit card, or they may be obtainable for free at a local library.

GENERAL PERIODICAL INDEXES

Most public libraries subscribe to database services such as InfoTrac and EBSCO that index articles from hundreds of general-interest periodicals (and some moderately specialized ones). The database can be searched by author name or by words in the title, subject headings, and sometimes by words found anywhere in the article text. Depending on the database used, "hits" can result in just a bibliographical description (author, title, pages, periodical name, issue date, and so on), a description plus an abstract (a paragraph summarizing the contents of the article), or the full text of the article. Before using such an index, it is a good idea to view the list of newspapers and magazines covered and determine the years of coverage.

Many libraries provide dial-in, Internet, or telnet access to their periodical databases as an option in their catalog menu. However, licensing restrictions usually mean that only researchers who have a library card for that particular library can access the database (by typing in their name and card number). Check with local public or school libraries to see what databases are available.

For periodicals not indexed by InfoTrac or another index (or for which only abstracts rather than complete text is available), check to see whether the publication has its own web site (most now do). Some scholarly publications are putting all or most of their articles online. Popular publications tend to offer only a limited selection of articles. Major newspapers typically offer current and recent articles (up to a week old perhaps) for free and provide an archive from which articles can be purchased for a few dollars.

JOURNALISM AND MEDIA PERIODICALS

There are many important periodicals in the fields of journalism and media studies. Today many periodicals have their own full-fledged web site (often with a sampling of current and past articles, as well as indexes). Some publications have more minimal pages on distributors' sites giving a description and information for ordering the publication. Following is a list of selected periodicals with the relevant Web addresses:

American Journalism Review (http://www.ajr.org/)
Columbia Journalism Review (http://www.cjr.org/)
Editor and Publisher (http://www.editorandpublisher.com/editor andpublisher/index.jsp)
Historical Journal of Film, Radio & Television (http://www.iamhist.org/ journal/)
Journal of Broadcasting & Electronic Media (http://www.beaweb.org/ publications.html)
Journal of Radio Studies (http://www.beaweb.org/publications.html)
Journal of Mass Media Ethics (http://jmme.byu.edu/)
Journal of Media Economics (http://www.catchword.com/erlbaum/ 08997764/contp1-1.htm)
Journalism History (http://scrippsjschool.org/journals.php?story_id=78)
News Photographer Magazine (http://www.nppa.org/members/magazine/ default.htm)

Nieman Report (http://www.nieman.harvard.edu/reports/contents.html)
Online Journalism Review (http://www.ojr.org/ojr/page_one/index.php)
Poynter Reports (http://poynteronline.org/subject.asp?id=53)
PR Week (http://www.prweekus.com/)
Public Relations Review (http://www.elsevier.com/inca/publications/store/6/2/0/1/8/8/)
The Quill (https://www.spj.org/quill_list.asp)
Women's Studies in Communication (http://www.cios.org/www/wommain.htm)

LEGAL RESEARCH

It is important for researchers to be able to obtain the text and summary of laws and court decisions relating to journalism and the media industry. Because of the specialized terminology of the law, legal research can be more difficult to master than bibliographical or general research tools. Fortunately, the Internet has also come to the rescue in this area, offering a variety of ways to look up laws and court cases without having to pore through huge bound volumes in law libraries (which may not be easily accessible to the general public, anyway).

FINDING LAWS AND REGULATIONS

When federal legislation passes, it eventually becomes part of the U.S. Code, a massive legal compendium. The U.S. Code can be searched online in several locations, but the easiest site to use is probably that of Cornell Law School (http://www4.law.cornell.edu/uscode/). The fastest way to retrieve a law is by its title and section citation, but phrases and keywords can also be used.

With regard to the print media, the high regard courts have for the First Amendment has meant that there are few laws directly related to a publication's content except for the application of defamation or libel laws (see Chapter 3 of this book for more details). For the broadcast and cable media industry, the source of specific regulations is the Federal Communications Commission (FCC) at http://www.fcc.gov. The link to the office of the General Counsel provides news and links for regulatory rulings and court cases.

KEEPING UP WITH LEGISLATIVE DEVELOPMENTS

The Library of Congress Thomas Web site (http://thomas.loc.gov/) includes files summarizing legislation by the number of the Congress. Each two-year session of Congress has a consecutive number: for example, the 108th Congress will be in session in 2003 and 2004. Legislation can be searched for by the name of its sponsor(s), the bill number, or by topical keywords. Laws that have been passed can be looked up under their Public Law number. For example, selecting the 106th Congress and typing in the phrase "cable television" into the search box will retrieve a number of bills pertaining to that subject. Clicking on the highlighted bill number brings up a display that includes the bill's status and text as well as further details including sponsors, committee action, and amendments.

FINDING COURT DECISIONS

The Supreme Court and state courts make important decisions every year that determine how the laws are interpreted. Like laws, legal decisions are organized using a system of citations. The general form is: *Party1* v. *Party2 volume reporter* [optional start page] *(court, year)*.
Here are some examples:

> *Brandenburg v. Ohio*, 395 U.S. 44 (1969): Here the parties are Brandenburg (the defendant who is appealing his case from a state court) and the state of Ohio. The case is in volume 395 of the U.S. *Supreme Court Reports*, beginning at page 44, and the case was decided in 1969. (For the Supreme Court, the name of the court is omitted.)
> *Fierro v. Gomez* 77 F.3d 301 (9th Cir. 1996): Here the case is in the 9th U.S. Circuit Court of Appeals, decided in 1996.

A state court decision can generally be identified because it includes the state's name. For example, in *State v. Torrance*, 473 S.E.2d. 703, S.C. (1996) *S.E.* refers to the appeals district, and *S.C.* to South Carolina.
Once the jurisdiction for the case has been determined, the researcher can then go to a number of web sites to find cases by citation and sometimes by the names of the parties or by subject keywords. Two of the most useful sites are:

- The Legal Information Institute (http://supct.law.cornell.edu/supct/) has all Supreme Court decisions since 1990 plus 610 of "the most important historic" decisions.
- Washlaw Web (http://www.washlaw.edu) has a variety of courts (including states) and legal topics listed, making it a good jumping-off place for many sorts of legal research. However, the actual accessibility of state court opinions (and the formats they are provided in) varies widely.

MEDIA LAW SITES

A number of useful web sites are devoted to First Amendment and media law issues. These often provide case summaries, current developments, and legal commentary. Some good starting points are:

- FindLaw Library: Communications Law (http://library.lp.findlaw.com/ communicationslaw.html)
- First Amendment Center Topics Summary (http://www.firstamendment center. org/topicssummary.aspx)
- Iowa State University Libraries: Media and Computer Law (http://bailiwick. lib.uiowa.edu/journalism/mediaLaw/media_law.html)
- Legal Information Institute: Law About Media (http://www.law.cornell. edu/topics/media.html)

LEXISNEXIS AND WESTLAW

LexisNexis and Westlaw are commercial legal databases that have extensive information, including an elaborate system of notes, legal subject headings, and ways to show relationships between cases. Unfortunately, these services are too expensive for use by most individual researchers unless they are available through a university or corporate library. Consult with a librarian on how to use these databases.

MORE HELP ON LEGAL RESEARCH

For more information on conducting legal research, see the "Legal Research FAQ" at http://www.cis.ohio-state.edu/hypertext/faq/usenet/law/ research/top.html. After a certain point, however, the researcher who lacks formal legal training may need to consult with or rely on the efforts of professional researchers or academics in the field.

EVALUATING INTERNET SOURCES

Thanks to the Web, there is more information from more sources available than ever before. There is also a greater diversity of voices since any person or group with a personal computer and Internet service can put up a web site—in some cases, a site that looks as polished and professional as that of an established group. Weblogs in particular offer an attractive format for original commentary and feedback. One benefit is that dissenting views can be found in abundance, including even sites maintained by radical groups or their supporters.

However, the other side of the coin is that the researcher—whether journalist, analyst, teacher, or student—must take extra care to try to verify facts and to understand the possible biases of each source. Some good questions to ask include:

• Who is responsible for this web site?
• What is the background or reputation of the person or group?
• Does the person or group have a stated objective or agenda?
• What biases might this person or group have?
• Do a number of high-quality sites link to this one?
• What is the source given for a particular fact? Does that source actually say what is quoted? Where did *they* get that information?

Increasingly, the skills of the journalist must also become the skills of the student and professional.

CHAPTER 8

ANNOTATED BIBLIOGRAPHY

This chapter presents a representative selection of books, articles, and Web (Internet) documents relating to journalism and the media industry, the power and social impact of the news media, and related issues. Materials have been selected where possible to be accessible, substantial, and diverse in viewpoint. The bibliography is divided into four broad categories that are further divided into subtopics as follows:

Reference and Background
Reference Works
Historical and Background

Structure and Operation of the News Media
Media Ownership and Corporate Influence
Reporting, News Coverage, Selection, and Bias
The New Media and Emerging Technology

Influence and Effects of the News Media
The Media and Public Attitudes
Media, Politics, and General Policy
The Media, Global Issues, and Foreign Policy
Media Coverage and Representation of Minorities
Media Literacy and Young People

Legal and Ethical Issues
General Legal Issues
Information Access and Sources
Libel and Privacy
Ethics and Standards in Journalism

Within each topic, the listings are divided according to books, articles, and Web documents. Note that although all Web addresses (URLs) have been checked, webpages are often moved or removed. If an address is not found, a keyword search using a search engine is recommended. See Chapter 7 for more information about Internet research and resources.

REFERENCE AND BACKGROUND

REFERENCE WORKS

This section includes reference books such as encyclopedias, dictionaries, and bibliographies.

Books

Asante, Clement E. *Press Freedom and Development: A Research Guide and Selected Bibliography.* Westport, Conn.: Greenwood Press, 1997. An overview and annotated bibliography of books and research articles on journalism and communications, including the relationship between the media and the government and press freedom issues. There is a strong emphasis on international perspectives, including those of developing nations.

Balnaves, Mark, James Donald, and Stephanie Hemelryk Donald. *The Penguin Atlas of Media and Information: Key Issues and Global Trends.* New York: Penguin Putnam, 2001. Compiles and interprets key information about various aspects of both traditional media (newspapers and television) and the Internet and e-commerce at the start of the 21st century, including long-term trends. Includes numerous maps and charts.

Bennett, James R. *Control of the Media in the United States: An Annotated Bibliography.* Garland, 1992. This bibliography is divided into chapters representing different aspects of control or influence of the media, including corporations, the military, and the presidency, as well as sectors of the media (broadcasting, print media, electronic media, music, and art).

Blum, Eleanor. *Mass Media Bibliography: An Annotated Guide to Books and Journals for Research and Reference.* Urbana: University of Illinois Press, 1990. Although it obviously does not include current material, this is a good reference for researching the development of media studies.

Bognar, Desi. *International Dictionary of Broadcasting and Film.* 2d ed. New York: Butterworth-Heinemann, 2000. In a global media world it is useful to have a dictionary that is likewise international in scope. This A–Z reference includes technical terms, acronyms, and organizations, and is updated to include "new media" developments.

Burt, Elizabeth. *Women's Press Organizations, 1881–1999.* Westport, Conn: Greenwood Press, 2000. This reference book profiles 40 significant women's press organizations, including their establishment, leadership, and activities.

Annotated Bibliography

Cates, Jo A. *Journalism: A Guide to the Reference Literature.* 2d ed. Westport, Conn.: Libraries Unlimited, 1997. The author, a former reference librarian at the Poynter Institute for Media Studies and other institutions, provides both a comprehensive, well-organized overview and an annotated bibliography of books on broadcast and print journalism.

Contemporary Authors: A Bio-Bibliographical Guide to Current Writers in Fiction, General Nonfiction, Poetry, Journalism, Drama, Motion Pictures, Television and Other Fields. Detroit: Gale Research, 1962–. This massive reference work can be used to find information on journalists, photographers, television commentators, producers, and people in other fields relating to the media.

Dansky, James P., ed. *African-American Newspapers and Editorials: A National Bibliography.* Harvard University Press, 1999. Includes entries on about 6,500 African-American periodicals from 1827 to 1998. The entries for this very diverse array of periodicals include bibliographical, library cataloguing, and contact information. There are also indexes by type of writing, names of editors and publishers, and state.

Dictionary of Literary Biography. Gale Group, 1978–. This massive work includes journalists in its coverage. Volumes are organized by field of writing. Relevant volumes for journalism include: Volume 23, American Newspaper Journalists, 1873–1900 (1983); Volume 25, American Newspaper Journalists, 1901–1925 (1984); Volume 29, American Newspaper Journalists, 1926–1950 (1984); Volume 43, American Newspaper Journalists, 1690–1872 (1985); Volume 127, American Newspaper Publishers (1993). This series is also available through the InfoTrac online information service.

Endres, Kathleen, ed. *Trade, Industrial, and Professional Periodicals of the United States.* Westport, Conn.: Greenwood Press, 1994. Profiles specialty publications including trade publications and professional journals. There is considerable detail about the ownership and production of each publication, as well as a bibliography.

Fischer, Heinz-Dietrich, and Erika J. Fischer, eds. *The Pulitzer Prize Archive: A History and Anthology of Award-Winning Materials in Journalism, Letters and Arts.* Munich, Germany: K. G. Saur, 1987. This series provides a complete compilation of Pulitzer Prize–winning writing. The volumes relevant to the study of journalism are Part A, Volume 1: Reportage Journalism: International Reporting, 1928–1985; Part A, Volume 2 Reportage Journalism: National Reporting 1941–1986; Part A, Volume 3: Reportage Journalism: Local Reporting, 1947–1987; Part B, Volume 4: Opinion Journalism: Political Editorial, 1916–1988; Part B, Volume 5: Opinion Journalism: Social Commentary, 1969–1989; Part B, Volume 6: Opinion Journalism: Cultural Criticism, 1969–1990; Part E: Volume 13: Editorial Cartoon Awards, 1922–1997; Part E, Volume 14: Press Photography Awards, 1942–1998. Each volume includes a complete listing of award winners and reprints of selected pieces. Volume 16 is a bibliographical encyclopedia of Pulitzer Prize winners.

Godfrey, Donald G. *Reruns on File: A Guide to Electronic Media Archives.* Mahwah, N.J.: Lawrence Erlbaum Associates, 1991. Describes a variety of archives of broadcast programming throughout the United States and Canada. Note that "electronic" here refers to the nature of the media, not to the archives being online.

Greenberg, Gerald S. *Tabloid Journalism: An Annotated Bibliography of English-Language Sources.* Westport, Conn.: Greenwood Press, 1996. An annotated bibliography of books and articles on popular, sensational, and tabloid journalism, including the early "penny press" and yellow journalism. Works dealing with related professional and legal issues are also included.

Henderson, Harry. *Privacy in the Information Age.* Library in a Book series. New York: Facts On File, 1999. This reference handbook discusses privacy and freedom-of-information issues, with special emphasis on how developments in the online world are forcing a reevaluation of traditional standards. The book includes an overview, chronology, biographical sketches, research guide, an extensive annotated bibliography, and other resources.

Jones, Steve, ed. *Encyclopedia of New Media: An Essential Reference to Communication and Technology.* Thousand Oaks, Calif.: Sage Publications, 2002. A comprehensive, readable guide to concepts and terms in use in the contemporary world of multimedia and the Internet. The 250 essay-length articles include biographies of significant figures and are accompanied by bibliographies.

Kanellos, Nicholas, and Helvetia Martell. *Hispanic Periodicals in the United States, Origins to 1960: A Brief History and Comprehensive Bibliography.* Houston, Tex.: Arte Publico Press, 2000. This is a comprehensive annotated bibliography that also serves as a reference handbook, with descriptions of the cultural and social history involved in the development of Hispanic journalism and publications.

Langman, Larry. *The Media in the Movies: A Catalog of American Journalism Films, 1900–1996.* Jefferson, N.C.: McFarland, 1998. This filmography describes more than 1,000 films, from silent to modern, that portray journalists and media people, often with the aid of common stereotypes (the hard-drinking, cynical reporter, and so on). A number of still photos are included, as is a bibliography.

McCoy, Ralph E. *Freedom of the Press: An Annotated Bibliography.* Carbondale: Southern Illinois University Press, 1968. Two supplements have been issued to bring this annotated bibliography up through 1992.

McKerns, Joseph P. *Biographical Dictionary of American Journalism.* Westport, Conn.: Greenwood Press, 1989. Provides biographical profiles of about 500 significant American journalists from 1690 to the 1980s. Entries are individually written by journalism historians; includes bibliographies and a table of categorization of journalists by field.

Murray, Michael D. *Encyclopedia of Television News.* Phoenix, Ariz.: Oryx Press, 1998. Contains about 300 entries describing significant people, companies, programs, and events in the history of television news. Includes bibliographies.

Passarelli, Eleanor. *Public Relations in Business, Government, and Society: A Bibliographic Guide.* Westport, Conn.: Libraries Unlimited, 1989. Serves as a historical bibliography for public relations, a field closely related to the news media. Includes annotations and material introducing various aspects of public relations.

Riley, Gail Blasser. *Censorship.* Library in a Book series. New York: Facts On File, 1998. The topic of censorship is closely related to journalism and the media, since censorship (such as by government agencies or courts) threatens to deprive both journalists and the public of vital information. This reference handbook includes an overview, chronology, biographical sketches, research guide, an extensive annotated bibliography, and other helpful information.

Roth, Mitchel. *Historical Dictionary of War Journalism.* Westport, Conn.: Greenwood Press, 1997. An extensive dictionary of terms, events, and correspondents relating to the coverage of wars, from the Mexican War of 1846 to the Gulf War. Extensive appendixes list the main correspondents who covered each conflict.

Signorielli, Nancy. *Women in Communication: A Biographical Sourcebook.* Westport, Conn.: Greenwood Press, 1996. Provides in-depth biographical profiles of 48 women who played an important role in communication, from Sarah Josepha Hale in the 18th century to modern media presences such as Barbara Walters. There is a good mixture of journalists, opinion columnists, correspondents, and news interviewers and anchors. An appendix provides additional short biographies.

Sloan, William. *American Journalism History: An Annotated Bibliography.* Vol. 1. Westport, Conn.: Greenwood Press, 1989. A comprehensive, extensively annotated bibliography of books, journal articles, and dissertations on American journalism history from colonial times through the 1980s. (No subsequent volume has appeared as of early 2004).

Stempel, Guido H., III. *Media and Politics in America: A Reference Handbook.* Santa Barbara, Calif.: ABC-CLIO, 2003. This reference handbook includes introductory overviews of the history and practice of "political communication," followed by a chronology, biographical sketches, legal documents and court cases, a list of associations and organizations, and an annotated bibliography. The focus is not on media power in general, but on the intersection between the media and politics.

Stempel, Guido H., David H. Weaver, and G. Cleveland Wilhoit, eds. *Mass Communication Research and Theory.* Boston: Allyn and Bacon, 2003. A handbook of methodology and theoretical background for researching various types and aspects of media, including broadcast, newspapers, public relations, and advertising.

Sterling, Christopher H., and John Michael Kittross. *Stay Tuned: A History of American Broadcasting.* 3d ed. Mahwah, N.J.: Lawrence Erlbaum Associates, 2002. An updated version of this massive but accessible single-volume history of American broadcasting. It includes historical developments, technical and business practices, and the latest developments in new media, the Internet, and media convergence. The extensive bibliography includes a comprehensive listing of broadcasting and media museums and archives.

Web Documents

Bowen, Jonathan. "Broadcasters." Virtual Library. Available online. URL: http://archive.museophile.sbu.ac.uk/broadcast/. Posted February 10, 2003. An international directory of links to information about broadcasting, including links to worldwide broadcasters, museums of broadcasting, and other sources.

"Global News Index." MediaChannel.org. Available online. URL: http://www.mediachannel.org/links/links-frameset.html. Updated May 19, 2001. Provides links to media outlets around the world.

"News Reporter's Handbook on Law and Courts." Missouri Press-Bar Commission. 2001 Revised ed. Available online. URL: http://mobar.org/handbook.index.htm. A comprehensive online guide to law as it affects journalists, including getting information about court proceedings, privacy, libel, and access to public records. Although some parts are specific to the state (such as the "Sunshine Law") most background material is generally applicable.

HISTORICAL AND BACKGROUND

This section covers the history of journalism and the media, giving general overviews as well as various topics and events that do not fit in a more specific category.

Books

Albarran, Alan B., and Gregory C. Pitts. *The Radio Broadcasting Industry.* Boston: Allyn & Bacon, 2001. A handbook describing the radio industry, including history, types of programming, ownership, regulation, and emerging technological developments.

Annotated Bibliography

Alexander, Alison, and Janice Hanson. *Taking Sides: Clashing Views on Controversial Issues in Mass Media and Society*. 7th ed. Guilford, Conn.: McGraw-Hill/Dushkin, 2003. A collection of readings organized in a debate-style format. Issues discussed include the mass media's role in society, media ethics, the media and politics, regulation of the media, the media industry, and implications of "the information society."

Armstrong, David. *Trumpet to Arms: Alternative Media in America*. Boston, Mass.: South End Press, 1984. Describes and provides excerpts from more than 200 alternative, dissident, or radical publications that contributed to a rich tradition of underground journalism. Selections range from pamphleteer Tom Paine *(Common Sense)* to the *Berkeley Barb* of the 1960s and early 1970s.

Brinkley, David. *11 Presidents, 4 Wars, 22 Political Conventions, 1 Moon Landing, 3 Assassinations, 2,000 Weeks of News and Other Stuff on Television and 18 Years of Growing Up in North Carolina*. New York: Alfred A. Knopf, 1995. The richly textured, engaging autobiography of David Brinkley, one of the great pioneers of television newscasting (together, of course, with Chet Huntley). Although Brinkley draws few 'sweeping conclusions' about history or the media, there are many wonderful anecdotes about covering the news or just socializing with presidents, military veterans, and other people.

Brown, Robert J. *Manipulating the Ether: The Power of Broadcast Radio in Thirties America*. Jefferson, N.C.: McFarland, 1998. The scholarly but accessible work describes the growing influence of radio in American life, from the effective use of the medium by President Franklin D. Roosevelt to Orson Welles's "War of the Worlds" hoax. Meanwhile, news broadcasts and commentary at that time became more sophisticated.

Campbell, W. Joseph. *Yellow Journalism: Puncturing the Myths, Defining the Legacies*. Westport, Conn.: Praeger, 2003. The author debunks many beliefs about yellow journalism that are shared by the public and media scholars alike. He says, for example, that William Randolph Hearst never vowed to "furnish the war" and is not responsible for pushing the United States into war with Spain in 1898. The results of Campbell's content analysis suggests that yellow journalism actually became mainstream journalism.

Chomsky, Noam. *Media Control: The Spectacular Achievements of Propaganda*. 2d ed. New York: Seven Stories Press, 2002. In this pamphlet Chomsky, a famed linguist and controversial political theorist, surveys the history of orchestrated American government propaganda campaigns starting with the effort to mobilize public sentiment for World War I. Chomsky believes the success of these campaigns is greatly aided by the lack of a robust media and other institutions that might equip the public with understanding and tools of critical thinking.

Power of the News Media

Cutlip, Scott M. *The Unseen Power: Public Relations, a History.* Mahwah, N.J.: Lawrence Erlbaum Associates, 1994. A detailed history of the field of public relations (PR) including the achievements of PR pioneers such as Edward Bernays, John Hill, Carl Byoir, and Ivy Lee. Public relations specialists provide source material for journalists, but the latter must adopt a critical attitude in order to maintain objectivity.

Day, James. *The Vanishing Vision: The Inside Story of Public Television.* Berkeley: University of California Press, 1995. Public broadcasting is often considered to be an alternative to corporate, commercial-driven media. This comprehensive history by a founder of San Francisco's television station KQED and former president of WNET in New York traces public television starting in the "educational television" days of the 1950s. He suggests that public broadcasting reached its nadir during the Nixon era when it was under intense assault from the administration. Since then, programs such as the *McNeil-Lehrer News Hour* have given public broadcasting a significant presence in the news sector. However, Day criticizes public broadcasters for lack of imagination and consistency compared to systems such as the BBC and suggests that a more comprehensive and independently funded public broadcasting sector is necessary.

Doss, Erika Lee, ed. *Looking at Life Magazine.* Washington, D.C.: Smithsonian Institution Press, 2001. Thirteen historians of media and popular culture look at the phenomenon of *Life* magazine, which became a major pictorial window on the world for U.S. readers during the middle part of the 20th century. The contributors analyze the style and themes of the magazine, as well as the social agenda it tried to promote—one of a unified, classless nation.

Downie, Leonard J., Jr., and Robert G. Kaiser. *The News About the News: American Journalism in Peril.* New York: Vintage Books, 2003. Two *Washington Post* editors assess the state of the news media at the opening of the 21st century. Topics include the effects of media concentration (mergers) and the superficial quality of local news coverage. At the same time, however, they also point to the boost in news-gathering resources and in attention to foreign affairs following the September 11, 2001, terrorist attacks and the effects of the Internet and new forms of expression.

Ferguson's Careers in Focus: Broadcasting. 2d ed. New York: Facts On File, 2002. One good way to get a basic grasp of the news and larger media worlds is to look at the many jobs involved with the media—thus a career guide can also serve as a useful introduction to the field.

Foerstel, Herbert N. *From Watergate to Monicagate: Ten Controversies in Modern Journalism and Media.* Westport, Conn.: Greenwood Press, 2001. A study of 10 major issues involving the practices of the modern media. Topics include media concentration, the relation between public relations and news professionals, media cooperation with intelligence agencies, press controls in wartime, tabloid journalism, the pursuit of celebrities by paparazzi, plagiarism scandals, privilege and the use of anonymous sources, the attempt to regulate the Internet, and a new form of broadcast media, local "microradio."

Friendly, Fred. *Due to Circumstances beyond Our Control.* New York: Times Books, 1999. This memoir of the pioneering producer provides much insight into how television news and particularly documentaries were developed in the 1950s. Friendly worked with Edward R. Murrow to produce *See It Now,* the documentary series that eventually took on Senator Joseph McCarthy at the height of his anticommunist hysteria. After Friendly quit CBS in disgust when the network decided to show *I Love Lucy* reruns instead of Senate hearings on the Vietnam War, he went on to PBS, and argued forcefully for an expansion of public noncommercial broadcasting.

Garner, Joe. *We Interrupt This Broadcast: The Events That Shaped Our Lives—From the Hindenburg Explosion to the Attacks of September 11.* 3d ed. Naperville, Ill.: Source Books, 2002. A collection of transcripts of the broadcasts that first told Americans that something terrible had just happened. An accompanying CD provides the audio. Includes a foreword by Walter Cronkite and narration by Bill Kurtis.

Goldstein, Tom, ed. *Killing the Messenger: 100 Years of Media Criticism.* New York: Columbia University Press, 1989. Although many people think criticism and complaints about the media are a modern phenomenon, this collection of readings reveals that there were several "waves" of intense criticism of the media during the 20th century, such as in the early 1920s when Walter Lippmann began exploring the complex relationship between the media and public opinion. The wide variety of materials—book excerpts, magazine articles, and reports—focuses on five themes: reporting on private matters, biased journalism, the power and limitations of the press, how to train better reporters, and the effects of different reporting and writing techniques on the portrayal of reality.

Halberstam, David. *The Powers That Be.* New York: Alfred A. Knopf, 1979. A classic, vivid narrative in which a popular historian recounts the giants of U.S. media in the mid-20th century, including figures such as Henry Luce *(Time),* Phil and Katherine Graham *(Washington Post),* and William Paley (CBS).

Henderson, Harry. *Communications and Broadcasting. Milestones in Discovery and Invention.* New York: Facts On File, 1997. Weaves together chapter-length biographies of key inventors including several related to the broadcast media: Guglielmo Marconi (radio), Edwin H. Armstrong (FM), and Philo T. Farnsworth (television) with narrative history and a variety of sidebars giving background information.

187

Hilmes, Michele. *Broadcast History Reader.* Belmont, Calif.: Wadsworth Publishing, 2001. Useful alone or as a complement to the author's textbook *(Only Connect)* this collection of readings provides a variety of materials arranged both chronologically, and thematically such as the development of radio, early television broadcasting, the eras of the television networks, and the era of multichannel cable and satellite television.

————. *Only Connect: A Cultural History of American Broadcasting.* Belmont, Calif.: Wadsworth Publishing, 2001. This textbook of the cultural history of broadcasting integrates the development of radio and television into general U.S. history. Each chapter shows how broadcasting responded to the particular crisis of a particular time, including the Great Depression and World War II. There is also good coverage of such current issues as violence on television, deregulation of broadcasting, and developments on the Internet.

Humphrey, Carol Sue. *The Press of the Young Republic, 1783–1833.* Westport, Conn.: Greenwood Press, 1996. Describes early stages of the development of the press in the new United States, including conflicts brought about by the Alien and Sedition Acts and the highly partisan press battles between Democratic-Republicans and Federalists. The book ends with the presidency of Andrew Jackson and a new surge of populism that would also be reflected in changes in journalism.

Huntzicker, William E. *The Popular Press, 1833–1865.* Westport, Conn.: Greenwood Press, 1999. A history of a tumultuous time in American journalism characterized by the "penny press" and a new focus on a popular audience, while at the same time abolitionists and other reformers were creating vigorous newspapers as platforms for their efforts. The book closes with coverage of Civil War journalism and its impact, and a full bibliography.

Hynes, Samuel. *Reporting World War II: American Journalism 1938–1946.* New York: Library of America, 2001. A collection of war reports by prominent journalists including William L. Shirer, Howard K. Smith, A. J. Liebling, and Edward R. Murrow. There is a preface by popular historian Stephen Ambrose.

Johnston, Lyle. *Good Night, Chet: A Biography of Chet Huntley.* Jefferson, N.C.: McFarland & Company, 2003. Recounts the pioneering news anchor's life from his boyhood on a farm to his early radio work, his television work for three networks, including, of course, the Huntley-Brinkley newscasts.

Levy, Beth, ed. *The Power of the Press.* New York: H. W. Wilson, 1999. A collection of reprinted articles and book excerpts organized into themes and with an editor's introduction. Topics include characterizations of the media, media ethics, failures of journalism, and the struggle for press freedom at home and abroad.

Lewis, Tom. *Empire of the Air: The Men Who Made Radio.* New York: Harper Perennial Library, 1993. This is a classic popular history of the development of the radio industry, told through vivid accounts of inventors such as Lee De Forest and Edwin Armstrong and pioneer entrepreneurs such as David Sarnoff.

Liebling, A. J. *The Press.* 2d ed. New York: Random House, 1975. One of the most respected critics of the American press in the early 20th century, Liebling wrote a column for the *New Yorker* from 1948 to 1963. Although the landscape of the media has changed considerably since then, the interplay of work pressure, prejudices, and corporate interests has not. Liebling predicted that declining competition among newspapers would result in less vigorous reporting of the news.

Lippmann, Walter. *Public Opinion.* New York: Simon & Schuster, 1997. Reissue of the classic 1922 work by one of the 20th century's most influential newspaper correspondents. Lippman lays out the parameters still followed today by political scientists who study the process of the formation of public opinion, including mechanisms of censorship or distribution of news, reader perception and, particularly, the problem of stereotyping.

McCay, Jenny. *The Magazine Handbook.* New York: Routledge, 2000. An introduction to and overview of the magazine industry, with a focus on the many positions and specialties available in the field. It includes a discussion of the historical development of magazines, numerous examples of work situations, and coverage of important journalistic and legal issues.

McLeish, Robert. *Radio Production: A Manual for Broadcasters.* 4th ed. Boston: Focal Press, 1999. Starting with the background and fundamental characteristics of the medium, this handbook provides basic information and procedures for producing various types of radio programming, including news reading, interviews, call-in talk shows, and music. With the recent interest in "micro radio" enabling more individuals and small groups to create local radio operations, as well as the development of Internet radio, there is likely to be a wider interest in this topic.

Nichols, Bill. *Introduction to Documentary.* Bloomington: Indiana University Press, 2001. A film scholar provides a comprehensive introduction to the development and craft of the film and television documentary. The treatment of facts and the use of persuasive techniques explored here is applicable also to other areas, including news and advertising.

Rabiger, Michael. *Directing the Documentary.* 2d ed. Boston: Focal Press, 1997. A handbook on how to research, produce, direct, and complete documentary films. Many examples from contemporary documentaries are included. The book includes a brief history of the genre and some career guidance. It would be useful to skim even for those not intending to produce their own documentaries.

Serrin, Judith, and William Serrin, eds. *Muckraking! The Journalism That Changed America.* New York: New Press, 2002. Although it includes the early 20th-century investigative style of journalism commonly called muckraking, this anthology covers a much broader scope in its more than 100 selections. These range from essays such as "Escape to Freedom" by Frederick Douglass (1834) to "AIDS Victims Seeking Help" by Randy Shilts (1985). The selections are grouped into sections by topics, including the poor, the working class, public health and safety, women's rights, race, and so on.

Smythe, Ted Curtis. *The Gilded Age Press, 1865–1900.* Westport, Conn.: Praeger Publishers, 2003. This history covers a key formative period in American journalism when the "new journalism" approach to covering the news, a shift from partisan to "objective" news (not editorial) coverage, and mass production and marketing of newspapers essentially created the modern newspaper.

Soan, William David, and Julie Hedgepeth Williams. *The Early American Press, 1690–1783.* Westport, Conn.: Greenwood Press, 1994. This history describes how the American press gradually became differentiated in practices and interests from its British parent. It also explores various theories and approaches to understanding the development of the American press and includes a bibliographical essay.

Thompson, Hunter S. *Fear and Loathing in Las Vegas.* 2d ed. New York: Vintage Books, 1998. This book is the canonical example of "gonzo journalism," using the language of surrealism and drug-fueled imagination to recount what happened when Thompson was sent to Las Vegas on what was supposedly a routine assignment to cover a motorcycle race.

Utley, Garrick. *You Should Have Been Here Yesterday: A Life in Television News.* New York: Public Affairs, 2001. After a long career as a foreign correspondent for NBC News, Utley also provides more than just a memoir, including many reflections on a correspondent's life and the demands of new technologies and changing corporate imperatives.

Walker, James R., and Douglas A. Ferguson. *The Broadcast Television Industry.* Boston: Allyn & Bacon, 1997. An overview of the television broadcasting industry (including cable), covering history, ownership and network operations, industry practices, audience, and social impact.

Walker, Jesse. *Rebels on the Air: An Alternative History of Radio in America.* New York: New York University Press, 2001. Describes radio "outside the box" from the earliest days when broadcasting was a highly individualistic enterprise to the alternative Pacifica Foundation to pirate and "micropower" radio activists who since the 1960s have tried to establish community alternatives to commercial radio while battling regulators.

Annotated Bibliography

Weaver, David H., and G. Cleveland Wilhoit. *The American Journalist: U.S. News People at the End of an Era*. Mahwah, N.J.: Lawrence Erlbaum Associates, 1996. Presents the results of the most comprehensive survey ever made of the demographics, backgrounds, working conditions, professional attitudes, and values of American journalists. There are separate sections on women and minority journalists. Results are compared with earlier surveys from the 1970s and 1980s.

White, Ted. *Broadcast News: Writing, Reporting, and Producing*. 3d ed. Boston: Focal Press, 2001. This is a detailed handbook on the many aspects of information gathering, writing, and presentation needed to produce a professional newscast. Contemporary news stories and broadcasts are used to illustrate each topic, and there are also excerpts from transcripts of historic broadcasts by Edward R. Murrow, Charles Kuralt, Eric Sevareid, and others.

Articles

Evans, Harold. "What a Century." *Columbia Journalism Review*, vol. 37, January/February 1999, p. 27. A panoramic view of what Americans would have been reading in their newspapers and magazines in 1900, including "snapshots" of a variety of publications. Public attitudes toward the press a century ago are compared with attitudes and concerns today. There is also a discussion of 20th-century journalistic achievements and failures and a chronology of events.

Hargreaves, Ian. "Spinning Out of Control." *History Today*, vol. 53, March 2003, p. 38ff. The author reviews the history of public relations—for example, John D. Rockefeller pioneered in hiring journalists to serve as his public relations specialists. Although public relations can be carried out with integrity, the pervasiveness of routine "spin" tactics is eroding trust in both the people who use it and the journalists who often get co-opted.

Harris, Roy J., Jr. "An Era of Crusaders: Without Much Fame or Glory, the Staff of One Paper Made Newspaper History." *The Quill*, vol. 91, May 2003, p. 10ff. Recounts a high point in crusading local journalism: the *St. Louis Post-Dispatch* of the mid-1930s to early 1950s, which embarked on a series of award-winning public service campaigns such as unmasking local "bosses" and election fraud, crusading against industrial pollution, and uncovering government corruption that had led to a deadly mine explosion.

McCabe, Carol. "Newspapers." *Early American Life*, vol. 25, June 1994, p. 40ff. Describes the origin of newspapers in colonial America. They started relatively late because of the strict government control on printing. Several early newspapers are described, including *Publick Occurrences* and the *New England Courant*.

"American Photography: A Century of Images." PBS Online. Available online: http://www.pbs.org/ktca/americanphotography. Downloaded on July 12, 2003. The web site for the PBS program of the same name, it includes transcripts, an interactive "Image Lab," and features on art, photography and war, digital truth, presidential image making, persuasion, social change, and cultural identity.

STRUCTURE AND OPERATION OF THE NEWS MEDIA

MEDIA OWNERSHIP AND CORPORATE INFLUENCE

This section deals with the ownership and control of the media, conglomeration and concentration in the media industry, and clashes between corporate agendas, economic pressures, and journalistic values.

Books

Albarran, Alan B. *Media Economics: Understanding Markets, Industries and Concepts.* 2d ed. Ames: Iowa State University Press, 2002. This textbook, which complements the *Global Media Economics* volume edited by the same author, focuses on the application of basic economic principles to the media industry. This requires a detailed look at industry practices and emerging trends in the various media sectors (radio, television, film, recording, Internet, newspapers, magazines, book publishing, and so on).

Albarran, Alan B., and Sylvia M. Chan-Olmsted. *Global Media Economics: Commercialization, Concentration, and Integration of World Media Markets.* Ames: Iowa State University Press, 1998. The contributors to this collection of essays provide a truly global survey of the impact of trends in the media industry and their impact on politics, society, and local economies around the world. Factors considered include mergers and acquisitions, regulations, and technological change.

Alexander, Alison, et al., eds. *Media Economics: Theory and Practice.* 3d ed. Mahwah, N.J.: Lawrence Erlbaum Associates, 2003. Best for professionals or students with some economics and business background, this collection of articles discusses the media as a business and how it responds to regulatory and economic pressures. After general considerations there are specific articles dealing with each sector of the media.

Allen, Craig M. *News Is People: The Rise of Local TV News and the Fall of News from New York.* Ames: Iowa State University Press, 2001. This book points to an interesting conundrum: at the same time that media power is increasingly being concentrated into national or global corporations, local news is generally winning out over national network news in the eyes and hearts of viewers. The author looks at the development of local news formats (such as "eyewitness news" in 1967–71) and the growing popularity of local newscasts. He suggests that a major reason for this popularity is that local newspeople tend to more closely reflect the values and interests of viewers than do the elite New York– or Washington, D.C.–based journalists.

Bagdikian, Ben. *The Media Monopoly.* 6th ed. Boston: Beacon Press, 2000. This latest edition of a classic study of media ownership trends suggests that the concentration of media ownership into a few large corporations continues to have serious negative consequences as the number of major players decreases from about 50 to only 10. The author focuses on the effects of such conglomerates as Gannett and Time/Warner on the diversity of media viewpoints available to readers and viewers—even while the corporate media has made some gains in diversity of employment and in addressing minority interests. He argues that lack of coverage of this issue in the corporate media itself, while not surprising, adds to the difficulty of addressing it. A new 2004 edition is expected.

Compaine, Benjamin M., and Douglas Gomery. *Who Owns the Media? Competition and Concentration in the Mass Media Industry.* 3d ed. Mahwah, N.J.: Lawrence Erlbaum Associates, 2000. This survey looks primarily at the business performance of the media rather than on the effects of its concentration on journalism. However, it provides an extensive collection of data that provides an in-depth look at the economic side of the media industry and the trends in each sector—newspapers, magazines, television, radio, the film industry, and so on.

Demers, David P. *Global Media: Menace or Messiah?* 2d ed. Creskill, N.J.: Hampton Press, 2001. Most works on media globalization and concentration emphasize its negative aspects. This study, however, attempts a more balanced approach. After describing current trends, it looks at the arguments of the critics and asks whether they are correct.

Hack, Richard. *Clash of the Titans: How the Unbridled Ambition of Ted Turner and Rupert Murdoch Created Global Empires That Control What We Read and Watch Each Day.* Beverly Hills, Calif.: New Millennium Press, 2003. A popular account of the battle between two powerful modern moguls for control of the media. The author suggests that the costly war between the two media giants has had a leveling effect on business and journalistic standards elsewhere in the industry. Using a weather metaphor, Hack describes Turner and Murdoch as "two storm fronts colliding. . . . Turner-the high front that swings erratic. . . . Murdoch-the low front that appears at rest, then moves with amazing speed, absorbing all in his path."

Herman, Edward S., and Noam Chomsky. *Manufacturing Consent: The Political Economy of the Mass Media*. New York: Pantheon Books, 2000. This book presents an updated version of the "Propaganda Model" proposed by Chomsky and his followers to explain the structure and behavior of the mass media. According to this theory, the structure, ownership, and practices of the media serve to maintain and reinforce the interests of the same dominant interests that make the news. Experts and pundits, for example, are selected to reinforce the dominant ideology; any views that might radically challenge it are marginalized. Decisions made by journalists about what is newsworthy and how to cover it "are frequently well explained by the incentives, pressures, and constraints incorporated into such a structural analysis."

Kung-Shankleman, Lucy. *Inside the BBC and CNN: Managing Media Organisations*. New York: Routledge, 2000. A study of the changing culture of broadcasting organizations that looks at two of the world's largest networks. The "continuous revolution" model is applied to the BBC, while CNN's business model was based on "reinventing the news." The concluding chapter argues that the management requirements of media organizations differ in crucial ways from mainstream business management.

McChesney, Robert W. *Corporate Media and the Threat to Democracy*. New York: Seven Stories Press, 1997. A short, rigorous exploration of the nature of ownership and control of the modern media and how it affects the journalistic process and product. McChesney emphasizes his belief that the functioning of democracy requires avoiding too great a disparity in wealth, fostering a sense of community, and providing for an accessible and effective method of political communication. Because corporate concentration of the media is degrading the last of these requirements, it is threatening the viability of democracy as a whole.

———. *Rich Media, Poor Democracy: Communication Politics in Dubious Times*. Champaign: University of Illinois Press, 1999. A liberal media scholar forthrightly argues that there is a fundamental conflict of interest between big business, profit-driven media, and the needs of democracy. His proposed solutions are equally forthright, if controversial. They include antitrust action to break up media conglomerates, reregulation of broadcasting, and large subsidies to nonprofit and alternative media.

McChesney, Robert W., and John Nichols. *Our Media, Not Theirs: The Democratic Struggle against Corporate Media*. New York: Seven Stories Press, 2002. Provides a diagnosis of the problems caused by corporate concentration of the U.S. and global media, surveys criticism of the corporate media from various sources, and describes facets of the movement that have risen to try to counter it. Includes forewords by Noam Chomsky, Barbara Ehrenreich, and Ralph Nader.

Soley, Lawrence. *Censorship, Inc.: The Corporate Threat to Free Speech in the United States*. New York: Monthly Review Press, 2002. Although the term *censorship* is usually thought of in connection with government action, this book looks at policies and tactics used by corporations to suppress speech that they find threatening. Some of these techniques include concealment of information (as with the tobacco companies), blacklisting employee whistleblowers, SLAPP (strategic lawsuits against public participation) suits, and restrictions of speech on commercial property. The final section deals with corporate control of the media and with legal and political strategies being used by activists to defend speech rights.

Articles

Auletta, Ken. "Synergy City." *American Journalism Review*, vol. 20, May 1998, p. 18ff. Describes how the Chicago Tribune Company (an old-line newspaper corporation) has responded to declining revenues and increased competition from other media by buying or investing in television, radio, cable, and online services. Although "synergy" may make sense as a business strategy, it threatens to diminish further the unique journalistic values of newspapers.

Coile, Zachary. "Limits on Media Ownership Eased." *San Francisco Chronicle*, June 3, 2003, pp. A1, A11. Summarizes the new, relaxed FCC media ownership restrictions. The same company may now be able to own several television and radio stations as well as a major newspaper in the same city. The article and an accompanying piece by Todd Wallack also profiles major media companies that are now poised to expand in the San Francisco Bay Area market.

Hartlaub, Peter. "Retired Broadcasters Lament the Diminished Diversity of Voices." *San Francisco Chronicle*, June 10, 2003, pp. D1, D7. Pioneer San Francisco Bay Area broadcasters James Gabbert and Bill Shaw react to recent FCC rulings allowing for greater media ownership consolidation. They argue that while news technology is better than ever before at providing information, there is less competition and diversity, and the new corporate culture makes radio work less satisfying.

Risser, James V. "Endangered Species." *American Journalism Review*, vol. 20, June 1998, p. 19ff. The author says that independent newspapers (those not belonging to a corporate chain) are definitely becoming an "endangered species." The selling of the Riverside (California) *Press-Independent* is the occasion for some somber analysis of what the loss of a vigorous independent newspaper sector means for journalism. A number of examples of the transition of local newspapers to corporate ownership are given. Some independent newspapers can be bad and selling them to a corporation might provide the management and resources needed to upgrade their quality. The article also includes 10 "standards of operation" developed by Nelson Poynter of the *St. Petersburg Times* in 1947 and later revised by Eugene Patterson.

Stern, Willy. "Grading the Daily." *Nashville Scene*, April 26–May 1, 2001, n.p. A five-part series of articles that investigates the pervasive changes in local journalism as newspapers are bought by national media chains. The prism for this examination is Nashville's daily newspaper *The Tennessean*. The series examines how the newspaper is being run, whether it is an economic success, and whose vision or agenda is being implemented. There is an indepth look at the newspaper's history as well as an explanation of how the reporters tried to ensure objectivity and avoid conflicts of interest by putting an outside editor in charge. (Note: this story can be viewed online at http://www.nashvillescene.com by using the search and browse facilities with the year 2001 and the five issues starting with April 26–May 1.)

Williams, Dmitri. "Synergy Bias: Conglomerates and Promotion in the News." *Journal of Broadcasting & Electronic Media*, vol. 46, September 2002, p. 453ff. The increasingly large corporations dominating the media are demanding "synergy" between their various divisions in order to reduce costs and improve efficiency. When a parent company demands such cooperation from a news media subdivision, the news content may be influenced, such as by having more frequent, detailed, or favorable mention of the company's other products in news coverage. However, the expected correlations do not always hold true and vary widely by type of industry.

Web Documents

"Diversity, Democracy, and Access: Is Media Concentration a Crisis?" MediaChannel.org. Available online. URL: http://www.mediachannel.org/ownership/index.shtml. Downloaded on July 13, 2003. Reports on media concentration around the world (including charts and tables) and the debate over whether media concentration imperils democracy.

Lehrer, Jim. "The New Age of Journalism." *PBS Online NewsHour.* Available online. URL: http://www.pbs.org/newshour/bb/media/jan-june00/new_journalism_1-19.html. Posted on January 19, 2000. PBS news commentator Jim Lehrer leads a panel discussion with liberal pundit and *Slate* founder Michael Kinsley, veteran journalist Haynes Johnson, and historians Michael Beschloss and Doris Kearns Goodwin. They discuss the impact of AOL/Time Warner and other media mergers on the practice of journalism. Two salient features mentioned are the sheer magnitude of these developments and the lack of public awareness and concern about them.

Moore, Aaron. "Who Owns What?" *Columbia Journalism Review.* Available online. URL: http://www.mediachannel.org/ownership/index.shtml. Downloaded on July 13, 2003. This interactive listing links media companies with their subsidiaries and with selected articles from the *Columbia Journalism Review* on media ownership.

Smith, Terence. "News Magazines." *PBS Online NewsHour.* Available online. URL: http://www.pbs.org/newshour/media/newsmags/newsmags_1-13. html. Posted on January 13, 1999. Smith, *NBC Dateline* producer Neil Shapiro, and other panelists discuss the burgeoning phenomenon of television "newsmagazines" during the three decades since CBS's pioneering *60 Minutes.* Shapiro suggests the format provides needed versatility and allows some stories to be covered in greater depth, but Smith points out that by "cloning" these shows, *Dateline* has created a profitable "news factory" with relatively low production costs that can earn considerable revenue by reselling stories to cable channels.

———. "Trouble at the L.A. Times." *PBS Online NewsHour.* Available online. URL:http://www.pbs.org/newshour/bb/media/july-dec99/la_times_ 12-16.html. Posted on December 16, 1999. Transcript of a *NewsHour with Jim Lehrer* report on the controversy surrounding the links between the *Los Angeles Times* and the Staples Center entertainment complex. The fact that the two companies had entered into an advertising revenue-sharing arrangement was felt by many journalists and experts on journalistic ethics to represent a fundamental conflict of interest that threatens the editorial independence of the newspaper.

Williams, Granville. "Bestriding the World." MediaChannel.org. Available online. URL: http://www.mediachannel.org/ownership/index.shtml. Downloaded on July 13, 2003. Provides details on media acquisitions and mergers and current holdings of media giants around the world. There is also a link to a large chart diagramming the ownership relationships.

REPORTING, NEWS COVERAGE, SELECTION, AND BIAS

This section deals with the process of gathering, selecting, and reporting news, techniques such as investigative reporting, the "gatekeeper" function of the journalist, and the possible effects of ideological or structural bias on the news.

Books

Alterman, Eric. *What Liberal Media? The Truth About Bias and the News.* New York: Basic Books, 2003. A refutation of Bernard Goldberg (author of *Bias*) and other critics who assert the media has a liberal bias. Alterman disputes many of the arguments for the media being liberal, finding it to be mainly (but not exclusively) conservative. He also suggests that conservatives have been effective in using the charge of media bias as a rallying cry and a way to intimidate the media.

Borjesson, Kristina. *Into the Buzzsaw: Leading Journalists Expose the Myth of a Free Press*. New York: Prometheus Books, 2002. The "buzzsaw" referred to in the title is the relentless institutional and other pressures that must be fought every day by often obscure journalists of integrity who fight to get truth into print or on the air. When the subject of the investigation is a powerful entrenched interest such as the military, the resistance becomes an almost visceral shock to the journalist. Each chapter gives a different journalist the opportunity to recount his or her struggles and suggest lessons from them.

Goldberg, Bernard. *Bias: A CBS Insider Exposes How the Media Distort the News*. Washington, D.C.: Regnery, 2002. A former CBS producer and winner of multiple Emmy Awards argues that the culture of the national broadcast media is strongly biased toward liberal views on social issues and is often intolerant or dismissive of opposing views. Material is often uncritically passed along from activist groups. Goldberg portrays veteran CBS anchor Dan Rather as petty and autocratic.

Graber, Doris A., Denis McQuail, and Pippa Norris, eds. *The Politics of News: The News of Politics*. Washington, D.C.: Congressional Quarterly Press, 1998. A collection of essays by distinguished scholars and media leaders (including Walter Cronkite and Kathleen Hall Jamieson) focusing on the factors and forces that determine what is selected as "news" and how stories are framed. The media functions as a multiple intermediary (between government and citizens, between special interest groups, and even between different factions in government).

Greenwald, Marilyn, and Joseph Bernt, eds. *The Big Chill: Investigative Reporting in the Current Media Environment*. Ames: Iowa State University Press, 2000. The contributors describe how investigative reporting developed and changed in substance, structure, and style. They go on to assess the current state of this form of journalism in a media world where corporate concentration brings intense pressures for profitability and at the same time technology pushes journalists toward immediate rather than in-depth reporting.

Herbert, John. *Global Journalism: Exploring Reporting Issues Worldwide*. Boston: Focal Press, 2000. An introduction to the global media marketplace and its players (news agencies and networks) and the types of sources journalists must use and evaluate (governmental and nongovernmental). There are comparative case studies about how similar issues are handled in different areas and full coverage of the use of the Internet.

Annotated Bibliography

Kuypers, Jim A. *Press Bias and Politics: How the Media Frame Controversial Issues.* Westport, Conn.: Praeger, 2002. Each chapter is a case study of how the media dealt with a controversial statement or initiative: The main topics focused on involve race and homosexuality. Examples include the Confederate flag controversy in Alabama, President Bill Clinton's Initiative on Race, and football star Reggie White's and Senator Trent Lott's comments in which they suggested that homosexuals be helped to deal with their "problem." The author argues that the media "operates within a narrow range of liberal belief," lashing out at anyone outside that range.

Meyer, Philip. *Precision Journalism: A Reporter's Introduction to Social Science Methods.* 4th ed. Lanham, Md.: Rowman & Littlefield, 2002. Precision journalism is a movement in journalism to adopt the more rigorous methods of science to the evaluation of information and events. While requiring some college-level statistics knowledge, this is a useful introduction to how journalists should approach studies, surveys, polls, and other tools that are used (and often misused) in sources encountered by reporters.

Murray, David, Joel Schwartz, and S. Robert Lichter. *It Ain't Necessarily So: How Media Make and Unmake the Scientific Picture of Reality.* Lanham, Md.: Rowman & Littlefield, 2001. The authors, all social scientists, use numerous case studies to suggest that the media often misstates or misuses statistics and scientific research findings. Often tentative conclusions based on insufficient evidence are treated as facts—and rallying cries—by politicians and interest groups. Readers need to take a critical approach to science stories reported in the media.

Olson, Walter K. *The Rule of Lawyers: How the New Litigation Elite Threatens America's Rule of Law.* New York: St. Martin's Press, 2003. The author, who has written several other books on litigation reform, attacks an elite group of lawyers whom he says are using novel theories (especially class action suits) to, in effect, redistribute a trillion or more dollars a year on the basis of dubious liability claims. He sees the media as often acting in synergy with activist lawyers by publicizing claims of risky products and sometimes even (as in the case of NBC and General Motors trucks) creating rigged "demonstrations" of accidents.

Salzman, Jason. *Making the News: A Guide for Activists and Nonprofits.* Revised ed. Boulder, Colo.: Westview Press, 2003. This handbook for activists and nonprofits provides a number of techniques for obtaining and shaping news coverage for an issue or program. Many of the tactics are imaginative and aggressive, and include Internet-related tools such as "viral e-mail." The book can also serve as an introduction for media students to public relations and media manipulation techniques commonly used by organizations of all types.

Power of the News Media

Schudson, Michael. *The Sociology of News.* New York: W. W. Norton, 2003. The author assesses current theories and issues about how the news media functions. Topics covered in the opening part include the definition of journalism, the effects of the media on society, allegations of media bias, the history of journalistic practice, as well as recent developments. The book then goes on to look at the components of the media structure, culture, and audience in more detail.

Seib, Philip. *Getting the News Right in a Real-Time, Online World.* Lanham, Md.: Rowman & Littlefield, 2002. Driven by the virtually real-time pace of the online world, other media such as television are also moving at an accelerating pace. Techniques from different fields are converging. The author explores the challenges to journalists who are under time pressure and have to sort through a torrent of information of uncertain authenticity and still "get it right."

Serrin, William. *The Business of Journalism: Ten Leading Reporters and Editors on the Perils and Pitfalls of the Press.* New York: New Press, 2000. A collection of essays by 10 leading journalists about the effects of changing corporate economics, other imperatives (such as the need for greater diversity), and pressures affecting story selection and treatment. Several contributors talk about their experience working with small, independent newspapers. (Only one contributor is from the broadcast media.)

Spark, David. *Investigative Reporting: A Study in Technique.* Boston: Focal Press, 1999. Using many real-life profiles and examples, the author explains what investigative reporting is and what techniques must be mastered to carry it out successfully. Besides discussion of research and writing techniques, there are also cautions about potentially dangerous situations, legal constraints, and other pitfalls.

Stauber, John, and Sheldon Rampton. *Toxic Sludge Is Good for You: Lies, Damn Lies and the Public Relations Industry.* Monroe, Maine: Common Courage Press, 1995. The authors, editors of the journal *PR Watch*, provide a scathing critique of the public relations (PR) industry, which is devoted to crafting messages and shaping perceptions. One of its favorite tools is euphemisms: sewer waste, for example, is now called "biosolids." Modern PR is closely related to the news media, which has come to depend for much of its daily fodder on neatly prepackaged PR releases.

Wilkins, Lee, and Philip Patterson, eds. *Risky Business: Communicating Issues of Science, Risk, and Public Policy.* Westport, Conn.: Greenwood Press, 1991. This volume tackles the difficult problems facing the portrayal of the process and conclusions of science in the media. The first contributions deal with the public perception of scientists and the hostile attitude many scientists have toward the media. The media tends toward a stereotyped approach to scientific issues, and there are always issues of accuracy and problems with limited access to data. A number of examples are drawn from coverage of medical developments, health risks, natural disasters, product safety, and other areas.

Articles

Barton, Gina. "What Is a Jour.Na.List? Despite Problems Surfacing from the Ambiguity of 'Journalism,' Many Professionals Are Reluctant to Define What We Do." *The Quill*, vol. 90, May 2002, p. 10ff. Journalists face a dilemma: They need some sort of definition of the profession in order to set standards and to receive credentials and the protection of "shield laws," but definitions can potentially be used by the government to shut out types of coverage they do not want. Various definitions of journalism and of its responsibilities are discussed.

Benaim, Daniel, Priyanka Motaparthy, and Vishesh Kumar. "TV's Conflicted Experts." *The Nation*, vol. 276, April 21, 2003, p. 6. Describes the potential conflicts of interest of many high-profile military experts who are called upon to analyze the war in Iraq for television news but often have connections with conservative advocacy groups or defense contractors.

Benoit, William L., and Heather Currie. "Inaccuracies in Media Coverage of the 1996 and 2000 Presidential Debates." *Argumentation and Advocacy*, vol. 38, Summer 2001, p. 28ff. Citing evidence that presidential debates can change voters' attitudes and voting intentions, the authors note that most voters only hear about the debates through news coverage (mostly in newspapers). The authors set out to determine the accuracy of that coverage. They found that statements characterized as attacks or defenses (rather than being focused on policy issues) were disproportionately featured in the media coverage. In 1996 (but not 2000) coverage emphasized character or personality issues more than policy differences. The newspaper coverage in 2000 dealt with only about 7 percent of the themes mentioned in the debate. The result is that media debate coverage is both distorted and highly selective.

Brady, Ray. "What Does Financial Reporting Look Like Today?" *Nieman Reports*, vol. 55, Summer 2001, p. 81. The price of pack journalism and "cheerleading" can be especially high when the subject is investments. During the boom times, financial writing took on the style of sports reporting and entertainment, but publications often did not identify the fact that their star analysts worked for companies that had a stake in the events being reported.

Brown, Fred. "Deciding Which Pieces to Leave Out: Part of a Journalist's Job Is to Exercise Judgment in Daily Coverage." *The Quill*, vol. 91, April 2003, p. 8ff. Journalists cannot be just passive conduits of information, so they need to think about what to leave out as well as what to put in. Examples

201

include situations involving public figures and personal acts that might be blown out of proportion. "Self-censorship" is not automatically bad.

De Moraes, Lisa. "CNN and Fox's Dueling Numbers." *Washington Post*, July 11, 2003, p. C7. Cable News Network (CNN) is preferred by many elite viewers, but Fox, with its populist approach, has surged out in front in viewing hours even though more people channel-surf to CNN. In watch terms, CNN thinks of itself as Rolex to Fox's Timex, but Fox thinks of CNN as "more like an antique hourglass."

Ewers, Justin. "Is the New News Good News?" *U.S. News & World Report*, vol. 134, April 7, 2003, p. 48. Assesses the impact and value of embedded journalists who traveled with military units in the 2003 Iraq war. Includes a historical overview of the relationship between journalists and the military in earlier wars such as World War II, Vietnam, and the Persian Gulf War.

Li, Xigen, and Ralph Izard. "9/11 Attack Coverage Reveals Similarities, Differences." *Newspaper Research Journal*, vol. 24, Winter 2003, p. 204ff. This content analysis study compares the coverage of the September 11 terrorist attacks by five television networks and eight newspapers. The study focuses on "framing," or the selection by journalists of what aspects of a story to emphasize. Generally, in a major crisis all outlets are working with the same facts; the differences show in the selection of sources and in the framing. Several hypotheses about framing differences between television and newspapers are proposed and tested; most were confirmed to some degree. For example, newspapers, which have to provide more in-depth coverage, tend to frame more for human interest, while television emphasizes immediate information.

Steiger, Paul E. "Not Every Journalist 'Missed' the Enron Story." *Nieman Reports*, vol. 56, Summer 2002, p. 10ff. The sheer complexity and opaqueness of the schemes set up by Enron made it almost impossible for outsiders to figure out what was going on. Professionals who had the ability to do such analysis—accounting firms like Arthur Andersen—had a conflict of interest because of the value of the business they were receiving from the company they were supposed to audit. A handful of journalists began to expose Enron's problems, but it was not until *Wall Street Journal* reporters Rebecca Smith and John Emshwiller made a sustained investigation that Enron's house of cards would tumble. The story suggests the difficult challenge that journalists face in dealing with the complexities of modern corporate structure.

Web Documents

Chinni, Dante. "Jessica Lynch: Media Myth-Making in the Iraqi War." Project for Excellence in Journalism. Available online. URL: http://www.journalism.org/resources/research/reports/war/postwar/lynch.asp. Posted on June 23, 2003. A detailed account of how the media covered the story of Private Jessica Lynch, who had been captured in the early days of the U.S.-Iraq war in April 2003. A chronology traces how various elements of the story (such as her being shot) developed and were questioned and how various media outlets gradually backed away from the story.

Croteau, David. "Examining the 'Liberal Media' Claim." Fairness and Accuracy in Reporting. Available online. URL: http://www.fair.org/reports/journalist-survey.html. Posted on June 1998. This survey and study refutes the claim that most journalists have left-wing attitudes and cover news in an ideologically biased way. The study concludes that, especially on important economic issues such as Social Security, Medicare, and global trade, the media is actually more conservative than the public. The coverage from business-oriented outlets is generally better and more effective than that of the general media.

"Media Bias Basics." Media Research Center. Available online. URL: http://secure.mediaresearch.org/news/MediaBiasBasics.html. Downloaded on July 4, 2003. A conservative media research group offers a well-organized introduction and compilation of survey statistics to support the assertion that media professionals are predominately liberal and biased toward liberal positions on policy issues.

Shafer, Jack. "The Varieties of Media Bias." *Slate.* Available online. URLs: http://slate.msn.com/id/2078200/, http://slate.msn.com/id/2078494/, and http://slate.msn.com/id/2078826/. Posted on February 5, 12, 18, 2003. A three-part series examines charges of ideological bias in the media. The author argues for a nuanced view, finding sampling flaws in both the Freedom Foundation survey (which found the majority of journalists to have a strongly liberal background) and the FAIR study, which concluded that there was a conservative bias. Rather, looking at the media in different ways might suggest both liberal and conservative biases, which are likely to roughly cancel each other out.

Smith, Terence. "A Changing Industry." *PBS Online NewsHour.* Available online. URLs: http://www.pbs.org/newshour/bb/media/july-dec98/ newnews_11-6.html and http://www.pbs.org/newshour/bb/media/july-dec98/newnews_11-13.html. Posted on November 6 and November 13, 1998. A two-part exploration of changes in the news industry. Former broadcaster and news analyst Marvin Kalb asserts that the networks now demand that news be profitable. However, David Talbot, editor of the online magazine *Salon*, suggests that the Internet, despite its excesses, is democratizing news, and Bill O'Reilly of Fox News points out that for all its faults, the aggressive multichannel media means that politicians and the government can no longer hide things for long.

———. "Death Watch." *PBS Online NewsHour.* Available online. URL: http://www.pbs.org/newshour/bb/media/july-dec98/suicide_11-

24.html. Posted on November 24, 1998. Smith, Dr. Jack Kevorkian, Catholic official Ned McGrath and *60 Minutes* anchor Mike Wallace discuss whether *60 Minutes's* broadcast of a videotaped assisted suicide represented bringing important, controversial news to the public or simply furthered Dr. Kevorkian's agenda. Wallace replies that the news media is "used" by nearly every important person who deals with it, but its job is to get material out in the open so there can be a public dialogue about it.

————. "Lowering the Bar?" *PBS Online NewsHour.* Available online. URL: http://www.pbs.org/newshour/bb/media/jan-june99/tabloid_2-3.html. Posted on February 3, 1999. Smith, together with journalist Todd Gitlin, former congresswoman Patricia Schroeder, and other panelists discuss the descent of the media into sleaze typified by coverage of the Clinton-Lewinsky scandal. Gitlin attributes this "long slide" to a "culture of confession," escalating leaks, and journalists apparently powerless to resist. Journalists will continue to struggle to find a way to draw a line between private and public behavior, perhaps with politicians perceived as hypocritical being treated more harshly.

THE NEW MEDIA AND EMERGING TECHNOLOGY

This section covers technological change—particularly the Internet and the use of digital media—and its effect on the news media

Books

Gunter, Barrie. *News and the Net.* Mahwah, N.J.: Lawrence Erlbaum Associates, 2003. The author focuses on the extension of newspapers into web sites in relation to the overall crisis facing the print news media, but also discusses Web-only news sites. He suggests that existing communication models are inadequate to capture the use, effectiveness, and impact of online news operations.

Hall, Jim. *Online Journalism: A Critical Primer.* Sterling, Va.: Pluto Press, 2001. The author provides a survey and critical evaluation of the advantages and disadvantages of online journalism as compared to traditional media. Many challenges await both journalists (who are faced with not only new technology but new corporate agendas) and readers (who must master new ways of interaction with and evaluation of media).

Herbert, John. *Journalism in the Digital Age: Theory and Practice for Broadcast, Print and Online Media.* Boston: Focal Press, 1999. This textbook focuses on the extension of traditional journalistic skills (and the development of new ones) appropriate to a world of changing technology. The convergence of different forms of media into a single enterprise is also explored, as are the changes required in management, journalistic practices, and ethical standards.

Houston, Brant. *Computer-Assisted Reporting: A Practical Guide.* 2d ed. New York: Bedford/St. Martin's, 1999. A guide to the use of computer data sources, tools, and techniques for investigative reporting. Besides providing material useful for students and researchers of all types, this book also gives a good indication of how technology is changing the practice of investigative journalism.

Kawamoto, Kevin, ed. *Digital Journalism: Emerging Media and the Changing Horizons of Journalism.* Lanham, Md.: Rowman & Littlefield, 2003. The contributors to this volume provide history and overviews of developments in digital and online journalism, as well as discussing such topics as media convergence, online activism, and the impact of accessibility to digital information on the relationship between citizens and government.

Kovach, Bill, and Tom Rosenstiel. *Warp Speed: America in the Age of the Mixed Media.* New York: Century Foundation Press, 1999. The excessive and sometimes bizarre coverage of the Clinton-Lewinsky scandal was seen by many media critics as a warning that the media no longer had effective mechanisms of self-restraint and evaluation of newsworthiness. The author explains how new technology and business demands have created this situation. With relentless time pressure to meet a news cycle measured in hours, journalists must increasingly rely on sources who have agendas of their own and cannot be verified. Competitive pressures demand big, sensational stories, so material is selected and skewed toward that objective.

Pavlik, John Vernon, and Seymour Topping. *Journalism and New Media.* New York: Columbia University Press, 2001. This nontechnical but thorough survey of online journalism and new media techniques is especially geared to working journalists who need to adapt to the online world and young people who are comfortable online and are seeking journalism careers. There are many examples comparing traditional and online approaches to particular kinds of stories.

Ward, Mike. *Journalism Online.* Boston: Focal Press, 2002. This handbook explains both the traditional and the "new media" skills needed for today's online journalism. These skills include online research techniques, editing audio and digital material, writing for the Web (with HTML and other tools), and appropriate online formats and writing style.

We've Got Blog: How Weblogs Are Changing Our Culture. Introduction by Rebecca Blood. Cambridge, Mass.: Perseus Publishing, 2002. A collection of essays exploring the development and implication of weblogs or "blogs," the regularly updated personal journals being published by many journalists (and other people) on the Web. Approaches of the essays range from commentary to personal accounts to how-tos.

Articles

Levy, Stephen. "Will the Blogs Kill Old Media?" *Newsweek*, May 20, 2002, p. 52. The author, a technology journalist and popular writer, says that the answer is no. He describes the remarkable growth of the "blogosphere" with its tens of thousands of pages of user-written commentary. Sites such as InstaPundit are providing a sorting and evaluation process, and many journalists are using their blogs as a supplement to their traditional journalism rather than a replacement for it. Prominent bloggers are starting to be coopted by major traditional media outlets.

Palser, Barb. "Free to Blog? Three Journalists Are Told by Their Employers to Cease their Web Musings." *American Journalism Review*, vol. 25, June–July 2003, p. 62. Many journalists see weblogs as an extension of their self-expression, but in three cases employers decided that the blogs were either distracting them from their regular work or creating a conflict of interest or compromising their objectivity. Policies balancing these considerations will need to be developed by media outlets.

———. "Online Advances: The Internet Lagged Far Behind Television and Newspapers as a Primary Source of News About Operation Iraqi Freedom." *American Journalism Review*, vol. 25, May 2003, p. 40ff. It was probably wrong to think that online reporting would displace 24-hour television news as the main source of information on the 2003 Iraq war. However, the Web showed its value in subtler ways, functioning as a tool for personal communication (weblogging) and allowing for experimentation in new ways to deliver the news.

Robertson, Lori. "The Romenesko Factor." *American Journalism Review*, vol. 22, September 2000, p. 28. Describes the effects of James Romenesko's MediaNews web site, which has become a forum for journalists to comment on news coverage and to react to developments in the industry. The site's impact is part of a larger online movement toward an interactive journalistic process.

Stein, Nicholas. "Slate vs. Salon." *Columbia Journalism Review*, vol. 37, January/February 1999, p. 56. The author compares two prominent online publications. Slate, founded by liberal pundit Michael Kinsley, emphasizes the selection and distillation of content to help readers navigate through the seas of online media. David Talbot's Salon, on the other hand, emphasizes direct reporting and a more personal and investigative approach, referring to Salon as a "smart tabloid." Both publications continue to face economic challenges.

Tucher, Andy. "Back to the Future." *Columbia Journalism Review*, vol. 40, November–December 2001, p. 165ff. Before the September 11 attacks it was commonplace for media experts to predict the continuing demise of the traditional media in favor of the Internet and the "New Media." However, in the wake of the attacks there has been a revival of traditional genres such as the news feature and the documentary. The war on terrorism will demand a much more substantive journalism, including a greater role for newspapers, which can convey high impact photojournalism with detail beyond that available to television.

Web Documents

Horrigan, John B., and Lee Rainie. "Counting on the Internet: Most Expect to Find Information Online, Most Find the Information They Seek, Many Now Turn to the Internet First." Pew Internet and American Life. Available online. URL: http://www.pewinternet.org/reports/toc.asp?Report=80. Posted on December 29, 2002. The title more or less states the report's conclusions. With more than 60 percent of Americans having online access, the Internet has become a mainstream information source and users have high expectations of finding news, health, and consumer information online.

Lenhart, Amanda. "The Ever-Shifting Internet Population: A New Look at Internet Access and the Digital Divide." Pew Internet and American Life. Available online. URL: http://www.pewinternet.org/reports/toc.asp?Report=88. Posted on April 16, 2003. Reports that Internet use is volatile especially when considering nonworkplace use. The statistics about nonusers are also interesting: 20 percent of nonusers live with users but resist going online; 17 percent of former users have "dropped out." About 24 percent of the American population has never been online and has no access. The report contains many demographic aspects of Internet access.

Miller, Adam S. CAR Talk: A Review of Computer-Assisted Reporting. Available online. URL: http://www.webcrossings.com/cartalk.html. Posted in 1999. A well-organized overview of computer-assisted journalism, which *Editor and Publisher* magazine called "the news-gathering tool of the 1990s." Different types of online database sources are described, along with the advantages and disadvantages of each. Includes links to information sources.

Murrie, Michael. "Local Web News: Case Study of Nine Local Broadcast Internet News Operations." Radio and Television News Directors Foundation Future of News Project. Available online. URL: http://www.rtndf.org/study/foreword.shtml. Posted in 2001. Describes the varying approaches of local broadcast stations in establishing a presence on the

Web. There is difficulty in sorting the extent to which the online operation is to be an extension of the broadcast coverage or an independent news source in its own right. Of the nine operations profiled, only some are profitable, but although many need improvement, the effectiveness of the Internet for local news has already been demonstrated.

Semonche, Barbara. "Computer-Assisted Journalism: An Overview." University of North Carolina School of Journalism. Available online. URL: http://www.ibiblio.org/journalism/cajinv.html. Posted in 1993. Despite its age, this excerpt from the author's *News Media Libraries* is a good introduction to the use of computer tools in journalism. This specialty, sometimes called computer-assisted reporting (CAR), has been an important tool for investigative reporters in recent years. This overview begins with some background on investigative reporting and the development of its techniques. A related technique, "precision journalism," is also defined. Many examples are given of how investigative reporters have used computers to obtain crucial information for a story. Librarians have also emerged as important resources in investigative journalism.

Smith, Terence. "Weblogging." *PBS Online NewsHour.* Available online. URL: http://www.pbs.org/newshour/bb/media/jan-june03/blog_04-28.html. Posted on April 28, 2003. Smith interviews webloggers, who create "blogs," or online diaries, commenting on personal and news events. It is suggested that blogs can indeed be journalism but work best when some judicious editing is used to help writers clarify their expression. Blogs are also credited with making Senator Trent Lott's remarks favoring Strom Thurmond's pro–state's rights and segregation 1948 presidential campaign into a national story, leading to Lott resigning as Senate majority leader.

INFLUENCE AND EFFECTS OF THE NEWS MEDIA

THE MEDIA AND PUBLIC ATTITUDES

This section covers assessment and characterization of public attitudes toward the news media, the nature of the media audience, how people use the media, and how the media affects public attitudes in general.

Books

Asher, Herbert B. *Polling and the Public: What Every Citizen Should Know.* 5th ed. Washington, D.C.: Congressional Quarterly, 2001. Because polls make news and, through the media, reflect the public's opinion back on itself, it is vital that people understand how polls work, as well as their uses, potential abuses, and limitations. The author describes all of these aspects and looks at how polls are used by the media and how they can create feedback effects.

Giles, David. *Media Psychology*. Mahwah, N.J.: Lawrence Erlbaum Associates, 2003. A comprehensive view of the psychological impact of various types of media on different audiences, drawing on both American and European research. It includes sections on the news media and on the growing influence of the Internet.

Lenart, Silvo. *Shaping Political Attitudes: The Impact of Interpersonal Communication and Mass Media*. Thousand Oaks, Calif.: Sage Publications, 1994. The author suggests that in focusing only on the effects of the mass media, researchers are missing half of the equation that creates political opinion. The other half is interpersonal communication, and the author constructs a model of "total information flow" that includes both mass and interpersonal communication, showing how together they shape perception and cognition.

Mutz, Diana C. *Impersonal Influence: How Perceptions of Mass Collectives Affect Political Attitudes*. New York: Cambridge University Press, 1998. The author describes the dynamics of "impersonal influence"—how people perceive and react to the collective experience and opinion of the public as reported in the media. Because of the effect of collective opinion on personal attitudes, the media as the channel of public opinion gains considerable power to shape individual attitudes, particularly toward crime and other social problems.

Mutz, Diana Carole, Richard A. Brody, and Paul M. Sniderman, eds. *Political Persuasion and Attitude Change*. Ann Arbor: University of Michigan Press, 1996. Contributors survey the latest findings on political persuasion, exploring its three main channels: the mass media, political elites, and individual citizens. Their approach is fine-grained, looking at the actual extent to which individuals' attitudes can be shifted in particular circumstances.

Perlmutter, David A. *Policing the Media: Street Cops and Public Perception of Law Enforcement*. Thousand Oaks, Calif.: Sage Publications, 2000. Much of the content of the nightly local news relates to crime and police activity. By gaining firsthand experience of riding with police, the author was able to study the discrepancies between the culture and work of policing and how it is portrayed in the media. Police themselves are aware of this discrepancy but find themselves having to adopt "TV- like" attitudes in order to relate to a public that has media-formed expectations.

Reese, Stephen D., ed. *Framing Public Life: Perspectives on Media and Our Understanding of the Social World*. Mahwah, N.J.: Lawrence Erlbaum

209

Associates, 2003. This collection of essays from interdisciplinary contributors explores how the media shape or frame the audience's perception of their social world. In doing so the news and entertainment media has a powerful effect on social relations and the resolution of social and political issues.

Sanford, Bruce. *Don't Shoot the Messenger: How Our Growing Hatred of the Media Threatens Free Speech for All of Us.* New York: Free Press, 1999. A First Amendment scholar, Sanford is concerned that widespread public disillusion with the media (and even hostility toward it) may be undermining public support for vital guarantees of free speech. Many politicians find it convenient to blame the media for various problems. In response to the souring public attitudes, courts are beginning to erode protection for aggressive news-gatherers. The corporate media may be adding to the problem by settling meritless libel or privacy claims rather than fighting them in court.

Wanta, Wayne. *The Public and the National Agenda: How People Learn About Important Issues.* Mahwah, N.J.: Lawrence Erlbaum Associates, 1997. An approach to agenda-setting that focuses on the individual media user rather than the content provider. By focusing on how individuals process information and attempt to use it to satisfy their needs, the author provides a useful new perspective.

Zaller, John R. *The Nature and Origins of Mass Opinion.* New York: Cambridge University Press, 1992. Working with specific issues in foreign and domestic policy, the author applies a comprehensive theory to explain how public opinion is formed, the role of the news media, and the influence of polls (including seemingly small variations in how questions are worded).

Articles

Greer, Jennifer D., and Joseph D. Gosen. "How Much Is Too Much? Assessing Levels of Digital Alteration as Factors in Public Perception of News Media Credibility." *News Photographer,* vol. 57, July 2002, p. S4ff. The authors conducted a study in which subjects were shown photographs altered to varying degrees. They found that the perceived credibility of the pictures dropped as alteration increased. However, other factors, such as the subject's age, income, and education, were more determinative of the degree of credibility.

Poniewozik, James. "Don't Blame It on Jayson Blair: Big Media's Big Problem Isn't Plagiarism—It's a Passion Deficit." *Time,* vol. 161, June 9, 2003, p. 90. The public's response to the Jayson Blair plagiarism scandal has been mostly a yawn. The author suggests it is because the public already thinks that most people in the media are "phonies" who lack commitment to their jobs.

Annotated Bibliography

Web Documents

"The American Radio News Audience Survey: Examining the Perception and Future of Radio News." Future of News and Journalism Ethics Projects, Radio and Television News Directors Foundation. Available online. URL: http://www.rtndf.org/radio. Posted in 2000. Presents results of extensive audience surveys of the effectiveness of various formats of radio news, audience listening patterns, and radio news in relation to other media formats.

"Examining Our Credibility." American Society of Newspaper Editors. Available online. URL: http://www.asne.org/kiosk/reports/99reports/ 1999examiningourcredibility/index.htm. Posted in 2003. A study of the public's attitudes toward journalism, focusing on concerns about accuracy, the relationship of newspapers to the community, and issues of perceived bias and sensationalism. Generally journalists share the public's concern with accuracy (particularly factual and grammatical errors) but are not as concerned about bias and sensationalism.

"The News Media/Communications." PollingReport.com. Available online. URL: http://www.pollingreport.com/media.htm. Posted in 2003. A compilation of polls and surveys on the public's use of attitudes toward the media.

"Public's News Habits Little Changed by September 11." Pew Research Center for the People and the Press. Available online. URL: http://people-press.org/reports/display.php3?ReportID=156. Posted on June 9, 2002. Reports that people's news habits have not been affected very much by the September 11 attacks and the subsequent war on terrorism. There has been a modest increase in interest in international news—16 percent followed it "very closely" in 1996 and 21 percent did so in 2002. The biggest reason for lack of interest in international news is that 65 percent said they lacked the background knowledge needed to make sense of world affairs. The overall trends remain unchanged: both network news viewership and newspaper readership generally increase with age.

MEDIA, POLITICS, AND GENERAL POLICY

This section covers the possible effects of the news media on politics, political campaigns, and debate on public policy issues. It also covers journalists' responses to shortcomings of the media in its political coverage and possible reforms such as civic (public) journalism.

Books

Bennett, W. Lance, and Doris Graber. *News: The Politics of Illusion.* 5th ed. New York: Longman, 2002. The latest edition of a classic historical overview and textbook detailing the historical evolution of the news industry and its changing political and social function. The text is enriched with numerous case studies, anecdotes, and excerpts from the media.

Bennett, W. Lance, and Robert M. Entman, eds. *Mediated Politics: Communication in the Future of Democracy.* New York: Cambridge University Press, 2000. Analyzes the effects of changes in media operation and technology on the functioning of democratic institutions. Factors discussed include the somewhat diminished role of newspapers and network television, the growing influence of cable and "new media" (including the Internet), and the blurring of distinctions between factual reporting, advertising, and fiction.

Bernstein, Carl, and Bob Woodward. *All the President's Men.* New York: Simon and Schuster, 1974. The classic recounting of the Watergate story by the two investigative reporters who brought it to light. They describe how they went about uncovering and verifying the story, as well as their dealings with their executive publisher on the *Washington Post*, Katharine Graham, and their editor, Ben Bradlee.

Cook, Timothy E. *Governing with the News: The News Media as a Political Institution.* Chicago: University of Chicago Press, 1998. People tend to think of the news media and government as quite distinct institutions, often cast in an adversarial role. The author shows that government has always shaped media (such as through postal subsidies starting in the late 18th century). Today, because reporters are so dependent on government sources, political leaders can shape the news more directly. The media has become an instrument of political power.

Corrigan, Don H. *The Public Journalism Movement in America: Evangelists in the Newsroom.* Westport, Conn.: Praeger, 1999. Public journalism, with its emphasis on involvement with the community and fostering of public discussion, has been hailed by advocates as a way to redeem journalism. The author strongly disagrees. After describing a number of approaches to public journalism and providing a useful overview, he argues that far from saving journalism, the movement is likely to harm journalism, not least by distracting from the field's real problems, including global corporate pressures.

Denton, Robert E. Jr., ed. *Political Communication Ethics: An Oxymoron?* Westport, Conn.: Praeger, 2000. This collection of essays focuses on the nuts and bolts of political communication and relationship to (and use of) the media. Areas discussed include campaign strategies, discourse and rhetoric, use of advertising, and exploitation of new technologies, including the Internet.

———. *The 2000 Presidential Campaign: A Communication Perspective.* Westport, Conn.: Praeger, 2002. A variety of experts analyze the political communication strategies used during the 2000 presidential campaign. Starting with the primaries, each key decision by the Bush and Gore campaigns is discussed in perspective. Aspects discussed include the orchestration of the party conventions, the presidential debates, and the use of the Internet. In general the contributors seem to conclude that Al Gore missed a number of opportunities to effectively challenge George W. Bush's tactics. (This book is part of a series of volumes about each presidential campaign, starting with 1992.)

Denton, Robert E., Jr., and Gary C. Woodward. *Political Communication in America.* 3d ed. Westport, Conn.: Praeger Publishers, 1998. Revised edition of a classic text on all aspects of political communication, including campaign management, communications and governing in the presidency and Congress, communication in the legal arena, and politics and popular culture.

Denton, Robert E., Jr., and Rachel L. Holloway, eds. *Images, Scandal, and Communication Strategies of the Clinton Presidency.* Westport, Conn.: Praeger, 2003. This collection of essays focuses on how Bill Clinton and his advisers dealt with the media during major scandals and challenges, including the Monica Lewinsky affair and the impeachment process. These events shed considerable light on how modern political professionals view and attempt to use the media today.

Eksterowicz, Anthony J., and Robert N. Roberts, eds. *Public Journalism and Political Knowledge.* Lanham, Md.: Rowman & Littlefield, 2000. Public (or civic) journalism attempts to transform journalists from passive recorders of events to active participants in promoting public discourse and community involvement. The contributors offer insights into the origin and development of the public journalism movement as well as considering its possible impact.

Fallows, James. *Breaking the News: How the Media Undermine American Democracy.* New York: Vintage Books, 1997. A passionate and wide-ranging criticism of the failures of American political journalism. The author argues that by succumbing to greed, intellectual laziness, and promotion of sales through sensationalism, the media reinforces the use of "spin," sound bites, and other tactics calculated to manipulate voters and shut out real debate on the issues. Many noted pundits and political talk show hosts are presented as examples of this behavior.

Fox, Roy F. *MediaSpeak: Three American Voices.* Westport, Conn.: Praeger, 2000. The author, who teaches classes in language, literacy, and culture at the University of Missouri at Columbia, argues that three voices predominate in popular media (including the news). They are "doublespeak," which appears to say something but is actually empty; "salespeak," which uses selective facts to persuade people to buy things; and "sensationspeak," which is a visceral substitute for thought. These voices need to be identified and counteracted if meaningful speech is to be restored.

Friedenberg, Robert C. *Communications Consultants in Political Campaigns: Ballot Box Warriors.* Westport, Conn.: Praeger, 1997. A thorough look at the little-known role played by communications or media consultants in modern political campaigns. Includes a variety of case studies showing typical situations.

Gelderman, Carol. *All the President's Words: The Bully Pulpit and the Creation of the Virtual Presidency.* New York: Walker, 1997. A study in the changing composition of presidential speech. Not only do modern presidents eschew complex rhetorical techniques and argument in favor of stringing together tested sound bites, but they also generally do not write their own speeches. Further, while the presidents from Franklin D. Roosevelt through Lyndon Johnson had speechwriters who were also active in policy making, Richard Nixon started a trend toward speechwriting specialists—a trend briefly interrupted only in the Clinton administration. This trend greatly reduces any possibility of a meaningful personal dialogue between a president and the nation.

Graber, Doris A. *Mass Media and American Politics.* 6th ed. Washington, D.C.: Congressional Quarterly Press, 2001. The latest edition of this respected handbook comprehensively discusses the role of the mass media in politics and its effects on shaping popular attitudes. Recent trends are highlighted, including the effects of media mega-mergers, deregulation, and the use of new technologies such as the Internet.

———. *Media Power in Politics.* 4th ed. A wide-ranging anthology of articles on issues in political communication and approaches to researching them. General areas covered include agenda-setting, the effect of the media on election outcomes, the conflict between politicians and the media, effects of media stories on public policy, and regulation and other ways in which the government seeks to constrain or manipulate the media.

———. *Processing Politics: Learning from Television in the Internet Age.* Chicago: University of Chicago Press, 2001. The author disagrees with the common assertion that the lack of public knowledge of policy matters comes from inherent defects in the medium (principally, television). Rather, television can be a very effective tool for conveying complex information, but modern politicians and media leaders usually do not use it that way. The use of television and the new medium of the Internet must therefore be rethought with learning theory in mind.

Jamieson, Kathleen Hall, and Karlyn Kohrs Campbell. *The Interplay of Influence: News, Advertising, Politics, and the Mass Media.* 5th ed. Belmont, Calif.: Wadsworth, 2000. Revised edition of an important study of how three different groups—journalists, politicians, and advertisers—interact to create political messages. The new edition includes additional case studies and expanded coverage of the Internet.

Jamieson, Kathleen Hall, and Paul Waldman. *The Press Effect: Politicians, Journalists, and the Stories That Shape the Political World.* New York: Oxford University Press, 2002. Using the massive Annenberg 2000 Survey of the media and popular opinion, the authors argue that, as shown in the 2000 presidential campaign, the media largely fails to penetrate the fabrications created by politicians and give voters the information they really need and want. Instead, the media cast the Gore-Bush contest as one "between Pinocchio and Dumbo."

Johnson, Thomas J., Carol E. Hays, and Scott P. Hays, eds. *Engaging the Public: How Government and the Media Can Reinvigorate American Democracy.* Lanham, Md.: Rowman & Littlefield, 1998. Following the 1996 election, a group of leading political and media scholars examined and identified the causes for lack of citizen involvement in politics. They offer a variety of ways to stimulate public engagement, including urging the media to take a more proactive approach to stimulating discussion of the issues that matter most.

Kendall, Kathleen. *Communication in the Presidential Primaries: Candidates and the Media, 1912–2000.* Westport, Conn.: Praeger, 2000. Besides being interesting in their own right, primary election campaigns are often decisive in determining who is ultimately elected president. This historical survey begins by describing the process of primary campaigns and the role played by speeches, debates, and media coverage. It then describes the role of political communication in the pretelevision era (1912–52) and the age of dominant network television (1972–92), then summarizes the communication patterns and their significance.

Kraus, Sidney. *Televised Presidential Debates and Public Policy.* 2d ed. Mahwah, N.J.: Lawrence Erlbaum Associates, 1999. The author, who has written previous books on the 1960 Kennedy-Nixon and 1976 Ford-Carter debates, argues that the debates can be of crucial importance in sharpening and highlighting policy differences between candidates. He also suggests ways to make the debates more engaging and useful to the voter.

Lipschiltz, Jeremy H., and Michael L. Hilt. *Crime and Local Television News: Dramatic, Breaking, and Live from the Scene.* Mahwah, N.J.: Lawrence Erlbaum Associates, 2002. The authors place crime coverage in the context of the highly competitive world of local television news, where sensational crime stories are often featured in an attempt to build ratings. Survey data is also included.

Paletz, David L. *The Media in American Politics: Contents and Consequences.* 2d ed. New York: Longman, 2001. Discusses recent developments in politics, media, and popular culture, including controversial topics such as crime, pornography, terrorism, and violence. The second edition adds coverage of the 2000 election and expanded discussion of the impact of the Internet on various areas of journalism.

Roberts, Gene, and Thomas Kunkel, eds. *Breach of Faith: A Crisis of Coverage in the Age of Corporate Newspapering*. Fayetteville: University of Arkansas Press, 2002. The second volume in the series begun with *Leaving Readers Behind*, the essays in this volume focus on how the changes in corporate ownership and control have affected the content of newspapers. On the one hand, bringing more newspapers into corporate networks has improved their technical resources and production quality. But when it comes to the news content, the pursuit of "safe" stories and the bottom line has increased coverage in areas such as sports and business at the expense of national politics and foreign affairs. Many contributors urge editors to work harder to get "hard news" into the paper rather than succumb to the self-fulfilling conclusions of focus groups.

Roberts, Gene, Thomas Kunkel, and Charles Layton, eds. *Leaving Readers Behind: The Age of Corporate Newspapering*. Fayetteville: University of Arkansas Press, 2001. Contributors to this collection trace the development of one of the biggest stories of the 1990s not to be covered in newspapers—the swallowing up of many newspapers by large multimedia corporations. The articles collected here and in the second volume, *Breach of Faith*, arise from the Project on the State of the American Newspaper. This first volume focuses on documenting the many developments that have led to the creation of the new corporate media.

Rosen, Jay. *What Are Journalists For?* New Haven: Yale University Press, 1999. A proponent of "public journalism" argues that today's dominant model of journalism as passive and supposedly objective is inadequate. Journalists need to actively learn what their community needs in terms of information and issues and to promote public discussion forums and other ways to involve citizens in election campaigns and other political processes.

Shogan, Robert. *Bad News: Where the Press Goes Wrong in the Making of the President*. Chicago: Ivan R. Dee, 2001. A veteran political reporter for the *Los Angeles Times* says that the press too often falls victim to the machinations of campaign media specialists. One reason is that with the virtually instant news cycle brought about by modern technology, the press no longer has time for independent analysis and evaluation of materials coming out of campaigns. As a result, crafted messages flow directly from candidates through the media to voters who are manipulated rather than being informed about the real issues.

Slotnick, Elliott E., and Jennifer A. Segal. *Television News and the Supreme Court: All the News That's Fit to Air?* New York: Cambridge University Press, 1998. A detailed analysis of national media coverage of Supreme

Court decisions, informed by detailed study of the videotaped coverage and in-depth interviews with prominent journalists on the Supreme Court beat. There are two main factors that lead to coverage of Supreme Court cases often being perfunctory and inaccurate. One is the culture of secrecy surrounding the Court itself (including the refusal to allow cameras into oral arguments), greatly limiting access to the court's work and to the justices. The other is the attitudes and practices of television news, with its emphasis on the visual and its need to boil complex stories down to a few sentences. The Court's custom of releasing several decisions simultaneously on a Monday also means that all but the most major rulings are unlikely to receive adequate coverage.

Sparrow, Bartholomew. *Uncertain Guardians: The News Media as a Political Institution.* Baltimore: Johns Hopkins University Press, 1999. The author, a professor of government, provides an accessible account of the factors that limit the news media's ability to serve as an independent source of accountability for politicians. Both the economic interests of the corporate media (and advertisers) and journalists' unwillingness to challenge conventional assumptions lead to one-sided coverage in many areas. Examples discussed include the Persian Gulf War of 1991, the AIDS crisis, and the savings and loan debacle of the late 1980s.

Traugott, Michael W., and Paul J. Lavrakas, eds. *Election Polls, the News Media, and Democracy.* New York: Chatham House Press, 2000. These essays examine the use of polls, particularly those heavily reported or sponsored by the media, and suggest ways to improve their accuracy.

Articles

Kennamer, David, and Jeff South. "Election Coverage Reflects Civic Journalism Values." *Newspaper Research Journal*, vol. 23, Fall 2002, p. 34ff. The authors compare the political coverage of two newspapers. The *Virginian-Pilot* practices "public" or "civic" journalism that emphasizes press involvement in the community, while the *Richmond Times-Dispatch* follows the traditional model of "objective" journalism. A study of their coverage in the 2000 election compared the numbers of stories featuring "citizen-based" rather than campaign-generated sources and the number of stories focusing on issues rather than competition between candidates. It also assessed the degree to which stories focused on the "horse race" aspect of the election and on differences between the candidates rather than areas of agreement and the use of polls to bring out attitudes on issues rather than support for candidates. In general, the two newspapers differed in their coverage in ways that would be expected based on the different agendas of civic journalism and traditional journalism.

Mooney, Chris. "John Zogby's Creative Polls: And a Closer Look at His Methods." *The American Prospect*, vol. 14, February 2003, p. 29ff. Critiques the Zogby polling organization, whose work is highly sought by interests at both ends of the ideological spectrum. Zogby provides highly regarded objective polling for media marketing departments, but according to the author, the Zogby polls marketed to political and policy groups use "creatively" phrased questions in order to elicit the results the client wants. The problem is then compounded by reporters' uncritical or exaggerated characterization of the poll results.

Pfau, Michael. "The Subtle Nature of Presidential Debate Influence." *Argumentation and Advocacy*, vol. 38, Spring 2002, p. 251ff. A survey and analysis of the research literature on the effects and importance of televised presidential debates. The ability of candidates to "relationally" connect with viewers and promote affection and trust as elements of persuasion seems to be much more crucial than success in conveying the substance of issues. This relational dimension also suggests that the debates have a longer impact on the outcome of the campaign than some scholars believe.

Rosentiel, Tom, and Dave Iverson. "Politics and TV Can Mix." *Los Angeles Times*, October 15, 2002, p. B15. Local television has largely ignored political coverage, with the general feeling being that it does not interest audiences. That conclusion, however, is based on flawed surveys that ask only perfunctory, general questions about interest in politics. A Pew Research Center survey found that when questions were asked about coverage of specific issues such as improving school performance, the number of people expressing interest was much higher. If television journalists focused more on politics connected to such pressing problems, greater coverage could be justified.

Tumulty, Karen. "I Want My Al TV: Liberals Look to Break the Conservative Stranglehold on Talk Radio and TV—But Will Anyone Tune In?" *Time*, vol. 161, June 30, 2003, p. 59. Reports on efforts by Al Gore and other liberal activists to create a liberal alternative to highly successful conservative media presences such as Rush Limbaugh and Fox News. Critics question the economic viability of such a network and suggest that the Left has to come up with compelling ideas before there would be an audience for liberal talk shows.

Wolper, Allan. "RIP, Civic Journalism." *Editor & Publisher*, vol. 136, April 14, 2003, p. 26. The author suggests that civic journalism, with its emphasis on forums, focus groups, and other interactions between journalists and the community, has simply served to mask the real problem—that the corporate media simply will not pay for adequate local coverage. There have also been serious ethical problems such as journalists becoming involved with, and even contributing to, the political campaigns they are covering.

Web Documents

Friedland, Lewis A., and Sandy Nichols. "Measuring Civic Journalism's Progress: A Report Across a Decade of Activity." Pew Center for Civil Journalism. Available online. URL: http://www.pewcenter.org/doingcj/research/measuringcj.pdf. Posted in September 2002. The study measured the extent to which civic (community-oriented) journalism was being practiced in U.S. newspapers, the types of practices being used, and what their effects have been. The report concluded that civic journalism is practiced in at least a fifth of all U.S. newspapers. Typically, newspapers using civic journalism progressed in coverage from elections to community issues and problems, and techniques became more interactive (often involving the Internet).

Smith, Terence. "Journalism and Patriotism." *PBS Online NewsHour.* Available online. URL: http://www.pbs.org/newshour/bb/media/july-dec01/patriotism_11-6.html. Posted on November 6, 2001. An interview and dialogue on how the media should relate to the post–September 11 world and the new emphasis on patriotism. Former Wyoming senator Alan Simpson suggests that the media needs to set aside cynicism, tone down skepticism, and put itself in the place of U.S. troops overseas who are looking for a united nation to support them. Media critic Geneva Overholser suggests that U.S. journalists can best show their patriotism by retaining their skepticism in the service of balanced, accurate information.

THE MEDIA, GLOBAL ISSUES, AND FOREIGN POLICY

This section deals with how the news media covers foreign affairs—particularly crises such as wars and terrorist attacks—and how the coverage affects public attitudes and the course of foreign policy.

Books

Ammon, Royce C. *Global Television and the Shaping of World Politics: CNN, Telediplomacy, and Foreign Policy.* Jefferson, N.C.: McFarland, 2001. In 1995 UN Secretary-General Boutros Boutros-Ghali remarked that "CNN is the sixteenth member of the Security Council." The author presents a groundbreaking look at how the information and perceptions being continually shaped by global networks such as CNN can interact with the efforts of diplomats to craft their own messages and can sometimes overwhelm diplomacy.

Bartimus, Tad, ed. *War Torn: Stories of War from the Women Reporters Who Covered Vietnam.* New York: Random House, 2002. Vivid personal accounts from nine women newspaper and television reporters who braved both the risks of war and the attitudes of a male-dominated profession to report harrowing events of the war.

Bernstein, Mark, and Alex Lubertozzi. *World War II on the Air: Edward R. Murrow and the Broadcasts That Riveted a Nation.* Naperville, Ill.: Sourcebooks, 2003. Describes and evaluates the broadcasting work of Edward R. Murrow, who became the best-known radio "voice from the front" during World War II. The account details how Murrow prepared to cover the war and appointed other talented journalists and producers who became pioneers in their own right. These pioneers of broadcast news had to cope with primitive equipment and uncertain transportation while creating a new form of journalism that would be further elaborated with the coming of network television. The book includes a CD with many excerpts of broadcast recordings, narrated by Dan Rather.

Cornebise, Alfred E. *Stars and Stripes: Doughboy Journalism in World War I.* Westport, Conn.: Greenwood Press, 1984. The development of a popular newspaper for the U.S. soldier was significant for the history of war reporting and the larger role of journalism in wartime. Under discipline, these military journalists also faced challenges different from those of their civilian counterparts.

De Beer, Arnold, and John C. Merrill, eds. *Global Journalism.* 2d ed. Boston: Allyn & Bacon, 2003. This thoroughly revised volume of essays by 28 international media scholars covers the main global issues confronting media organizations and journalists, then surveys the media in eight major regions to see how these issues are being played out. Coverage also includes technological changes, trends in various kinds of reporting (such as of military affairs or sporting activities), and illustrative international media stories as diverse as Princess Diana's death, Nelson Mandela's imprisonment and release, and the scandals of Monica Lewinsky.

Gilbert, Allison, et al., eds. *Covering Catastrophe: Broadcast Journalists Report September 11.* Chicago: Bonus Books, 2002. Television journalists and producers recount how they covered the September 11, 2001, terrorist attacks, starting with the first few moments of shock as the first plane hit in New York. These quite personal accounts often show journalists working at their best under pressure.

Gilboa, Eytan. *Media and Conflict: Framing Issues, Making Policy, Shaping Opinions.* Ardsley, N.Y.: Transnational Publishers, 2003. Twenty-two contributors from around the world and from a variety of disciplines and perspectives present their research into how the media has dealt with various types of conflicts in many areas. The actions of the media are coordinated to various stages of each conflict, and examples include not only wars between nations but insurgencies and global movements such as environmentalism and antiglobalism.

Hachten, William A., and James Francis Scotton. *The World News Prism: Global Media in an Era of Terrorism.* 6th ed. Ames: Iowa State University Press, 2002. This well-established textbook on the dynamics of world media coverage is updated to reflect the worldwide response to the attacks of September 11, 2001. The many facets considered include the role of the Internet, global information distribution channels, and public diplomacy and information warfare carried out by competing governments.

Hammond, William H. *Reporting Vietnam: Media and Military at War.* Lawrence: University Press of Kansas, 1998. During the Vietnam War, the media and military both went to war—but the focus of this heavily documented but somewhat opaque study is on the war *between* the media and military. The military exercised considerable control and manipulation of the media until popular perception of the war began to shift, the political fortunes of the administration began to reverse, and the media grew in skepticism and boldness.

Hess, Stephen. *International News and Foreign Correspondents.* Washington, D.C.: Brookings Institution, 1996. A scholar in government studies with the Brookings Institution, Hess describes how foreign correspondents (both regular and freelance) work, their decision-making process, and the media culture in which they operate. He includes in-depth profiles of selected correspondents as well as statistics about the field as a whole.

Lembecke, Jerry. *CNN's Tailwind Tale: Inside Vietnam's Last Great Myth.* Lanham, Md.: Rowman & Littlefield, 2003. The author explores the origins of a later discredited story that claimed that U.S. forces used nerve gas against civilians and U.S. defectors in Laos in 1970. He suggests that a culture of conspiracy theories and paranoia was responsible and that it infected investigating journalists.

MacArthur, John R. *Second Front: Censorship and Propaganda in the Gulf War.* Berkeley: University of California Press, 1993. An impassioned, often harsh depiction of the U.S. military's policy toward and management of the media during the Persian Gulf War of 1990–91. The author criticizes the military for essentially imprisoning the press pool in an army base far behind the lines, resulting in censorship by suffocation, or what he calls "Operation Desert Muzzle."

Malek, Abbas. *The News Media and Foreign Relations: A Multifaceted Perspective.* Norwood, N.J.: Ablex Publishing, 1996. A collection of essays providing clear theoretical frameworks and analyzing case studies of media coverage of important foreign events of the 1970s through the early 1990s, including Botswana, Iran, Central America, and the Persian Gulf War.

Nacos, Brigitte L. *Mass-Mediated Terrorism: The Central Role of the Media in Terrorism and Counterterrorism.* Lanham, Md.: Rowman & Littlefield, 2002. The author points out the increasing sophistication of terrorists in creating maximum media coverage for their actions, as well as for transmitting fear through the media. For that reason, effective counterterrorism requires an equally sophisticated strategy for dealing with the mass media following a terrorist attack.

Perlmutter, David D. *Photojournalism and Foreign Policy: Icons of Outrage in International Crises.* Westport, Conn.: Praeger, 1998. Using many examples, including the televised execution of a prisoner in Saigon during the Vietnam War and images of starvation from Somalia, the author documents how powerful photographic images ("icons of outrage") have played an important role in bringing distant crises to public attention and thus putting pressure on governments and diplomats.

Reporting Vietnam: American Journalism: Part One, 1959–1969 and *Part Two, 1969–1975.* New York: Library of America, 2000. A two-volume collection of reportage from the Vietnam War. Material ranges from accounts of combat to news analysis, essays, and interviews. Some of the better known contributors include David Halberstam, Neil Sheehan, Norman Mailer, and Tom Wolfe. In addition to the primary sources, the volumes contain a chronology of the war, maps, profiles of the journalists included, and a glossary of military terms.

Robinson, Piers. *The CNN Effect: The Myth of News Media, Foreign Policy, and Intervention.* New York: Routledge, 2002. Explores the connection between media attention to foreign conflicts and humanitarian disasters and the willingness of the United States to intervene in the situation. Using examples such as Iraq, Somalia, Bosnia, Kosovo, and Rwanda, the author suggests that the media, rather than passively reporting news, can often focus and drive attention to various areas of the world and influence the outcome of key decisions.

Seib, Philip. *Headline Diplomacy: How News Coverage Affects Foreign Policy.* Westport, Conn.: Praeger, 1996. Using examples such as the Tet Offensive in Vietnam (1968), the Iran hostage crisis (1979–81), and the Gulf War (1991) the author argues that how the media labels and frames each situation, and what it does with the information it obtains, has a strong influence on the course of foreign policy

Smith, Hedrick. *The Media and the Gulf War: The Press and Democracy in Wartime.* Washington, D.C.: Seven Locks Press, 1992. A critique of the media coverage of the Gulf War of 1990–91 with documentary materials, including Senate hearings and legal briefs. The author decries the tight

Annotated Bibliography

military and Defense Department control of access to information needed to enable the American public to truly judge the military and political campaign.

Washburn, Philo C. *Broadcasting Propaganda: International Radio Broadcasting and the Construction of Political Reality.* Westport, Conn.: Praeger, 1992. Although television may have a more immediate impact, international radio broadcasting has long been the way in which people around the world, particularly in remote areas and less developed countries, encounter the culture of the United States and other developed countries. The author shows how official broadcasting and propaganda helps shape international perceptions and relationships.

Articles

Baker, Russ. "'Scoops' and Truth at the *Times:* What Happens When Pentagon Objectives and Journalists' Needs Coincide." *The Nation,* vol. 276, June 23, 2003, p. 18. The author critiques the recent work of Judith Miller, a veteran correspondent who, he alleges, uncritically used sources referred to her by the Pentagon. Further, the military exercised prepublication control over what would be written. The underlying problem is that it is easy for journalists to find themselves being manipulated in such a situation and the resulting stories can be as pernicious as the wholly fabricated reports of a Jayson Blair—but more subtly so.

Gitlin, Todd. "Embed or In Bed?: The Media and the Truth." *The American Prospect,* vol. 14, June 2003. p. 43ff. The coverage of the Iraq War is critiqued. According to Gitlin, the problem with the "embedded" reporters was not so much their lack of objectivity, but that "they saw what they saw and they couldn't see what they couldn't see." The media and the military both got what they wanted—dramatic but sanitized footage—and the reporting was replete with euphemisms. The many discrepancies between the justifications for the war and what has actually been found to be true have been largely smoothed over.

Hickey, Neil. "Access Denied: Pentagon's War Reporting Rules Are Toughest Ever." *Columbia Journalism Review,* vol. 40, January–February 2002, p. 26ff. Reports that restrictions on press coverage of U.S. military operations in Afghanistan in 2001–02 were tighter than ever. Journalists had little official access to the combat theater, although those willing to risk it could enter the area unescorted. Journalists were denied the opportunity to interview Special Forces troops. Access to generals and high-ranking Pentagon officials has also been restricted. Pentagon spokesperson Victoria Clarke is interviewed and defends the Pentagon's policies toward information access.

Nacos, Brigitte. "Accomplice or Witness? The Media's Role in Terrorism." *Current History*, April 2000, pp. 174–178. Explores the fundamental problem that the free press, which properly must give extensive coverage to terrorist attacks and threats, is also fulfilling the goals of terrorists who want to achieve recognition and publicity for their cause(s) as well as spreading fear. In addition, new media, ranging from handheld video cameras to the Internet, is making it easier for small terrorist or radical groups to spread their messages.

Richelson, Jeffrey T. "Planning to Deceive: How the Defense Department Practices the Fine Art of Making Friends and Influencing People." *Bulletin of the Atomic Scientists*, vol. 59, March–April 2003, p. 64ff. The author, a senior researcher with the National Security Archive, looks back at Pentagon efforts to manipulate the news and public perception, from the Iranian hostage crisis of 1979–81 (examined with the aid of recently declassified documents) to recent crises in North Korea and Iraq. In the Iranian crisis, a secret proposal suggested a campaign of deceptive information to convince the Iranians that the United States would not attempt to rescue the hostages. Similarly, a plan was actually enacted to convince Libyan leader Mu'ammar Gadhafi that a major U.S. attack and/or coup attempt was imminent. The creation of a Pentagon Office of Strategic Influence in 2002 proved short-lived because of opposition by journalists and the public.

Smolkin, Rachel. "Thinking About the (No Longer) Unthinkable: When News Breaks, the Journalistic Instinct Is to Respond Quickly and in Force. But Are the Rules Different When the News Is a Chemical, Biological, or Radiological Attack?" *American Journalism Review*, vol. 25, May 2003, p. 52ff. The realities of such terrorist attacks require that journalists not follow their instinct to run to a story. Experts suggest that reporters take a cautious, observant approach. The different types of toxic agents and recommended responses are explained.

Taylor, Philip. "Spin Laden." *The World Today*, December 2001, pp. 6–8. The author suggests that the media can sometimes exacerbate misperceptions at home and anger toward the United States abroad and thus contribute to terrorism and unrest. For example, the Internet spread rumors such as that "4,000 Jews failed to turn up for work at the World Trade Center" the morning of September 11. Footage of a Palestinian celebration during the 1991 Gulf War was mistakenly labeled as showing them celebrating the attacks on the World Trade Center in 2001. To many Islamic fundamentalists in the Middle East, global broadcast networks such as CNN have become not neutral sources of news but symbols of U.S. imperialism. To counter such negative images and rhetoric, the United States needs to have a serious, wide-ranging program of public diplomacy that can reach not only local elites but the person in the street.

Web Documents

"Weblogs and Diaries from Embedded Journalists." Cyberjournalist.net. Available online. URL: http://www.cyberjournalist.net/features/moreiraq coverage.html#embeds. Downloaded on October 27, 2003. A compilation of links to Internet writing from journalists during their service as embedded journalists with U.S. armed forces during the 2003 Iraq War.

Smith, Terence. "Covering the War." *PBS Online NewsHour.* Available online. URL: http://www.pbs.org/newshour/bb/media/jan-june00/vietnam_4-20.html. Posted on April 20, 2000. A panel of news experts discusses the media coverage of the war in Vietnam and its impact on subsequent journalistic attitudes toward the government and military. H. D. S. Greenway of the *Boston Globe* summarizes that impact as "we don't take things for granted; we don't take things as face value; we don't believe officials, as we did before Vietnam." Christiane Amanpour describes her experience of "pool coverage" in the 1991 Gulf War, when the military, reacting to perceived media hostility, tightly restricted and micromanaged media contacts.

MEDIA COVERAGE AND REPRESENTATION OF WOMEN AND MINORITIES

This section deals both with the news coverage of women and minority communities and with how such communities are represented in the journalism profession and media industry.

Books

Beadle, Mary E., and Michael D. Murray. *Indelible Images: Women of Local Television.* Ames: Iowa State Press, 2001. These profiles highlight the often little appreciated roles women have played and continue to play in local television as programmers, producers, directors, and writers.

Carter, Cynthia, Gill Branston, and Stuart Alan, eds. *News, Gender, and Power.* New York: Routledge, 1998. A variety of contributors explore the complex relationship between gender perceptions and media practice, using such cases as the coverage of the O. J. Simpson trial, child sexual abuse, "false memory syndrome," and other issues.

Entman, Robert M., and Andrew Rojecki. *The Black Image in the White Mind: Media and Race in America.* Chicago: University of Chicago Press, 2001. The authors, professors of communications and journalism, survey and analyze the perceptions and portrayals of blacks in contemporary media. They believe that such portrayals remain predominately negative, as well as including subtle new forms of "racial differentiation"—for example, in the types of products promoted by blacks and whites in commercials. Although the media gives more coverage to black views than it used to, black experts tend to be "ghettoized" into certain topics, primarily having to do with race relations. True integration into the mainstream in both media and society has not been achieved.

Gallagher, Margaret. *Gender Setting: New Media Agendas for Monitoring and Accuracy.* New York: Zed Books, 2001. Provides a status report on the representation of women in the media and detailed guidance for women's groups around the world who are monitoring media portrayal of women and women's issues and advocating for reform.

Heider, Don. *White News: Why Local News Programs Don't Cover People of Color.* Mahwah, N.J.: Lawrence Erlbaum Associates, 2000. To try to answer the title question, the author closely observed the activities in two television newsrooms serving moderate-sized, culturally diverse markets. He suggests that the problem is not conscious racism but the fact that most news content is selected and framed by white producers even if it is increasingly delivered by a diverse on-air staff. The unconscious biases of the content providers and the increasing reliance on uniform corporate news distribution are reflected in the news remaining largely "white."

Hunt, Darnell M. *Screening the Los Angeles "Riots": Race, Seeing, and Resistance.* New York: Cambridge University Press, 1997. Compares the perceptions of news professionals to the 1992 civil disturbances in Los Angeles and those of 15 groups of viewers. Explores the relationship between race and the ability to "see" certain aspects and resist stereotypes.

Keever, Beverley, Ann Deepe, Carolyn Martindale, and Mary Ann Weston. *U.S. Coverage of Racial Minorities: A Sourcebook, 1934–1996.* Westport, Conn.: Greenwood Press, 1997. An extensive compilation of scholarly studies of how each of the racial and ethnic minority groups in the United States has been covered. For each group it focuses on significant, pivotal events and finds common patterns in the coverage.

Law, Ian. *Race in the News.* New York: Palgrave Macmillan, 2002. This comprehensive look at how racial and ethnic groups and issues relevant to them are covered in the media in Great Britain can provide a useful comparative perspective to similar American studies.

McGowan, William. *Coloring the News: How Crusading for Diversity Has Corrupted American Journalism.* San Francisco: Encounter Books, 2001. Argues for the pervasive and negative effects of "political correctness" in shaping (and distorting) news that might offend minority groups, as well as the deleterious effects of policies giving preferences to minority journalists.

Annotated Bibliography

O'Dell, Cary. *Women Pioneers in Television: Biographies of Fifteen Industry Leaders.* Jefferson, N.C.: McFarland, 1997. The biographies are presented in chronological order and cover a few well-known and many little-known women who made a significant mark on television. On the news side they include Judith Waller, who developed the first children's educational television show; pioneer foreign correspondent Pauline Frederick; and actress and television personality Betty Furness.

Reporting Civil Rights: American Journalism, Vol. 1, 1941–1963 and *Vol. 2, 1963–1973.* New York: Library of America, 2003. A chronologically organized two-volume compilation of newspaper and magazine articles, photographs, speeches, and essays dealing with the Civil Rights movement. The second volume continues the coverage to include the urban riots and the growing split between then Civil Rights and Black Power movements.

Robertson, Nan. *The Girls in the Balcony: Women, Men, and the New York Times.* New York: Random House, 2000. A former *Times* staffer recounts how women (who had been relegated to the balcony at National Press Club meetings) organized and fought discrimination at the paper during the 1970s, suing for equal pay for equal work.

Rush, Ramona R., Carol E. Oukrop, and Pamela J. Creedon, eds. *Seeking Equity for Women in Journalism and Mass Communication Education: A 30-Year Update.* Mahwah, N.J.: Lawrence Erlbaum Associates, 2003. The book begins with a review of the landmark 1972 study of the status of women in journalism. Contributors then assess the results of three decades of women's struggle for equity in the profession, identify trends, and suggest what remains to be done.

Sebba, Anne. *Battling for News: The Rise of the Woman Reporter.* London: Hodder & Stoughton, 1995. Tells the stories of women who struggled to be allowed to practice journalism, starting in Victorian times. The author is a former Reuters reporter.

Articles

Berardi, Gayle K., and Thomas W. Segady. "The Development of African-American Newspapers in the American West: A Sociohistorical Perspective." *The Journal of Negro History,* vol. 75, Summer–Fall 1990, p. 96ff. Describes the functions of African-American newspapers in the West and their relationship to the community. During the later 19th century, the papers began carrying more diverse content and were no longer limited to reacting to the white community or crusading for civil rights. They also reflected growing black migration even in the face of harsh treatment.

Rhra, Shawn. "Pressing Ahead." *Black Enterprise*, vol. 30, November 1999, p. 98ff. Describes how black-owned community newspapers are coping with technological, economic, and social changes. The growing awareness of the black community on the part of national advertisers offers potential revenue.

Web Documents

"2002 Women and Minorities Survey." Radio-Television News Directors Association and Foundation. Available online. URL: http://rtnda.org/research/womin.shtml. Posted in 2003. This annual survey tracks the representation of women and minorities in the television news industry. There are numerous charts broken down into media, specific positions, and specific minority groups. There are also links to organizations working to improve diversity in the newsroom.

"The Great Divide: Female Leadership in U.S. Newsrooms." American Press Institute and Pew Center for Civic Journalism. Available online. URL: http://www.americanpressinstitute.org/curtis/Great_Divide.pdf. Posted in September 2002. This survey conducted by Setzer & Company for the Pew Center reports that "the great divide" in newsrooms is not between men and women but between two approaches taken by women to advancing their careers. About 45 percent of women journalists are termed "career-conflicted"—they want to advance but report being troubled about concerns such as sexism and lack of higher opportunities. The 55 percent, the "career-confident" women, are surer of their path, in part because they have had a good relationship with a career mentor as well as with their superiors. The survey provides a detailed breakdown of job satisfactions, feeling about advancement, and style of relationships for each of these groups.

"Minority Newsroom Employment Inches Up in 2003." American Society of Newspaper Editors. Available online. URL: http://www.asne.org/index.cfm?id=4446. Posted on April 8, 2003. Reports the American Society of Newspaper Editors' annual survey of diversity in newspaper employment. Although minority employment representation is up, it is not keeping up with the growth in the minority population.

MEDIA LITERACY AND YOUNG PEOPLE

This section covers the promotion of media literacy—knowledge and tools to help young people and others evaluate the information they are receiving. It also covers the possible effects of the news media on young people.

Annotated Bibliography

Books

Cohn, Victor, and Lewis Cope. *News and Numbers: A Guide to Reporting Statistical Claims and Controversies in Health and Other Fields.* 2d ed. Ames: Iowa State University Press, 2001. Two science writers explain to general journalists how to evaluate the competing statistics often found in stories about health, product safety, and other science-related topics. Many examples are drawn from the health field. This is also a good source for helping general readers evaluate reporting on matters involving statistics.

Fisherkeller, Joellen. *Growing Up with Television: Everyday Learning Among Young Adolescents.* Philadelphia: Temple University Press, 2002. Numerous commentators have analyzed (or just viewed with alarm) the impact of television on young people. Other writers have conducted surveys of young people and made inferences from them. This book takes a different approach: a variety of young adults are asked in detail how they use television, what they think it is good for, and what conclusions about life and the world they have drawn from it.

Kundanis, Rose M. *Children, Teens, Families, and Mass Media: The Millennial Generation.* Mahwah, N.J.: Lawrence Erlbaum Associates, 2003. A survey and review of research into the effects of the mass media on children of different age groups and backgrounds. Besides covering psychological/developmental and educational aspects, the author provides numerous sidebars, including interviews with teens who work in youth media and people who make policy for or develop media for children.

Spring, Joel. *Educating the Consumer-Citizen: A History of the Marriage of Schools, Advertising, and Media.* Mahwah, N.J.: Lawrence Erlbaum Associates, 2003. The central focus of this study is on consumerism as an ideology that has become increasingly preeminent not only in the mass media and advertising but even in images and role models presented in the schools. According to the author, even the liberating social movements (Civil Rights, women's rights) resulted only in integration of these previously excluded groups into the omnipresent consumer.

Articles

Considine, David. "An Introduction to Media Literacy: The What, Why and How To's" *Telemedium, The Journal of Media Literacy,* vol. 41, Fall 1995, n.p. Also available online. URL: http://www.ci.appstate.edu/programs/edmedia/medialit/article.html. A good overview of media literacy—what it involves, who teaches it, and why it is important. Several approaches are introduced, including media esthetics, introducing media production techniques to children, protecting children from negative media influence, and creating better citizens.

Maynard, Nancy. "The Age Factor I: How Gray Is Your Newsroom?" *Columbia Journalism Review*, vol. 39, September 2000, p. 68. The author presents demographic statistics about journalists. The average age of staffers in newspapers and, to a somewhat lesser extent, the television networks increased through the 1990s. This is at least partly due to there being less upward mobility in the profession. Media companies need to consider what might be the connection between the graying of their newsrooms and the diminishing appeal of their product to young people.

Scharrer, Erica. "Making a Case for Media Literacy in the Curriculum: Outcomes and Assessment." *Journal of Adolescent & Adult Literacy.* Vol. 46, December 2002, p. 354ff. *Media literacy* is an important buzzword, but its definition and expectations need to be outlined, and the results of media literacy programs measured. Several perspectives on media literacy are explained.

Serchuk, David. "All the News That's Fit to Click? More Teens Are Turning to Nontraditional Sources for News." *New York Times Upfront*, vol. 135, May 9, 2003, p. 24ff. Recent observation suggests that teenagers and young adults no longer trust traditional "authoritative" sources of news, such as the television networks. They still watch them but only as part of an eclectic mix of other sources, including an increasing number of web sites. Teenagers also feel that the people presenting news on television are not relating to them.

Zill, Karen. "Media Literacy: Television Meets the Internet." *Multimedia Schools*, vol. 9, March–April 2002, p. 24ff. Describes the development of MedaSmart, a media literacy program developed by WETA, Washington, D.C.'s public television station. The program's goals are to help students understand the power and influence of the media and to help them become informed, discriminating, and literate media consumers. The program requires training teachers and then students how to use not only media technology but journalistic techniques.

Web Documents

Anderson, Neil. "Making a Case for Media Literacy in the Classroom." Center for Media Literacy. Available online. URL: http://www.medialit.org/ reading_room/article98.html. Downloaded on July 13, 2003. The author argues that because of the central role of the media in students' lives, media literacy is no longer separable from the objectives of general education. However, it must take into account the fact that most young people are primarily engaged with visual media, not printed media such as newspapers. Not only students' knowledge but also their learning styles and abilities have been profoundly shaped by their exposure to media.

Hobbs, Renee. "The Seven Great Debates in the Media Literacy Movement—Circa 2001." Center for Media Literacy. Available online. URL: http://www.medialit.org/reading_room/article2.html. Downloaded on July 13, 2003. Describes the varying ideologies and agendas that are being applied to the task of promoting media literacy. Some of these controversies include: whether media education aims to protect young people from negative media influences; whether students should learn media production techniques in order to truly understand the media; whether media literacy should be linked to a broader study of popular culture; and whether media literacy should have a political or ideological agenda. The author argues for a thoughtful debate to bring clarity and resolution to these and other issues.

Meade, Robin, and Carl Gottlieb. "Searching for Youth." *PBS Online NewsHour.* Available online. URL: http://www.pbs.org/newshour/forum/march02/news.html. Posted in March 2002. CNN anchor Robin Meade and Carl Gottlieb of the Project for Excellence in Journalism respond to a number of questions from young people. For example, they agree that new technology (particularly the Internet and wireless communications) is changing the old picture of the media as "gatekeeper" of information. Today people, particularly younger people, have become used to interacting with several "streams" of information simultaneously, multitasking between TV, radio, and web sites. Meade and Gottlieb also respond to a teenager who complains about the "boring" tone of most television news.

Zukin, Cliff. "Generation X and the News." News in the Next Century Project, Radio and Television News Directors Foundation. Available online. URL: http://www.rtndf.org/resources/genx/index.html. Posted in 1997. Profiles "Generation X" as a television audience that is intensely engaged with a variety of media but generally disengaged from the news. Describes how Gen Xers watch television—they are visually oriented, tend to channel surf, and tend to multitask (watch while doing other things). The author suggests that media outlets that want to counteract declining news viewing will have to find ways to adapt their presentation to the very different ways in which the young generation watches and relates to news.

LEGAL AND ETHICAL ISSUES

GENERAL LEGAL ISSUES

This section includes works that deal with comprehensive coverage of media and communications law, including general freedom of the press.

Books

Alexander, S. L. *Covering the Courts: A Handbook for Journalists.* 2d ed. Lanham, Md.: Rowman & Littlefield, 2003. This comprehensive guide provides a complete overview of the judicial process to help journalists understand what is going on at each stage and an overview of issues that arise with regard to pretrial publicity and the conflict between the free press and fair trials.

Fiss, Owen M. *The Irony of Free Speech.* Cambridge, Mass.: Harvard University Press, 1996. The author, who is in the broad communitarian tradition, suggests a paradox: when speech is "free" without regulation or intervention, the speech of the rich and powerful drowns out the views of others. Therefore, Fiss argues for government intervention, such as subsidies or mandates for media to air dissenting views, or restricting the influence of the powerful through limitations on campaign funding.

Jasper, Margaret C. *The Law of Speech and the First Amendment.* Dobbs Ferry, N.Y.: Oceana Publications, 1999. A well-organized outline of First Amendment law, including content-based restrictions on speech, prior restraint doctrine, seditious speech, symbolic speech, obscenity, speech in schools, and hate speech.

Paraschos, Emmanuel E. *Media Law and Regulation in the European Union: National, Transnational, and U.S. Perspectives.* Ames: Iowa State University Press, 1998. When evaluating media regulation (and proposed changes) in the United States it can be useful to see what many other advanced democracies are doing. This book serves as a country-by-country reference guide to constitutional rights, legislation, censorship, libel, information access, and other issues.

Russomanno, Joseph. *Speaking Our Minds: Conversations with the People Behind Landmark First Amendment Cases.* Mahwah, N.J.: Lawrence Erlbaum Associates, 2002. The participants in 10 key cases in First Amendment law describe what it was like to be involved in the litigation. The cases run the gamut of First Amendment issues, including free expression, hate speech, libel, privacy, confidential news sources, the clash between press freedom and a fair trial, and cases involving the new media of the Internet.

Siegel, Paul. *Cases in Communication Law.* Boston: Allyn and Bacon, 2002. A survey of key cases affecting the rights and responsibilities of the media. Topics include the First Amendment, common law and constitutional considerations for libel, invasion of privacy, copyright and trademark, access to government and judicial information, protecting news sources, regulation of broadcasting, sexually oriented speech, and the Internet.

Tillinghast, Charles H. *American Broadcast Regulation and the First Amendment: Another Look.* Ames: Iowa State University Press, 2000. Reviews the history of broadcast media regulation from the original Radio Act of 1927 to regulation of television networks and cable. Throughout the account, the First Amendment implications are always kept in mind. While some regulatory provisions may limit broadcasters' First Amendment rights more than those of the print media, failure to use regulation to make media accountable and to prevent excessive corporate concentration may also undermine the effectiveness of the First Amendment rights of the media and its audience.

Wagman, Robert J. *The First Amendment Book.* New York: Pharos Books, 1991. A collection celebrating the bicentennial of the Bill of Rights. Includes overviews and narrative accounts relating to the history of press and speech freedom, limits on freedom, and the other First Amendment guarantees (religion, petition, assembly, and association).

Articles

Bull, John V. R. "The Legal Community and the Press: Access to Information and Libel." *Vital Speeches,* vol. 63, May 15, 1997, p. 464ff. Transcript of a speech by the assistant to the editor of the *Philadelphia Enquirer.* Bull advocates closer cooperation between the press and the legal community in order to resolve contentious issues involving the media's access to court proceedings. He gives a number of examples of judges or officials arbitrarily denying the press access to public information. Bull also acknowledges abuses of privacy and shady tactics used by the media. He suggests that courts can protect the integrity of trials by means other than denying media access—such as restraining the lawyers in a case from making public statements.

INFORMATION ACCESS AND SOURCES

This section covers works that focus on issues relating to free access to information by journalists and the public and on clashes between journalists' need to protect sources and confidential information and competing interests such as fair trials.

Books

Campbell, Douglas S. *Free Press v. Fair Trial.* Westport, Conn.: Praeger Publishers, 1993. A detailed reference on 30 Supreme Court cases dealing with the major legal clash between journalists' desire to protect sources while obtaining information and judges' concern about either the withholding of source information or the promulgation of prejudicial information making a fair trial impossible.

Friendly, Fred W. *Minnesota Rag: Corruption, Yellow Journalism, and the Case that Saved Freedom of the Press.* Minneapolis: University of Minnesota Press, 2003. Pioneering television producer Fred Friendly vividly recounts the Minnesota case that began with a clash between corrupt officials and a crusading (though admittedly racist) "yellow journalist" named Jay Near. When the Supreme Court decided *Near v. Minnesota*, it established the right of the press to have robust criticism of government and access to public information.

Kupferman, Theodore R., ed. *Censorship, Secrecy, Access, and Obscenity.* Westport, Conn.: Meckler Publishing, 1990. A collection of articles from the quarterly journal *Communications and the Law.* Topics covered include shield laws, secondary information sources, censorship, and closed judicial proceedings.

Articles

Allen, Teresa. "A Thin Line: How Far Should Journalists Go to Protect At-Risk Sources." *The Quill*, vol. 91, February 2003, p. 8ff. Deciding how far to go in protecting a source who assured the journalist she was safe created an ethical dilemma for the author. Another problem arises in dealing with people who, if revealed in a story, might suffer severe psychological effects or even commit suicide. Part of ethics is determining whether the source is competent to agree to reveal information and to be as honest as possible.

Cochran, Barbara. "Access Denied: The Sniper Case Illustrated an Ominous Post–September 11 Trend of Trying to Keep Information Away from Journalists—and the Public." *American Journalism Review*, vol. 24, December 2002, p. 32ff. The Washington, D.C., sniper case illustrates a troubling problem: Law enforcement agencies want to use the media to reassure the public and to enlist its aid in obtaining information, but they also seek to block the media from obtaining information that is deemed to be sensitive, such as certain details about a crime scene or roadblocks. Fear of terrorism following the September 11 attacks has at least temporarily increased the public's willingness to accept secrecy about the prosecution of the war on terrorism, but this will not serve us well in the long run. The news media and authorities must learn to cooperate better in order to get vital information to the public.

Kirtley, Jane. "No Campus Censors: Prior Restraint Acceptable in High School Doesn't Apply to University Publications." *American Journalism Review*, vol. 25, June–July 2003, p. 66. Reports a recent conflict between officials and student journalists at an Illinois state university—even though the Supreme Court has ruled that college students, unlike those in high school, have full First Amendment rights. The students have gone to court, where they have a good chance of winning.

Web Documents

Gaines, Bill. "Deep Throat Uncovered: How Students Uncovered One of America's Top Mysteries." Department of Journalism, University of Illinois at Champaign. Available online. URL: http://deepthroatuncovered. com. Posted in 2003. Report by a group of journalism students who exhaustively investigated Watergate coverage and came to the conclusion that Deep Throat, the mysterious source used by Bob Woodward and Carl Bernstein, was Fred Fielding, former counsel to President Richard Nixon. Bernstein and others have criticized the investigative reporting of media sources.

Smith, Terence. "Free Press vs. Fair Trial." *PBS Online NewsHour.* Available online. URL: http://www.pbs.org/newshour/bb/media/july-dec99/cbs_11-12a .html. Posted on November 12, 1999. Smith, Dan Rather, First Amendment advocate Bruce Sanford, and Texas prosecutor Guy James Gray debate whether CBS should have been forced to turn over the transcript of an interview with a murder suspect.

———. "Thirty Years Later." *PBS Online NewsHour.* Available online. URL: http://www.pbs.org/newshour/bb/media/jan-june02/watergate_6-17.html. Posted on June 17, 2002. A 30-year retrospective on the Watergate scandal and the work of reporters Bob Woodward, Carl Bernstein, and *Washington Post* managing editor Ben Bradlee, who join Smith in conversation. They debate the pros (the creation of a powerful new specialty of investigative journalism) and the cons (a "gotcha" attitude between some reporters and the subjects of their investigation).

LIBEL AND PRIVACY

This section deals with intrusion by the media on private individuals, legal issues of defamation or libel, and clashes between aggressive reporting and privacy.

Books

Calvert, Clay. *Voyeur Nation: Media, Privacy, and Peering in Modern Culture.* Boulder, Colo.: Westview Press, 2000. The author explores "mediated voyeurism," a cultural development evident in such phenomena as confessional television (such as *Jerry Springer*) and "reality TV." He suggests that the wide scope given by the First Amendment, instead of helping the media properly cover politics and public issues, has largely facilitated the systematic exploitation of privacy to create profitable entertainment and quasi news.

Campbell, Douglas S. *The Supreme Court and the Mass Media: Selected Cases, Summaries, and Analyses.* Westport, Conn.: Praeger Publishers, 1990. Presents summaries of major media and First Amendment cases; despite the general title this volume actually complements Campbell's *Free Press v. Fair Trial* by focusing on libel and privacy cases.

Kupferman, Theodore R., ed. *Defamation: Libel and Slander.* Westport, Conn.: Meckler, 1990. A collection of articles from the quarterly journal *Communications and the Law.* They discuss the court precedents and laws affecting common journalistic practices, including what constitutes reporting protected by the First Amendment and how to safely work with sources.

———. *Privacy and Publicity.* Westport, Conn.: Meckler, 1990. A collection of articles from the quarterly journal *Communications and the Law* on aspects of privacy and the conflict between privacy rights, freedom of the press, and the public's right to know. Specific topics include the Freedom of Information Act, use of photography, public records, and cameras in the courtroom.

LaMay, Craig, ed. *Journalism and the Debate over Privacy.* Mahwah, N.J.: Lawrence Erlbaum Associates, 2003. This collection of essays focuses on the gap between the intrusions on privacy that are allowed by U.S. libel laws (which offer almost no recourse for public figures) and what the professed ethics of journalism demands. The collection begins with a theoretical legal overview and then proceeds to practical clashes between journalistic interests and privacy rights. Privacy is presented as a multifaceted right that is both legal and social and that is undergoing constant change.

Putnam, William Lowell. *John Peter Zenger and the Fundamental Freedom.* Jefferson, N.C.: McFarland, 1997. A biography not only of John Peter Zenger, the pioneer colonial printer who was acquitted of libel by a defiant jury, but of the ancestry of the First Amendment and other guarantees of freedom of speech and of the press.

Rosini, Neil J. *The Practical Guide to Libel Law.* Westport, Conn.: Greenwood Press, 1994. This practical guide for journalists explains how to research and present stories in such a way as to minimize potential legal liability. The author starts by dispelling some common myths, such that a journalist quoting another person has no liability for the statement quoted. Although journalists do have considerable protection when dealing with public figures, even unsuccessful legal action can be devastating to smaller media outlets.

Annotated Bibliography

Articles

Hoyt, Michael. "Peripheral Vision and Wen Ho Lee." *Columbia Journalism Review*, vol. 39, November 2000, p. 10. The author suggests that the underlying problem with the coverage that portrayed Chinese-American physicist Wen Ho Lee as a sort of master spy for China resulted in part from reporters starting with dubious assumptions and framework for analysis. For example, they ignored evidence that China did not really need espionage to make progress with its nuclear weapons miniaturization program.

Kaplan, David A. "Smoke Gets in CBS's Eye: Under Fear of Lawsuits, the Network Kills a Tough '60 Minutes' Report on the Tobacco Industry." *Newsweek*, vol. 126, November 20, 1995, p. 96. Reports how fear of litigation led CBS executives to kill a tobacco industry exposé. In part they feared that they would be sued for interfering with nondisclosure contracts between tobacco executives and scientists and their employers. The author suggests that media should be given "qualified immunity" from liability for publishing such information if they did not actively solicit it.

Wolper, Joanna, and Alan Wolper. "Papering Over the Joel Rose Case in Cleveland?" *Editor & Publisher*, December 18, 2000, p. 34. After the *Cleveland Plain Dealer* named local TV and radio celebrity Joel Rose as a sexual stalking suspect, Rose committed suicide. Rose's attorney had tried to get the paper to hold the story until actual charges (if any) were filed. Neither the DNA on stamps from harassing letters or the typewriter used turned out to match Rose's. The question is whether the paper acted too hastily in writing the story under perceived competitive pressure and whether prosecutors prolonged the investigation too long after learning that the key evidence did not match.

Web Documents

"Hidden Cameras, Hidden Microphones: At the Crossroads of Journalism, Ethics and the Law." News in the Next Century Project, Radio and Television News Directors Foundation. Available online. URL: http://www.rtndf.org/resources/hiddencamera/index.html. Posted 1998. A collection of essays giving both news directors' and attorneys' perspectives on the use of hidden cameras and microphones in investigative journalism. Some contributors believe that these tools can be essential for uncovering vital information of public interest, while others focus on their misuse, which cheapens journalism and fosters negative public attitudes toward the media. There is also a glossary and compilation of federal and state court cases.

ETHICS AND STANDARDS IN JOURNALISM

This final section covers the development of standards of fairness, accuracy, and ethics by journalists, and instances of plagiarism, fabrication, and other forms of journalistic malfeasance.

Books

Baird, Robert M., Stuart E. Rosenbaum, and William E. Loges, eds. *The Media and Morality*. Amherst, N.Y.: Prometheus Books, 1999. This collection steps back from the nuts and bolts of the media business and of reporting and considers basic moral questions. Journalists must weigh their responsibilities to employers, the subjects of their stories, and the general public. A number of contemporary examples of intrusive and even potentially dangerous media coverage are discussed, including the coverage of President Bill Clinton, Princess Diana, and Richard Jewell.

Berkman, Robert I., and Christopher A. Shumway. *Digital Dilemmas: Ethical Issues for Online Media Professionals*. Ames: Iowa State University Press, 2003. The authors of this comprehensive textbook begin by surveying traditional codes of ethics in journalism, noting where and how they can be applied to the new online media. The next part of the book examines privacy, freedom of speech, and enforcement of intellectual property as key issues in the online media. Finally, there is an examination of the procedures online journalists need to employ to validate often uncertain Internet sources and maintain quality control often while under intense time pressure.

Bivins, Thomas. *Mixed Media: Moral Distinctions in Advertising, Public Relations and Journalism*. Mahwah, N.J.: Lawrence Erlbaum Associates, 2003. Designed for journalism and business ethics students but accessible to general readers, this text develops a framework for determining obligations and making moral decisions and then applies in different ways to various types of media activity.

Bugeja, Michael J. *Living Ethics: Developing Values in Mass Communication*. Boston: Allyn and Bacon, 1996. A systematic handbook for helping journalists in all media develop values and practices in journalistic ethics. Includes case studies and exercises as well as a variety of background essays by numerous well-known journalists.

Christians, Clifford G., ed. *Media Ethics: Cases and Moral Reasoning*. 6th ed. New York: Longman, 2000. This comprehensive textbook begins by offering a framework for "moral reasoning" and then applies it to the areas of news, advertising, public relations, and entertainment. More than 80 real and hypothetical cases are used to make the issues concrete.

Commission on Freedom of the Press. *A Free and Responsible Press*. Chicago: University of Chicago Press, 1947. This commission, headed by Robert

M. Hutchins, chancellor of the University of Chicago, was tasked with addressing growing concerns about whether the media was meeting its responsibilities to the public interest. The commission's recommendations to the media, the government, and the public were quite controversial at the time and have continued to spur debate on many issues, including media accuracy, recourse for victims of media errors, and the need for public interest journalism.

Fuller, Jack. *News Values: Ideas for an Information Age.* Chicago: University of Chicago Press, 1996. The author, the Pulitzer Prize–winning publisher of the *Chicago Tribune*, addresses fundamental questions about the duties and obligations of journalists. These include the need for truthful, complete, and accountable reporting versus the duty to sources that had been promised protection and finding a balance between meeting the needs of the community and challenging the community's prejudices and preconceptions. He also addresses the impact of new digital media technology on journalistic practices.

Glasser, Theodore L., and James Ettema. *Custodians of Conscience: Investigative Journalism and Public Virtue.* New York: Columbia University Press, 1998. Two media critics go beyond discussions of technique to explore the moral and social implications of investigative journalism. Through interviews with leading investigative reporters and analysis of their stories, the authors question the simplistic traditional standard of objectivity and the conventional understanding of fact and narrative. They argue that values with social implications are necessarily bound up with the journalistic endeavor.

Kovach, Bill, and Tom Rosenthal. *The Elements of Journalism: What Newspeople Should Know and the Public Should Expect.* New York: Crown Publishers, 2001. Although the title makes it sound like a handbook, this book is actually a synthesis of principles of good journalism, drawing on the results of the work of the Committee of Concerned Journalists, which conducted extensive studies, surveys, and public forums. The principles include obligation to tell the truth, responsibility for verification of sources and information, the need to hold the powerful accountable and "offer voice to the voiceless," and the need to make the news "comprehensive and proportional."

Mitchell, Amy, ed. *Thinking Clearly: Cases in Journalistic Decision-Making.* New York: Columbia University Press, 2002. This well-organized textbook discusses issues involved with the selection and reporting of the news where growing economic and time pressures can compromise standards and ethics. Historical and contemporary example cases include Watergate, the Richard Jewell case, and the Columbine school shootings.

Patterson, Philip, and Lee Wilkins, eds. *Media Ethics: Issues & Cases.* 4th ed. Boston: McGraw-Hill, 2002. A variety of issues in media ethics are explored

239

by a number of contributors. Topics covered include objectivity, treatment of sources, privacy, involvement in political reform, economic imperatives, use of images, and journalism in cyberspace.

Smith, Ron F. *Groping for Ethics in Journalism.* 4th ed. Ames: Iowa State University Press, 1999. More vivid and direct than most journalism ethics texts, this work focuses on basic principles and uses dozens of real stories to illustrate the ethical questions facing journalists. Topics covered include accountability, truth and objectivity, errors and corrections, the temptation to fake facts and sources, and the growing claims of diversity.

Articles

Dowd, Ann Reilly. "The Great Pretender: How a Writer Fooled His Readers." *Columbia Journalism Review*, vol. 37, July–August 1998, p. 14ff. Until Jayson Blair came along, Stephen Glass was probably the best-known example of a journalist accused of fabricating large amounts of his work. The author gives examples of many of Glass's stories that passed through perfunctory editorial checking despite occasional misgivings. Although the lack of sufficient fact-checking staff may have played a role, the main reason for Glass being undetected so long was that he "games the system," knowing that it largely relied on trust.

Ellen, Sue. "New Directions in Ethics: Educators Consider Shifting the Focus of Classroom Ethics Discussions." *The Quill*, vol. 91, April 2003, p. 11ff. Experts suggest that the teaching of journalism ethics focus more on the subtle dilemmas that beginning journalists often have to face, rather than the "big picture" issues dealt with by managing editors or news directors. Journalists need to think about how they use sources and quotes—perhaps more attention to the nuts and bolts of journalism would help prevent further plagiarism and fabrication scandals.

Goldstein, Tom. "Wanted: More Outspoken Views: Coverage of the Press Is Up, But Criticism is Down." *Columbia Journalism Review*, vol. 40, November–December 2001, p. 144ff. A review of media criticism through the 20th century. It begins by showing that there have often been unflattering portrayals of the press in literature and popular culture. In mid-century the number of scholarly reviews of journalism and the media increased, including partisan groups (Accuracy in Media and Fairness and Accuracy in Reporting), as well as publications for journalists, such as *Quill* and *Nieman Reports*. The media also covers itself, but "self-criticism remains rare" and is badly needed.

Hanson, Christopher. "Weighing the Costs of a Scoop: How a Sniper Story Trapped the Press in an Ethical No-Man's Land." *Columbia Journalism Review*, vol. 41, January–February 2003, p. 34ff. Practical lessons in ethical reasoning are revealed in examples such as the Washington, D.C. sniper case, where reporters had to decide whether to reveal details that police thought might compromise the investigation. A common problem in ethics is that people tend to pick only one of two opposing principles to resolve an ethics question. A real solution, however, must involve both principles.

Hickey, Neil. "Ten Mistakes That Led to the Great CNN/Time Fiasco." *Columbia Journalism Review*, vol. 37, September–October 1998, p. 26ff. Outlines the chronology of the investigation and retraction of the CNN/*Time* "Operation Tailwind" story about alleged use of nerve gas by U.S. forces in Cambodia in 1970. The author identifies what he says are 10 key mistakes CNN and *Time* made in the course of developing and checking the story, including failure to submit the story for evaluation by their regular military experts.

Kornbluh, Peter. "Crack, Contras, and the CIA: The Storm over 'Dark Alliance.'" *Columbia Journalism Review*, vol. 35, January/February 1997, p. 33ff. A detailed account of Gary Webb's sensational and controversial piece linking the CIA to the Contras, to drug-running, and to America's crack cocaine epidemic. Although many investigators concluded that the story was deeply flawed, the issues it has raised have given it continued life as a "metastory," and the outcry in the black community helped force congressional investigations into other CIA activities.

Lieberman, Trudy. "Plagiarize, Plagiarize, Plagiarize . . . Only Be Sure to Call It Research." *Columbia Journalism Review*, July/August 1995, p. 1ff. Also available online. URL: http://www.cjr.org/year/95/4/plagiarize.asp. Although plagiarism is considered by some to be the one unforgivable sin in journalism, in reality punishment has varied from firing to ... nothing. Some editors will decide that a journalist's talent outweighs their going too close to (or over) the line. A number of examples are given.

Madrick, Jeffrey. "A Good Story Isn't Always the Right One to Tell." *Nieman Reports*, vol. 56, Summer 2002, p. 6ff. The author charges the business media with not giving timely and appropriate warnings during the boom times in the Internet economy, and thus not preparing investors for the bust to come. Enron was only one example of the media's inability to investigate and expose dubious accounting practices that were encouraging unwarranted confidence in the "new economy." Indeed, the media went out of its way to praise Enron for being innovative and vastly overstated its real earnings.

Mnookin, Seth, et al. "The *Times* BOMB." *Newsweek*, vol. 141, May 26, 2003, p. 40ff. A detailed account of the events leading to the dismissal of Jayson Blair and the resignation of executive editor Howell Raines in the *New York Times* journalistic fabrication scandal, including profiles of both men. Describes Blair's struggles with psychological problems, his downward trajectory, and the tumultuous meetings following the revelation of the scandal.

Pollitt, Katha. "White Lies." *The Nation,* vol. 276, June 16, 2003, p. 9. Pollitt argues that the reason why Jayson Blair duped so many of his editors and colleagues at the *New York Times* was not forbearance arising from affirmative action (Blair is black) but his ability to be charming, flattering, and brilliantly deceptive. He shares these characteristics with Stephen Glass, a white writer for the *New Republic.* Now both are reinventing themselves and making lucrative book deals. Giving other examples of journalistic malfeasance, Pollitt suggests that it is a more serious threat to journalistic integrity when a reporter such as Judith Miller lets the army vet her article about Iraqi weapons of mass destruction, as well as control the timing of its publication.

Poniewozik, James, et al. "Mutiny at the *Times.*" *Time,* vol. 16, June 16, 2003, p. 49ff. Profiles and reports on the resignation of *New York Times* editors Howell Raines and Gerald Boyd, who resigned in the wake of the alleged journalistic fabrications by Jayson Blair and Rick Bragg. The scandal was the occasion for a staff revolt against the editors, whose management style was unpopular with many.

Rosen, Joel. "All About the Retrospect: Jayson Blair Charmed and Dazzled the Right People on His Rapid Rise from Cocky College Student to *New York Times* National Reporter. But He Left Plenty of Clues About the Serious Problems That Lay Beneath the Surface." *American Journalism Review,* vol. 25, June–July 2003, p. 32ff. People who encountered Blair at school and in his early career describe the powerful impression he made on them but also point out misgivings that in retrospect should have been taken seriously. At his college newspaper, Blair was amazingly productive and excelled at making contacts, but even then he seemed to have a chronically high error rate. When Blair went to the *Times,* other disturbing perceptions about his personality and behavior began to surface.

Shaw, David. "Medical Miracles or Misguided Media?" *Los Angeles Times,* February 13, 2000, p. A1ff. This two-part series describes how news stories about medical breakthroughs are often exaggerated and overhyped— both because many general reporters and editors lack the necessary scientific background to ask critical questions and because the scientists being interviewed often have an agenda of their own that is not properly taken into consideration.

Shepard, Alicia C. "The Web That Gary Spun." *American Journalism Review,* vol. 19, January–February 1997, p. 34ff. An account of the aftermath of *San Jose Mercury News* reporter Gary Webb's account of alleged CIA-

Contra drug-running. Despite the explosion of controversy over the accuracy of the story, Webb received a Journalist of the Year award.

Web Documents

Bingham, Barry, Jr. "Journalism Ethics Cases Online." Indiana University–Bloomington School of Journalism. Available online. URL: http://www. journalism.indiana.edu/Ethics/ Updated on October 27, 2003. A database containing a variety of cases involved with topics such as handling and naming sources, acceptable techniques for getting stories, and invasion of privacy.

Code of Ethics." Society of Professional Journalists. Available online. URL: http://www.spj.org/ethics_code.asp. Posted in 1996. A detailed set of guidelines voluntarily embraced by thousands of professional journalists. The guidelines are divided into the following aspects: "Seek Truth and Report It," "Minimize Harm," "Act Independently," and "Be Accountable."

Habib, Lisa. "Plugged In: Using the Internet for High School (and Professional) Journalism." Radio and Television News Directors Foundation. Available online. URL: http://www.rtndf.org/resources/pluggedin.pdf. Posted in 2002. A guide for journalists of all levels in researching and pursuing stories on the Web. Includes chapters on evaluating the credibility of online sources, watching for ethnic and racial stereotypes, legal constraints on freedom of expression for youth, the First Amendment and defamation, proper crediting of sources and observance of copyright, and general journalistic ethics.

Haiman, Robert J. "Best Practices for Newspaper Journalists: A Handbook for Reporters, Editors, Photographers and Other Newspaper Professionals on How to be Fair to the Public." Freedom Forum. Available online. URL: http://www.freedomforum.org/publications/diversity/bestpractices/ bestpractices.pdf. Posted in 1999. The chapters of this guide each cover a way in which newspapers can be unfair. Newspapers are unfair when: they get the facts wrong, they refuse to admit errors, they will not name names, they have ignorant or incompetent reporters, they prey on the weak, they concentrate on bad news, they lack diversity, they allow editorial bias in news stories, or they cannot admit that sometimes there is no story. There is also an overview of the history of public perception of unfairness in the media, and a summary of First Amendment considerations.

"National Press Photographers Association Code of Ethics." The National Press Photographers Association. Available online. URL: http://www. asne.org/ideas/codes/nppa.htm. Posted on October 26, 1999. States nine ethical principles for press photographers, including that "it is wrong to alter the content of a photo in any way (electronically or in the darkroom) that deceives the public."

Smith, Terence. "Troubled Times." *PBS Online NewsHour.* Available online. URL: http://www.pbs.org/newshour/bb/media/jan-june03/nytimes_06-05.html. Posted on June 5, 2003. Smith and two media analysts, Geneva Overholser and Alex Jones, discuss the journalistic lapses at the *New York Times* and the subsequent resignation of senior editors Howell Raines and Gerald Boyd. Overholser suggests that the story has been kept alive largely by the new web sites that feature criticism and commentary on the media and journalism. The struggle to find ways to restore the paper's credibility is also discussed.

CHAPTER 9

ORGANIZATIONS AND AGENCIES

Following are listings for selected organizations and agencies involved with journalism, the media industry, and related issues. They are divided into the following categories: Industry and Trade Groups, Journalism and Media Organizations, Legal and Advocacy Interests, Media Research and Criticism, and Diversity Interests.

INDUSTRY AND TRADE GROUPS

American Press Institute
URL: http://www.
  americanpressinstitute.org
E-mail: info@
  americanpressinstitute.org
Phone: (703) 620-3611
11690 Sunrise Valley Drive
Reston, VA 22091-1498
This newspaper industry group emphasizes continuing education and development for print journalists. The group holds extensive training programs (including the use of computerized decision-making simulations) as well as seminars and conferences.

Association of Alternative
  Newsweeklies (AAN)
URL: http://aan.org

E-mail: chris@aan.org
Phone: (202) 822-1955
1020 Sixteenth Street, NW
Fourth Floor
Washington, DC 20036-5702
This is a trade association for the free nondaily newspapers circulated in many communities. There were 116 member publications as of mid-2003. The group holds a convention each summer in which editors and other professionals working in alternative newspapers can share ideas and techniques that often differ from those employed by the conventional paid-circulation press.

National Association
  of Broadcasters (NAB)
URL: http://www.nab.org
Email: nab@nab.org
Phone: (202) 429-5300
1771 N Street, NW
Washington, DC 20036

The National Association of Broadcasters is the national trade association for television and radio broadcasters. It provides resources and research to the industry, as well as advocating for its interests.

National Newspaper Association (NNA)
URL: http://www.nna.org
E-mail: info@nna.org
Phone: (800) 829-4662
127-129 Neff Annex
Columbia, MO 65211-1200
Originally founded as the National Editorial Association in 1885, the NNA today functions as a trade association for community-based newspapers. It advocates for industry interests in the legislative and public policy arenas.

Newspaper Association of America (NAA)
URL: http://www.naa.org
E-mail: info@naa.org
Phone: (703) 902-1600
1921 Gallows Road
Suite 600
Vienna, VA 22182-3900
The NAA is the main trade association for the newspaper industry as a whole. The association "focuses on six key strategic priorities that collectively affect the newspaper industry: marketing, public policy, diversity, industry development, newspaper operations and readership."

Radio-Television News Directors Association and Foundation (RTNDA)
URL: http://www.rtndf.org
E-mail: rtnda@rtnda.org
Phone: (202) 659-6510
1600 K Street, NW
Suite 700
Washington, DC 20006-2838
The Radio-Television News Directors Association is the world's largest organization devoted exclusively to broadcast and other electronic journalism. It represents news directors and other media executives in more than 30 countries. The group does research and establishes standards for broadcast news gathering and reporting.

JOURNALISM AND MEDIA ORGANIZATIONS

American Library Association (ALA)
URL: http://www.ala.org
E-mail: library@aol.org
Phone: (800) 545-2433
50 E. Huron
Chicago, IL 60611
As "gateways" to knowledge, libraries are closely related to journalism and the media industry. Among its many functions in the service of the field of librarianship and promoting better libraries, the ALA zealously advocates for protecting library patrons' right to information access and privacy. Recently the group took part in the unsuccessful Supreme Court challenge to a law mandating that federally funded libraries install Internet

content filtering software. The ALA has also resisted government attempts to get more information about patrons' book borrowing for purposes of investigating possible terrorist links.

**American Society
of Newspaper Editors (ASNE)
URL: http://www.asne.org
E-mail: asne@asne.org
Phone: (703) 453-1122
11690B Sunrise Valley Drive
Reston, VA 20191-1409**
ASNE is the main organization for newspaper editors in the United States. It provides a forum for sharing ideas, undertakes research projects, and strongly advocates for First Amendment rights and for freedom of the press around the world.

**International Center
for Journalists (ICFJ)
URL: http://www.icfj.org
E-mail: editor@icfj.org
Phone: (202) 737-3700
1616 H Street, NW
Third Floor
Washington, DC 20006**
This organization "was established in 1984 to improve the quality of journalism in nations where there is little or no tradition of independent journalism."

**Investigative Reporters
and Editors, Inc. (IRE)
URL: http://www.ire.org
E-mail: info@ire.org
Phone: (573) 882-2042
138 Neff Annex**

**Missouri School of Journalism
Columbia, MO 65211**
IRE provides educational resources and services to reporters, editors, and other people interested in investigative journalism. The organization works to develop and maintain high professional standards for this type of reporting. It also maintains the National Institute for Computer-Assisted Reporting (NICAR) in a joint program with the Missouri School of Journalism. It offers practical training courses to help journalists with "the practical skills of finding, prying loose and analyzing electronic information."

**National Press Club
URL: http://www.press.org
E-mail: info@press.org
Phone: (202) 662-7500
529 14th Street, NW
Washington, DC 20045**
The National Press Club is best known for the events it holds where prominent newsmakers speak. The club also sponsors seminars and offers a directory and other services to members.

**National Press Foundation
URL: http://www.
nationalpress.org
Phone: (202) 663-7280
1211 Connecticut Avenue, NW
Suite 310
Washington, DC 20036**
The National Press Foundation promotes excellence in journalism and honors it through awards. It holds conferences that strengthen

journalists' background in important subjects behind the news, and provides fellowships. In 1993 the organization merged with the Washington Journalism Center.

National Press Photographers Association (NPPA)
URL: http://www.nppa.org/default.cfm
Email: info@ppa.org
Phone: (919) 383-7246
3200 Croasdaile Drive
Suite 306
Durham, NC 27705
This organization is dedicated to the advancement of all aspects of photojournalism, advocacy of freedom of expression, and the development of ethical standards for the field.

National Scholastic Press Association
URL: http://www.studentpress.org
E-mail: info@studentpress.org
Phone: (612) 625-8335
2221 University Avenue, SE
Suite 121
Minneapolis, MN 55414
This group helps high school students become better reporters, editors, and photographers at their high school papers. The organization also has a collegiate division called Associated College Press.

Nieman Foundation for Journalism
URL: http://www.nieman.harvard.edu
E-mail: niemanweb@harvard.edu
Phone: (617) 495-2237
Harvard University
Lippmann House
One Francis Avenue
Cambridge, MA 02138
This foundation, based at Harvard University, focuses on high-quality continuing education for journalists. Through its Nieman Fellowships it has provided career-enhancing opportunities for more than 1,000 journalists. It also publishes the quarterly *Nieman Reports*, an important forum for discussing current journalism and media issues.

Public Relations Society of America (PRSA)
URL: http://www.prsa.org
E-mail: membership@prsa.org
Phone: (212) 995-2230
33 Irving Place
New York, NY 10003-2376
PRSA is the world's largest organization for public relations practitioners. It seeks to advance the public relations profession, provide professional development services, and establish high standards for the field.

Society of Professional Journalists (SPJ)
URL: http://www.spj.org
E-mail: questions@spj.org
Phone: (317) 927-8000
Eugene S. Pulliam National Journalism Center
3909 N. Meridian Street
Indianapolis, IN 46208
SPJ is a major professional organization for journalists in all fields

and media. It promotes and protects freedom of expression, the free flow of and access to information, and other freedoms needed for the effective practice of journalism. At the same time SPJ also promotes high standards and ethical behavior by journalists.

LEGAL AND ADVOCACY INTERESTS

American Civil Liberties Union (ACLU)
URL: http://www.aclu.org
E-mail: (form) http://www.aclu.org/feedback/feedback.cfm
Phone: (888) 567-ACLU
125 Broad Street
18th Floor
New York, NY 10004
ACLU is one of the nation's oldest and most formidable advocates for civil liberties. It has a particularly strong emphasis on First Amendment issues, including freedom of the press and the right to access public information. See the website "Issues" link under "Free Speech" for coverage of current issues.

Center for Democracy and Technology (CDT)
URL: http://www.cdt.org
E-mail: webmaster@cdt.org
Phone: (202) 637-9800
1634 Eye Street, NW
Suite 1100
Washington, DC 20006

This civil liberties group works to "promote democratic values and constitutional liberties in the digital age." A number of the issues it monitors have relevance to journalism and the media, including freedom of speech and access to government information online.

Electronic Frontier Foundation (EFF)
URL: http://www.eff.org
E-mail: ask@eff.org
Phone: (415) 436-9333
454 Shotwell Street
San Francisco, CA 94110
This organization was formed in 1990 to maintain and enhance intellectual freedom, privacy, and other values of civil liberties and democracy in networked communications. It publicizes and campaigns against legislation that threatens free expression, access to information, fair use of media, and privacy, such as laws requiring that public libraries that receive federal funds block access to "undesirable" web sites. The group publishes newsletters, Internet guidebooks, and other documents; provides mailing lists and other online forums; and hosts a large electronic document archive.

Federal Communications Commission (FCC)
URL: http://www.fcc.gov
Email: fccinfo@fcc.gov
Phone: (888) 225-5322
445 12th Street, SW
Washington, DC 20554

The FCC is the federal agency charged with regulating television and radio broadcasting as well as various aspects of telecommunications. Of its subdivisions, the Media Bureau regulates commercial broadcasting and the Enforcement Bureau deals with violations. Applicable regulations and rulings of the agency can be viewed on its web site. See also the page for the Office of General Counsel at http://www.fcc.gov/ogc.

First Amendment Foundation
URL: http://www.floridafaf.org
E-mail: foi@vashti.net
Phone: (800) 337-3518
336 East College Avenue
Tallahassee, FL 32301
This Florida-based organization seeks to strengthen First Amendment rights and to educate the public about their importance. It has expressed serious concerns about the 1996 Anti-Terrorism Act, publishing a book *Terrorism & The Constitution*, which detailed concerns about the legislation and reviewed the history of abuses of the rights of dissident groups and immigrants by the Federal Bureau of Investigation (FBI) and other federal agencies.

The Media Institute
URL: http://www.
  mediainstitute.org
E-mail: info@mediainstitute.org
Phone: (202) 298-7512
1000 Potomac Street, NW
Suite 201
Washington, DC 20007

This is a nonprofit research foundation specializing in communications policy and the First Amendment. Two recent activities are the Cornerstone Project, an effort to promote public awareness and education with regard to the First Amendment, and a colloquium on copyright and intellectual property.

Reporters Committee
  for Freedom of the Press
  (RCFP)
URL: http://www.rcfp.org
E-mail: rcfp@rcfp.org
Phone: (800) 336-4243
1815 N. Fort Myer Drive
Suite 900
Arlington, VA 22209
This organization provides news, resources, and legal help to journalists concerning issues of freedom of the press, access to information, and legal protection for journalists. Its web site has many current stories relating to these issues.

MEDIA RESEARCH AND CRITICISM

Accuracy in Media (AIM)
URL: http://www.aim.org
Phone: (202) 364-4401
E-mail: ar1@aim.org
4455 Connecticut Avenue, NW
Suite #330
Washington, DC 20008
This conservative media watchdog organization was founded in 1972 by Reed Irvine with the intent of expos-

ing media bias. It provides a media monitor and weekly column, as well as highlighting current stories and special reports on its web site.

American Journalism Historians Association (AJHA)
URL: http://www.ajha.org
Phone: (405) 878-2221
E-mail: carolhumphrey@mail. okbu.edu
500 West University
Shawnee, OK 74804-2590
This organization was founded by a group of journalism history professors in 1981 in order to foster the teaching of journalism history (embracing all types of media). It also includes scholars in related disciplines, graduate students, archivists, and journalists.

Center for Media Literacy
URL: http://www.medialit.org
E-mail: cml@medialit.org
Phone: (310) 581-0260
3101 Ocean Park Boulevard #200
Santa Monica, CA 90405
This nonprofit educational organization promotes media literacy and develops and distributes resources to help educators in this field. Through effective media literacy programs, students and citizens will learn both necessary critical thinking skills and media production skills.

Fairness and Accuracy in Reporting (FAIR)
URL: http://www.fair.org
E-mail: fair@fair.org

Phone: (212) 633-6700
112 West 27th Street
New York, NY 10001
This media watch group explores and documents cases of media bias. FAIR also broadly researches factors that cause the mainstream media to "marginalize public interest, minority and dissenting viewpoints." FAIR is a self-described progressive group that advocates reform "to break the dominant media conglomerates."

Poynter Institute
URL: http://www.poynter.org
Phone: (888) 769-6837
801 Third Street South
St. Petersburg, FL 33701
The Poynter Institute is a prestigious and innovative school of journalism that sponsors extensive surveys and studies on the media and society. Through its web site and publications it provides a wide variety of research and resources to the journalism community and to the general public.

Project Censored
URL: http://www. projectcensored.org
E-mail: censored@sonoma.edu
Phone: (707) 664-2500
Sonoma State University
Rohnert Park, CA 94928
Project Censored searches for stories about significant issues that have not been reported (or adequately reported) in the media. It publicizes these stories and issues and also explores the forces or factors that may be responsible for de

facto censorship. It encourages journalists to be more proactive in pursuing such stories and encourages the public to demand better coverage from the media.

DIVERSITY INTERESTS

American Jewish Press Association (AJPA)
URL: http://www.ajpa.org
E-mail: info@ajpa.org
Phone: (202) 785-2282
1828 L Street, NW
Suite 1000
Washington, DC 20036
This organization promotes journalism in the Jewish community and provides a forum for Jewish journalists. More than 150 newspapers, other publications, and journalists are affiliated with the group.

American News Women's Club (ANWC)
URL: http://www.anwc.org
E-mail: anwclub@qwest.net
Phone: (202) 332-6770
1607 22nd Street, NW
Washington, DC 20008
This professional organization for women journalists was founded in 1932. Today it covers women working in all forms of media work, providing professional development workshops and seminars.

American Women in Radio and Television (AWRT)
URL: http://www.awrt.org

E-mail: info@awrt.org
Phone: (703) 506-3290
8405 Greensboro Drive
Suite 800
McLean, VA 22102
This group, now more than 50 years old, is a professional organization for women working in radio and television. It works to improve the quality of broadcast programming through advancing the effectiveness and impact of women in the field. There is also a related educational foundation.

Asian American Journalists Association (AAJA)
URL: http://www.aaja.org
E-mail: National@aaja.org
Phone: (415) 346-2051
1182 Market Street
Suite 320
San Francisco, CA 94102
This group encourages Asian Pacific Americans to enter the field of journalism, and promotes fair and accurate coverage of Asian Pacific Americans in the media.

Association for Women in Communication
URL: http://womcom.org
E-mail: nancy@womcom.org
Phone: (410) 544-7442
780 Ritchie Highway
Suite 28-S
Severna Park, MD 21146
This organization seeks to bring together women working in all forms of communications, including print and broadcast journalism, television and radio production, film, adver-

tising, public relations, and design. It emphasizes helping its members develop competence across multiple fields in order to enhance career advancement.

International Women's Media Foundation (IWMF)
URL: http://www.iwmf.org
E-mail: info@iwmf.org
Phone: (202) 496-1992
1726 M Street, NW
Suite 1002
Washington, DC 20036
IWMF works to strengthen the role of women in the news media around the world, "based on the belief that no press is truly free unless women share an equal voice."

National Association of Black Journalists (NABJ)
URL: http://www.nabj.org
E-mail: carolyn@nabj.org
Phone: (301) 445-7100
University of Maryland
8701-A Adelphi Road
Adelphi, MD 20783-1716
The NABJ brings together journalists, students, and media-related professionals and provides resources and services on behalf of black journalists worldwide. It currently has 3,300 members in dozens of professional and student chapters.

National Association of Hispanic Journalists (NAHJ)
URL: http://www.nahj.org
E-mail: membership@nahj.org
Phone: (202) 662-7145
1000 National Press Building
Washington, DC 20045-2001
The NAHJ promotes the recognition and professional advancement of Hispanics in the news industry. It seeks to encourage Hispanics to enter the field and to communicate Hispanic concerns to the journalism and media professions.

National Lesbian & Gay Journalists Association (NLGJA)
URL: http://www.nlgja.org
E-mail: info@nlgja.org
Phone: (202) 588-9888
1420 K Street, NW
Suite 910
Washington, DC 20005
The NLGJA tries to promote fair coverage in the media for issues such as same-sex marriage, gay parenting and adoption, gays in the military, and antigay violence. It provides briefings to members on proposed legislation affecting gays and lesbians.

Native American Journalists Association (NAJA)
URL: http://www.naja.com
E-mail: info@naja.com
Phone: (605) 577-5282
University of South Dakota
414 East Clark Street
Vermillion, SD 57069
According to its web site, "The Native American Journalists Association serves and empowers Native journalists through programs and actions designed to enrich journalism and promote Native cultures."

UNITY: Journalists of Color, Inc.
URL: http://www.
  unityjournalists.org
E-mail:
  info@unityjournalists.org
Phone: (703) 469-2100
1601 North Kent Street
Suite 1003
Arlington, VA 22209

This organization seeks to retain and increase the numbers of journalists of color by promoting fairer treatment and representation. It also strives to improve the media coverage of people of color through dispelling stereotypes and increasing understanding of diverse cultures.

PART III

APPENDICES

APPENDIX A

NEWS MEDIA DATA AND TRENDS

The following summaries and charts help provide a sense of how the news media has developed and changed in the late 20th century as well as suggesting the attitudes and concerns of today's media audience.

THE MEDIA INDUSTRY

MEDIA EMPLOYMENT

In 1983 there were 204,000 reporters and editors in the United States. Of these, 48.4 percent were female, 2.9 percent were black, and 2.1 percent Hispanic. By 2001 there were 309,000 workers in the same category, with 5.2 percent black and 4.3 percent Hispanic. According to the American Society of Newspaper Editors, women in 2001 were 37 percent of newsroom staffs, including 49 percent of reporters and 22 percent of editors or supervisors.

In terms of total employees in various media fields in 2000, 412,600 were in newspapers, 132,200 in television broadcasting, and 121,500 in radio broadcasting. Another 212,700 worked in cable television programming and distribution, which has been growing very rapidly (an increase of about 25 percent between 1999 and 2000). Another rapidly growing category has been online information services, which employed 177,300 persons in 2000, up from 98,900 in 1999. However, the Internet shakeout of 2001–02 has considerably reduced employment in parts of this sector.

Power of the News Media

MEDIA REVENUE

According to various tables in the *Statistical Abstract of the United States 2002*, the total estimated revenue for newspapers in 2000 was about $52 billion. Of this, $38 billion (about 75 percent) came from sales of advertising, not sales of the newspapers themselves. Broadcast television revenue in 2000 was about $38 billion with radio revenue about $15 billion. Cable networks and program distribution earned about $68 billion. Online information services had an estimated revenue of $27 billion in 2000, of which about 45 percent came from selling Internet access, which only indirectly reflects the marketability of content.

OWNERSHIP OF THE MEDIA

The following table summarizes the holdings of major news media conglomerates as of mid-2003. Note that it does not include entertainment media.

Conglomerate	News-Related Media Holdings
Clear Channel	More than 1,200 radio stations nationwide
Cox Enterprises	Discovery Communications, Cox Interactive Media, 17 daily and 30 other newspapers, 15 TV stations, 79 radio stations
Disney	ABC, ESPN (80 percent), History Channel (with Hearst and GE), 10 television stations, 66 radio stations or services
Dow Jones Co.	*Wall Street Journal* and 10 other business publications or information services, 20 daily or weekly newspapers, CNBC (co-owned with General Electric)
General Electric	NBC, CNBC (co-owned with Dow Jones), MSNBC (co-owned with Microsoft), History Channel (With Disney and Hearst), News 12 (regional, co-owned with Cablevision), 13 TV stations, various international broadcast services
Hearst Corporation	20 newspapers, 17 magazines, Hearst News Service, 15 TV stations, two radio stations A&E and AETN, History Channel (with Disney and GE), New England Cable News (with MediaOne)
Knight-Ridder	More than 60 daily or weekly newspapers, interests in several newspaper agencies and services
Liberty Group Publishing	66 daily and about 240 other newspapers

Appendix A

Conglomerate	News-Related Media Holdings
Media General	24 newspapers and 100 other periodicals, 26 television stations, Media General Financial services
MediaNews Group	47 daily newspapers, several newspaper operating companies, one television station, four radio stations
Morris Communications Corp.	26 daily and 12 other newspapers, 29 radio stations or services, magazines
New York Times Co.	*New York Times* and 18 other newspapers, eight television stations, two radio stations
News Corp. (Rupert Murdoch)	Fox News, 34 television stations, broadcasting interests in UK and Australia, five magazines, 26 newspapers Including *New York Post* and the *Times* and *Sun* in London, 20 Australian newspapers
Pulitzer, Inc.	14 daily and 37 other newspapers and periodicals
E. W. Scripps Co.	21 daily newspapers, Scripps Howard News Service, 10 TV stations
Sinclair Broadcast Group	62 TV stations
Tribune Co.	12 major newspapers, including the *Los Angeles Times* and *Chicago Tribune,* plus local newspapers, 26 stations
Time Warner	CNN, America Online, CompuServe, Time-Life Books, *Time, Fortune,* and more than 70 other magazines
Viacom	CBS, UPN, TNN, 40 stations, Infinity Broadcasting (about 180 radio stations), Simon & Schuster, Pocket Books, Scribner, six other imprints
Washington Post Co.	*Washington Post* and about 30 local and miscellaneous newspapers, *Newsweek* magazine, seven TV stations

Sources: "Who Owns What," *Columbia Journalism Review.* Available online. URL:http://www.cjr.org/owners/; various company web sites.

MEDIA USAGE

NEWSPAPERS

Total daily newspaper readership has declined overall during the second half of the 20th century, as shown in chart "Newspaper Readership Has Been Declining":

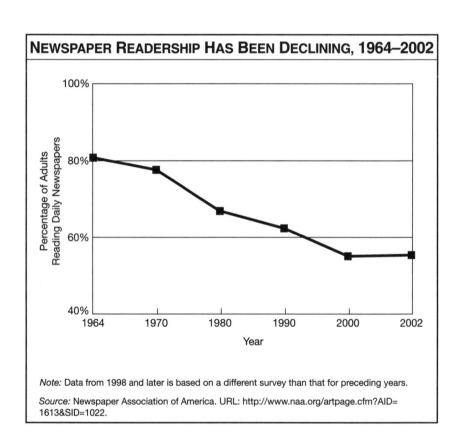

NEWSPAPER READERSHIP HAS BEEN DECLINING, 1964–2002

Note: Data from 1998 and later is based on a different survey than that for preceding years.

Source: Newspaper Association of America. URL: http://www.naa.org/artpage.cfm?AID=1613&SID=1022.

Appendix A

As shown in the chart "Newspaper Readership and Age," newspaper readership overall increases with age, with peaks at around 40 and 50 years.

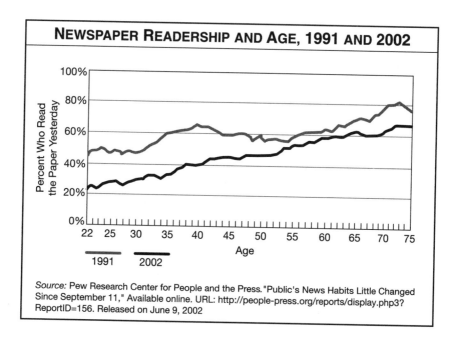

NEWSPAPER READERSHIP AND AGE, 1991 AND 2002

1991 — 2002

Source: Pew Research Center for People and the Press. "Public's News Habits Little Changed Since September 11," Available online. URL: http://people-press.org/reports/display.php3? ReportID=156. Released on June 9, 2002

TELEVISION

The chart "Cable vs. the Broadcast Networks" indicates that during the 1990s cable displaced the broadcast networks as accounting for the largest viewer share:

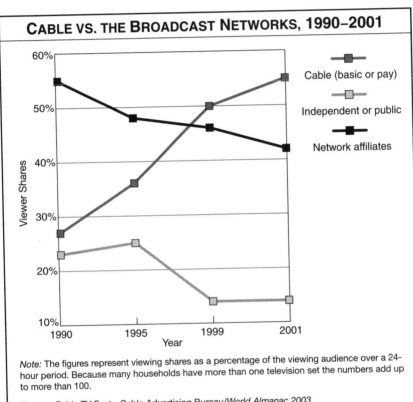

CABLE VS. THE BROADCAST NETWORKS, 1990–2001

Note: The figures represent viewing shares as a percentage of the viewing audience over a 24-hour period. Because many households have more than one television set the numbers add up to more than 100.

Source: Cable TV Facts, Cable Advertising Bureau/*World Almanac 2003.*

According to the chart "Network News Viewership," the percentage of people who watch network news regularly also tends to increase with age:

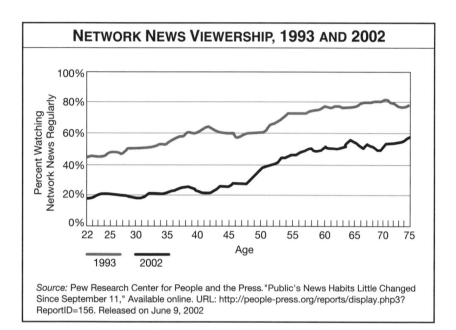

NETWORK NEWS VIEWERSHIP, 1993 AND 2002

Percent Watching Network News Regularly

Age

1993   2002

Source: Pew Research Center for People and the Press. "Public's News Habits Little Changed Since September 11," Available online. URL: http://people-press.org/reports/display.php3? ReportID=156. Released on June 9, 2002

INTERNET

Each of the major information media (print, radio, television, and Internet) has in turn taken a shorter time to pervade our society. Although the Internet has existed in some form since the 1970s, it became accessible to the general user starting in the mid-1990s. The chart "Percent of U.S. Households with Internet Access" summarizes the percentage of Americans with Internet access in 2001, by income and by race or Hispanic origin.

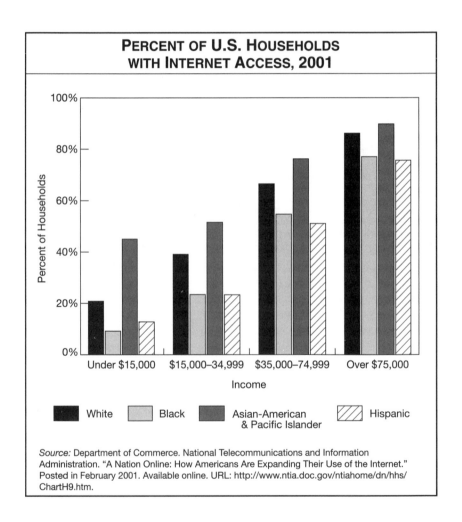

PERCENT OF U.S. HOUSEHOLDS WITH INTERNET ACCESS, 2001

Source: Department of Commerce. National Telecommunications and Information Administration. "A Nation Online: How Americans Are Expanding Their Use of the Internet." Posted in February 2001. Available online. URL: http://www.ntia.doc.gov/ntiahome/dn/hhs/ChartH9.htm.

Appendix A

WHERE DO PEOPLE GO FOR NEWS?

Today there are a number of widely available sources of news. The chart "Trend in Regular News Consumption" breaks down news use by medium or format, showing trends between 1993 and 2002.

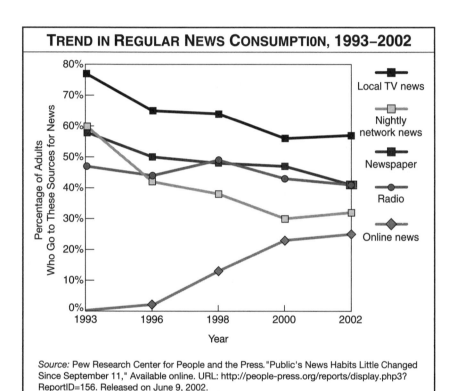

TREND IN REGULAR NEWS CONSUMPTION, 1993–2002

Source: Pew Research Center for People and the Press. "Public's News Habits Little Changed Since September 11," Available online. URL: http://people-press.org/reports/display.php3? ReportID=156. Released on June 9, 2002.

The following Gallup poll gives a breakdown of how often respondents use various sources for news and information:

"Now thinking for a moment about the news media, please indicate how often you get your news from each of the following sources: every day, several times a week, occasionally, or never. How about...?"

Source	Every Day %	Several Times a Week %
"Local television news from TV stations in your area"	57	16
"Local newspapers in your area"	47	13
"Nightly network news programs on ABC, CBS or NBC"	43	16
"Cable news networks such as CNN, Fox News Channel and MSNBC"	41	15
"Public television news"	35	12
"Morning news and interview programs on the national TV networks"	29	10
"Radio talk shows"	22	10
"National Public Radio"	22	9
"News on the Internet"	15	8
"National newspapers such as *The New York Times, Wall Street Journal, USA Today*"	11	5

"And how often do you get your news from each of the following weekly sources of news: every week, several times a month, occasionally, or never. How about...?"

Source	Every Week %	Several Times a Month %
"TV news magazine shows during the evenings, such as *60 Minutes, 20-20, Dateline,* and others"	23	12
"Television news programs on Sunday mornings"	18	5
"Weekly news magazines"	12	5

Note: The "occasionally" and "never" categories were eliminated from these tables because the current discussion focuses on the extent to which the various sources are being used regularly.

Source: Gallup Poll, December 5–8, 2002.

PUBLIC ATTITUDES
TOWARD THE MEDIA

While people are consuming many forms of news and rely particularly on television news and newspapers in these times of fear of terrorism and anxiety about war, according to a Pew Center for the People and the Press survey, the public has serious concerns about both the accuracy and possible bias of the news.

Respondents Who Agree That News Organizations ...	Percentage Who Agree
Usually get facts straight	36
Often report inaccurately	56
Don't know	8
Willing to admit mistakes	27
Try to cover up mistakes	62
Neither/don't know	11
Are politically biased	53
Are careful not to be biased	29
Neither/don't know	18

Source: Pew Center for People and the Press survey, July 2003. Available online.
URL: http://people-press.org/reports/display.php3?ReportID=188. Released July 13, 2003.

When asked to characterize bias, a larger percentage of respondents say the media is more liberal than that it is conservative, although this margin is less among Democrats (who might be expected to be more liberal themselves).

Respondents Who Agree That the Press Is ...	Party Affiliation			
	Total	Republican	Democrat	Independent
Liberal	51	65	41	30
Conservative	26	22	33	25
Neither applies	14	7	16	18
Don't know	2	6	10	7

Source: Pew Center for People and the Press survey, July 2003. Available online.
URL: http://people-press.org/reports/display.php3?ReportID=188. Released July 13, 2003.

Respondents strongly believe that the news tends to favor one side or another and that the news is most influenced by "powerful" interests.

Respondents Who Agree That News Organizations . . .	Percentage Who Agree
Deal fairly with all sides	26
Tend to favor one side	66
Don't know	8
Pretty independent	23
Influenced by the powerful	70
Don't know	7

Source: Pew Center for People and the Press survey, July 2003. Available online.
URL: http://people-press.org/reports/display.php3?ReportID=188. Released July 13, 2003.

Respondents tend to believe that media professionals do not empathize much with the people they cover.

Respondents Who Agree That Journalists Care About People They Report On . . .	Percentage Who Agree
Yes	31
No	56

Source: Pew Center for People and the Press survey, July 2003. Available online.
URL: http://people-press.org/reports/display.php3?ReportID=188. Released July 13, 2003.

However, the public has a higher regard for journalists' professionalism and the ultimate value of their work.

Respondents Who Agree That News Organizations . . .	Percentage Who Agree
Are highly professional	62
Are not professional	24
Neither/don't know	14
Care about how good a job they do	68
Don't care about job	22
Neither/don't know	10
Protect democracy	52
Hurt democracy	28
Neither/don't know	20

Source: Pew Center for People and the Press survey, July 2003. Available online.
URL: http://people-press.org/reports/display.php3?ReportID=188. Released July 13, 2003.

PRESS FREEDOM VS. SECURITY

An *ABC News/Nightline* poll asked respondents where they stood on some of the contentious issues involving media conduct. Respondents strongly support the right to a free press in general and oppose government control of the media. However, when it is wartime or military secrets are involved, respondents support the government's security interests more than they do freedom of the press.

"How important to you is the right to a free press in this country? Would you say it's essential, very important, somewhat important or not especially important?"

Respondents	Percentage
Essential	38
Very important	49
Somewhat important	10
Not especially important	3
No opinion	1

"In general, do you think the government should or should not have the right to control what information the news media can report?"

Respondents	Percentage
Should	28
Should not	58
Depends on the subject (vol.)	13
No opinion	1

Note: "vol." means volunteered by respondent.

"If you had to pick, which of these would you say is more important: the right to a free press in this country OR the government's ability to keep military secrets in wartime?"

Respondents	Percentage
Right to free press	34
Keeping military secrets	60
No opinion	6

"Specifically in a time of war, do you think the news media have more of an obligation to support how the government carries out the war OR more of an obligation to question how the government carries out the war?"

Respondents	Percentage
Support the government	56
Question the government	36
No opinion	8

"Again, specifically in time of war, do you think the government should or should not have the right to prohibit the news media from reporting sensitive military information?"

Respondents	Percentage
Should have right to prohibit	66
Should not have right to prohibit	31
No opinion	4

Source: "The News Media/Communications," *ABC News Nightline.* Available online. URL: http://www.pollingreport.com/media.htm. January 8–12, 2003.

VIOLENCE AND THE NEWS MEDIA

Although the majority of concern about violence in the media has focused on the entertainment media, according to a Pew Research Center poll, the public also generally feels that too much violence is depicted on television news.

Respondents' opinion when asked "Do you think that TV news is too full of violence, or not?"

Respondents Who Felt It Was . . .	February 1993	May 1999
Too full	52%	63%
Not too full	44%	33%
Don't know	4%	4%

Source: "Bradley Boxes Out Political Center." Pew Research Center for People and the Press. Conducted May 12–16, 1999. Available online. URL: http://people-press.org/reports/print.php3?PageID-298.

APPENDIX B

NEW YORK TIMES V. SULLIVAN, 1964

The following are excerpts from the decision of the Supreme Court. Footnotes have been omitted.

NO. 39
SUPREME COURT
OF THE UNITED STATES
376 U.S. 254
ARGUED JANUARY 6, 1964
DECIDED MARCH 9, 1964

Together with No. 40, *Abernathy et al. v. Sullivan,* also on certiorari to the same court, argued January 7, 1964.

SYLLABUS

Respondent, an elected official in Montgomery, Alabama, brought suit in a state court alleging that he had been libeled by an advertisement in corporate petitioner's newspaper, the text of which appeared over the names of the four individual petitioners and many others. The advertisement included statements, some of which were false, about police action allegedly directed against students who participated in a civil rights demonstration and against a leader of the civil rights movement; respondent claimed the statements referred to him because his duties included supervision of the police department. The trial judge instructed the jury that such statements were "libelous per se," legal injury being implied without proof of actual damages, and that, for the purpose of compensatory damages, malice was presumed, so that such damages could be awarded against petitioners if the statements were found to have been published by them and to have related to respondent. As to punitive damages, the judge instructed that mere negligence was not evidence of actual malice, and would not justify an award of punitive damages; he refused to instruct that actual intent to harm or recklessness had to be found before punitive damages could be awarded, or that a verdict for respondent should differentiate between compensatory and punitive damages. The jury found for respondent, and the State Supreme Court affirmed.

Held: A State cannot, under the First and Fourteenth Amendments, award damages to a public official for defamatory falsehood relating to his official conduct unless he proves "actual malice"—that the statement was made with knowledge of its falsity or with reckless disregard of whether it was true or false. Pp. 265–292.

(a) Application by state courts of a rule of law, whether statutory or not, to award a judgment in a civil action, is "state action" under the Fourteenth Amendment. P. 265.

(b) Expression does not lose constitutional protection to which it would otherwise be entitled because it appears in the form of a paid advertisement. Pp. 265–266.

(c) Factual error, content defamatory of official reputation, or both, are insufficient to warrant an award of damages for false statements unless "actual malice"—knowledge that statements are false or in reckless disregard of the truth—is alleged and proved. Pp. 279–283.

(d) State court judgment entered upon a general verdict which does not differentiate between punitive damages, as to which, under state law, actual malice must be proved, and general damages, as to which it is "presumed," precludes any determination as to the basis of the verdict, and requires reversal, where presumption of malice is inconsistent with federal constitutional requirements. P. 284.

(e) The evidence was constitutionally insufficient to support the judgment for respondent, since it failed to support a finding that the statements were made with actual malice or that they related to respondent. Pp. 285–292.

273 Ala. 656, 144 So.2d 25, reversed and remanded.

MR. JUSTICE BRENNAN delivered the opinion of the Court.
We are required in this case to determine for the first time the extent to which the constitutional projection for speech and press limit a State's

power to award damages in a libel action brought by a public official against critics of his official conduct. . . .

It is uncontroverted that some of the statements contained in the two paragraphs [of the advertisement] were not accurate descriptions of events which occurred in Montgomery. Although Negro students staged a demonstration on the State Capitol steps, they sang the National Anthem and not "My Country, 'Tis of Thee." Although nine students were expelled by the State Board of Education, this was not for leading the demonstration at the Capitol, but for demanding service at a lunch counter in the Montgomery County Courthouse on another day. Not the entire student body, but most of it, had protested the expulsion, not by refusing to register, but by boycotting classes on a single day; virtually all the students did register for the ensuing semester. The campus dining hall was not padlocked on any occasion, and the only students who may have been barred from eating there were the few who had neither signed a pre-registration application nor requested temporary meal tickets. Although the police were deployed near the campus in large numbers on three occasions, they did not at any time "ring" the campus, and they were not called to the campus in connection with the demonstration on the State Capitol steps, as the third paragraph implied. Dr. King had not been arrested seven times, but only four, and although he claimed to have been assaulted some years earlier in connection with his arrest for loitering outside a courtroom, one of the officers who made the arrest denied that there was such an assault.

On the premise that the charges in the sixth paragraph could be read as referring to him, respondent was allowed to prove that he had not participated in the events described. Although Dr. King's home had, in fact, been bombed twice when his wife and child were there, both of these occasions antedated respondent's tenure as Commissioner, and the police were not only not implicated in the bombings, but had made every effort to apprehend those who were. Three of Dr. King's four arrests took place before respondent became Commissioner. Although Dr. King had, in fact, been indicted (he was subsequently acquitted) on two counts of perjury, each of which carried a possible five-year sentence, respondent had nothing to do with procuring the indictment.

Respondent made no effort to prove that he suffered actual pecuniary loss as a result of the alleged libel. . . .

Alabama law denies a public officer recovery of punitive damages in a libel action brought on account of a publication concerning his official conduct unless he first makes a written demand for a public retraction and the defendant fails or refuses to comply. Alabama Code, Tit. 7, § 914. Respondent served such a demand upon each of the petitioners. None of the individual petitioners responded to the demand, primarily because each took the position that he had not authorized the use of his name on the advertisement, and therefore had not published the statements that respondent alleged had libeled him. . . .

The trial judge submitted the case to the jury under instructions that the statements in the advertisement were "libelous per se," and were not privileged, so that petitioners might be held liable if the jury found that they had published the advertisement and that the statements were made "of and concerning" respondent. The jury was instructed that, because the statements were libelous per se, "the law . . . implies legal injury from the bare fact of publication itself," "falsity and malice are presumed," "general damages need not be alleged or proved, but are presumed," and "punitive damages may be awarded by the jury even though the amount of actual damages is neither found nor shown." An award of punitive damages—as distinguished from "general" damages, which are compensatory in nature—apparently requires proof of actual malice under Alabama law, and the judge charged that "mere negligence or carelessness is not evidence of actual malice or malice in fact, and does not justify an award of exemplary or punitive damages." He refused to charge, however, that the jury must be "convinced" of malice, in the sense of "actual intent" to harm or "gross negligence and recklessness," to make such an award, and he also refused to require that a verdict for respondent differentiate between compensatory and punitive damages. The judge rejected petitioners' contention that his rulings abridged the freedoms of speech and of the press that are guaranteed by the First and Fourteenth Amendments.

In affirming the judgment, the Supreme Court of Alabama sustained the trial judge's rulings and instructions in all respects. 273 Ala. 656, 144 So.2d 25. It held that, "where the words published tend to injure a person libeled by them in his reputation, profession, trade or business, or charge him with an indictable offense, or tend to bring the individual into public contempt," they are "libelous per se"; that "the matter complained of is, under the above doctrine, libelous per se, if it was published of and concerning the plaintiff", and that it was actionable without "proof of pecuniary injury . . . such injury being implied." *Id.* at 673, 676, 144 So.2d at 37, 41. . . .

Because of the importance of the constitutional issues involved, we granted the separate petitions for certiorari of the individual petitioners and of the Times. 371 U.S. 946. We reverse the judgment. We hold that the rule of law applied by the Alabama courts is constitutionally deficient for failure to provide the safeguards for freedom of speech and of the press that are required by the First and Fourteenth Amendments in a libel action brought by a public official against critics of his official conduct. We further hold that, under the proper safeguards, the evidence presented in this case is constitutionally insufficient to support the judgment for respondent.

I

We may dispose at the outset of two grounds asserted to insulate the judgment of the Alabama courts from constitutional scrutiny. The first is the proposition relied on by the State Supreme Court—that "The Fourteenth Amendment is directed against State action, and not private action." That proposition has no application to this case. Although this is a civil lawsuit between private parties, the Alabama courts have applied a state rule of law which petitioners claim to impose invalid restrictions on their constitutional freedoms of speech and press. It matters not that that law has been applied in a civil action and that it is common law only, though supplemented by statute. See, e.g., Alabama Code, Tit. 7, §§ 908–917. The test is not the form in which state power has been applied but, whatever the form, whether such power has, in fact, been exercised. See *Ex parte Virginia*, 100 U.S. 339, 346–347; *American Federation of Labor v. Swing*, 312 U.S. 321.

The second contention is that the constitutional guarantees of freedom of speech and of the press are inapplicable here, at least so far as the Times is concerned, because the allegedly libelous statements were published as part of a paid, "commercial" advertisement. The argument relies on *Valentine v. Chrestensen*, 316 U.S. 52, where the Court held that a city ordinance forbidding street distribution of commercial and business advertising matter did not abridge the First Amendment freedoms, even as applied to a handbill having a commercial message on one side but a protest against certain official action, on the other. The reliance is wholly misplaced. The Court in Chrestensen reaffirmed the constitutional protection for "the freedom of communicating information and disseminating opinion"; its holding was based upon the factual conclusions that the handbill was "purely commercial advertising" and that the protest against official action had been added only to evade the ordinance.

The publication here was not a "commercial" advertisement in the sense in which the word was used in Chrestensen. It communicated information, expressed opinion, recited grievances, protested claimed abuses, and sought financial support on behalf of a movement whose existence and objectives are matters of the highest public interest and concern. See *NAACP v. Button*, 371 U.S. 415, 435. That the Times was paid for publishing the advertisement is as immaterial in this connection as is the fact that newspapers and books are sold. *Smith v. California*, 361 U.S. 147, 150; cf. *Bantam Books, Inc., v. Sullivan*, 372 U.S. 58, 64, n. 6. Any other conclusion would discourage newspapers from carrying "editorial advertisements" of this type, and so might shut off an important outlet for the promulgation of information and ideas by persons who do not themselves have access to publishing facilities—who wish to exercise their freedom of speech even though they are not members of the press. Cf. *Lovell v. Griffin*, 303 U.S. 444, 452; *Schneider v. State*, 308 U.S. 147, 164. The effect would be to shackle the First Amendment in its attempt to secure "the widest possible dissemination of information from diverse and antagonistic sources." *Associated Press v. United States*, 326 U.S. 1, 20. To avoid placing such a handicap upon the freedoms of expression, we hold that, if the allegedly libelous statements would otherwise be constitutionally protected from the present judgment, they do not forfeit that protection because they were published in the form of a paid advertisement.

II

Under Alabama law, as applied in this case, a publication is "libelous per se" if the words "tend to injure a person . . . in his reputation" or to "bring [him] into public contempt"; the trial court stated that the standard was met if the words are such as to "injure him in his public office, or impute misconduct to him in his office, or want of official integrity, or want of fidelity to a public trust..." The jury must find that the words were published "of and concerning" the plaintiff, but, where the plaintiff is a public official, his place in the governmental hierarchy is sufficient evidence to support a finding that his reputation has been affected by statements that reflect upon the agency of which he is in charge. Once "libel per se" has been established, the defendant has no defense as to stated facts unless he can persuade the jury that they were true in all their particulars. . . . Unless he can discharge the burden of proving truth, general damages are presumed, and may be awarded without proof of pecuniary injury. A showing of actual malice is apparently a prerequisite to recovery of punitive damages, and the defendant may, in any event, forestall a punitive award by a retraction meeting the statutory requirements. Good motives and belief in truth do not negate an inference of malice, but are relevant only in mitigation of punitive damages if the jury chooses to accord them weight. *Johnson Publishing Co. v. Davis, supra*, 271 Ala., at 495, 124 So.2d at 458. [268]

The question before us is whether this rule of liability, as applied to an action brought by a public official against critics of his official conduct, abridges the freedom of speech and of the press that is guaranteed by the First and Fourteenth Amendments.

Respondent relies heavily, as did the Alabama courts, on statements of this Court to the effect that the Constitution does not protect libelous publications. Those statements do not foreclose our inquiry here. None of the cases sustained the use of libel laws to impose sanctions upon expression critical of the official conduct of public officials. . . . In *Beauharnais v. Illinois*, 343 U.S. 250, the Court sustained an Illinois criminal libel statute as applied to a publication held to be both defamatory of a racial group and "liable to cause violence and disorder." But the Court was careful to note that it "retains and exercises authority to nullify action which encroaches on freedom of utterance under the guise of punishing libel"; for "public men, are, as it were, public property," and "discussion cannot be denied and the right, as well as the duty, of criticism must not be stifled. . . .

The general proposition that freedom of expression upon public questions is secured by the First Amendment has long been settled by our decisions . . . Those who won our independence believed . . . that public discussion is a political duty, and that this should be a fundamental principle of the American government. They recognized the risks to which all human institutions are subject. But they knew that order cannot be secured merely through fear of punishment for its infraction; that it is hazardous to discourage thought, hope and imagination; that fear breeds repression; that repression breeds hate; that hate menaces stable government; that the path of safety lies in the opportunity to discuss freely supposed grievances and proposed remedies, and that the fitting remedy for evil counsels is good ones. Believing in the power of reason as applied through public discussion, they eschewed silence coerced by law—the argument of force in its worst form. Recognizing the occasional tyrannies of governing majorities, they amended the Constitution so that free speech and assembly should be guaranteed.

Thus, we consider this case against the background of a profound national commitment to the principle that debate on public issues should be uninhibited, robust, and wide-open, and that it may well include vehement, caustic, and sometimes unpleasantly sharp attacks on government and public officials. See *Terminiello v. Chicago*, 337 U.S. 1, 4; *De Jonge v. Oregon*, 299 U.S. 353, [271] 365. The present advertisement, as an expression of grievance and protest on one of the major public issues of our time, would seem clearly to qualify for the constitutional protection. The question is whether it forfeits that protection by the falsity of some of its factual statements and by its alleged defamation of respondent.

Authoritative interpretations of the First Amendment guarantees have consistently refused to recognize an exception for any test of truth—whether administered by judges, juries, or administrative officials—and especially one that puts the burden of proving truth on the speaker. Cf. *Speiser v. Randall*, 357 U.S. 513, 525–526. The constitutional protection does not turn upon "the truth, popularity, or social utility of the ideas and beliefs which are offered." . . .

That erroneous statement is inevitable in free debate, and that it must be protected if the freedoms of expression are to have the "breathing space" that they "need . . . to survive" . . .

Cases which impose liability for erroneous reports of the political conduct of officials reflect the obsolete doctrine that the governed must not criticize their governors. . . . The interest of the public here outweighs the interest of appellant or any other individual. The protection of the public requires not merely discussion, but information. Political conduct and views which some respectable people approve, and others condemn, are constantly imputed to Congressmen. Errors of fact, particularly in regard to a man's mental states and processes, are inevitable. . . . Whatever is added to the field of libel is taken from the field of free debate.

Injury to official reputation affords no more warrant for repressing speech that would otherwise be free than does factual error. Where judicial officers are involved, this Court has held that concern for the dignity and reputation of the courts does not justify the punishment as criminal contempt of criticism of the judge or his decision. . . . surely the same must be true of other government officials, such as elected city commissioners. Criticism of their official conduct does not lose its constitutional protection merely because it is effective criticism, and hence diminishes their official reputations.

If neither factual error nor defamatory content suffices to remove the constitutional shield from criticism of official conduct, the combination of the two elements is no less inadequate. . . .

What a State may not constitutionally bring about by means of a criminal statute is likewise beyond the reach of its civil law of libel. The fear of damage awards under a rule such as that invoked by the Alabama courts here may be markedly more inhibiting than the fear of prosecution under a criminal statute. . . .

The state rule of law is not saved by its allowance of the defense of truth. A defense for erroneous statements honestly made is no less essential here than was the requirement of proof of guilty knowledge which, in *Smith v. California*, 361 U.S. 147, we held indispensable to a valid conviction of a bookseller for possessing obscene writings for sale. . . .

A rule compelling the critic of official conduct to guarantee the truth of all his factual assertions—and to do so on pain of libel judgments virtually unlimited in amount—leads to a comparable "self-censorship." Allowance of the defense of truth, with the burden of proving it on the defendant, does not mean that only false speech will be deterred. . . .

The constitutional guarantees require, we think, a federal rule that prohibits a public official from recovering damages for a defamatory falsehood relating to his official conduct unless he proves that the statement was made with "actual malice"—that is, with knowledge that it was false or with reckless disregard of whether it was false or not.

It is of the utmost consequence that the people should discuss the character and qualifications of candidates for their suffrages. The importance to the state and to society of such discussions is so vast, and the advantages derived are so great, that they more than counterbalance the inconvenience of private persons whose conduct may be involved, and occasional injury to the reputations of individuals must yield to the public welfare, although at times such injury may be great. The public benefit from publicity is so great, and the chance of injury to private character so small, that such discussion must be privileged. . . .

Such a privilege for criticism of official conduct is appropriately analogous to the protection accorded a public official when he is sued for libel by a private citizen. In *Barr v. Matteo*, 360 U.S. 564, 575, this Court held the utterance of a federal official to be absolutely privileged if made "within the outer perimeter" of his duties. The States accord the same immunity to statements of their highest officers, although some differentiate their lesser officials and qualify the privilege they enjoy. But all hold that all officials are protected unless actual malice can be proved. The reason for the official privilege is said to be that the threat of damage suits would otherwise "inhibit the fearless, vigorous, and effective administration of policies of government" and "dampen the ardor of all but the most resolute, or the most irresponsible, in the unflinching discharge of their duties." *Barr v. Matteo, supra,* 360 U.S. at 571. Analogous considerations support the privilege for the citizen-critic of government. It is as much his duty to criticize as it is the official's duty to administer. See *Whitney v. California,* 274 U.S. 357, 375 (concurring opinion of Mr. Justice Brandeis), quoted *supra,* p. 270. As Madison said, see *supra* p. 275, "the censorial power is in the people over the Government, and not in the Government over the people." It would give public servants an unjustified preference over the public they serve, if critics of official conduct did not have a fair equivalent of the immunity granted to the officials themselves.

We conclude that such a privilege is required by the First and Fourteenth Amendments.

III

We hold today that the Constitution delimits a State's power to award damages for libel in actions brought by public officials against critics of their official conduct. . . .

Applying these standards, we consider that the proof presented to show actual malice lacks the convincing clarity which the constitutional standard demands, and hence that it would not constitutionally sustain the judgment for respondent under the proper rule of law. The case of the individual petitioners requires little discussion. Even assuming that they could constitutionally be found to have authorized the use of their names on the advertisement, there was no evidence whatever that they were aware of any erroneous statements or were in any way reckless in that regard. The judgment against them is thus without constitutional support. . . .

We think the evidence against the Times supports, at most, a finding of negligence in failing to discover the misstatements, and is constitutionally insufficient to show the recklessness that is required for a finding of actual malice. . . .

The present proposition would sidestep this obstacle by transmuting criticism of government, however impersonal it may seem on its face, into personal criticism, and hence potential libel, of the officials of whom the government is composed. There is no legal alchemy by which a State may thus create the cause of action that would otherwise be denied for a publication which, as respondent himself said of the advertisement, "reflects not only on me but on the other Commissioners and the community." Raising as it does the possibility that a good faith critic of government will be penalized for his criticism, the proposition relied on by the Alabama courts strikes at the very center of the constitutionally protected area of free expression. We hold that such a proposition may not constitutionally be utilized to establish that an otherwise impersonal attack on governmental operations was a libel of an official responsible for those operations. Since it was relied on exclusively here, and there was no other evidence to connect the statements with respondent, the evidence was constitutionally insufficient to support a finding that the statements referred to respondent.

The judgment of the Supreme Court of Alabama is reversed, and the case is remanded to that court for further proceedings not inconsistent with this opinion.

Reversed and remanded.

MR. JUSTICE BLACK, with whom MR. JUSTICE DOUGLAS joins, concurring.

. . . I base my vote to reverse on the belief that the First and Fourteenth Amendments not merely "delimit" a State's power to award damages to "public officials against critics of their official conduct" but completely prohibit a State from exercising such a power. The Court goes on to hold that a State can subject such critics to damages if "actual malice" can be proved against them. "Malice," even as defined by the Court, is an elusive, abstract concept, hard to prove and hard to disprove. The requirement that malice be proved provides at best an evanescent protection for the right critically to discuss public affairs and certainly does not measure up to the sturdy safeguard embodied in the First Amendment. Unlike the Court, therefore, I vote to reverse exclusively on the ground that the Times and the individual defendants had an absolute, unconditional constitutional right to publish in the Times advertisement their criticisms of the Montgomery agencies and officials. . . .

In my opinion the Federal Constitution has dealt with this deadly danger to the press in the only way possible without leaving the free press open to destruction—by granting the press an absolute immunity for criticism of the way public officials do their public duty. Compare *Barr v. Matteo*, 360 U.S. 564. Stopgap measures like those the Court adopts are in my judgment not enough. This record certainly does not indicate that any different verdict would have been rendered here whatever the Court had charged the jury about "malice," "truth," "good motives," "justifiable ends," or any other legal formulas which in theory would protect the press. Nor does the record indicate that any of these legalistic words would have caused the courts below to set aside or to reduce the half-million-dollar verdict in any amount. . . .

We would, I think, more faithfully interpret the First Amendment by holding that at the very least it leaves the people and the press free to criticize officials and discuss public affairs with impunity . . . This Nation, I suspect, can live in peace without libel suits based on public discussions of public affairs and public officials. But I doubt that a country can live in freedom where its people can be made to suffer physically or financially for criticizing their government, its actions, or its officials. "For a representative democracy ceases to exist the moment that the public functionaries are by any means absolved from their responsibility to their constituents; and this happens whenever the constituent can be restrained in any manner from speaking, writing, or publishing his opinions upon any public measure, or upon the conduct of those who may advise or execute it." An unconditional right to say what one pleases about public affairs is what I consider to be the minimum guarantee of the First Amendment.

I regret that the Court has stopped short of this holding indispensable to preserve our free press from destruction.

MR. JUSTICE GOLDBERG, with whom MR. JUSTICE DOUGLAS joins, concurring in the result.

The Court today announces a constitutional standard which prohibits "a public official from recovering damages for a defamatory falsehood relating to his official conduct unless he proves that the statement was made with 'actual malice'—that is, with knowledge that it was false or with reckless disregard of whether it was false or not." *Ante*, at 279–280. The Court thus rules that the Constitution gives citizens and newspapers a "conditional privilege" immunizing nonmalicious misstatements of fact regarding the official conduct of a government officer. The impressive array of history and precedent marshaled by the Court, however, confirms my belief that the Constitution affords greater protection than that provided by the Court's standard to citizen and press in exercising the right of public criticism.

In my view, the First and Fourteenth Amendments to the Constitution afford to the citizen and to the press an absolute, unconditional privilege to criticize official conduct despite the harm which may flow from excesses and abuses. . . . The theory of our Constitution is that every citizen may speak his mind and every newspaper express its view on matters of public concern

282

and may not be barred from speaking or publishing because those in control of government think that what is said or written is unwise, unfair, false, or malicious. In a democratic society, one who assumes to act for the citizens in an executive, legislative, or judicial capacity must expect that his official acts will be commented upon and criticized. Such criticism cannot, in my opinion, be muzzled or deterred by the courts at the instance of public officials under the label of libel. . . .

This is not to say that the Constitution protects defamatory statements directed against the private conduct of a public official or private citizen. Freedom of press and of speech insures that government will respond to the will of the people and that changes may be obtained by peaceful means. Purely private defamation has little to do with the political ends of a self-governing society. The imposition of liability for private defamation does not abridge the freedom of public speech or any other freedom protected by the First Amendment. This, of course, cannot be said "where public officials are concerned or where public matters are involved. . . . [O]ne main function of the First Amendment is to ensure ample opportunity for the people to determine and resolve public issues. Where public matters are involved, the doubts should be resolved in favor of freedom of expression rather than against it." Douglas, The Right of the People (1958), p. 41. . . .

If the government official should be immune from libel actions so that his ardor to serve the public will not be dampened and "fearless, vigorous, and effective administration of policies of government" not be inhibited, *Barr v. Matteo, supra,* at 571, then the citizen and the press should likewise be immune from libel actions for their criticism of official conduct. Their ardor as citizens will thus not be dampened and they will be free "to applaud or to criticize the way public employees do their jobs, from the least to the most important." If liability can attach to political criticism because it damages the reputation of a public official as a public official, then no critical citizen can safely utter anything but faint praise about the government or its officials. The vigorous criticism by press and citizen of the conduct of the government of the day by the officials of the day will soon yield to silence if officials in control of government agencies, instead of answering criticisms, can resort to friendly juries to forestall criticism of their official conduct . . .

For these reasons, I strongly believe that the Constitution accords citizens and press an unconditional freedom to criticize official conduct. It necessarily follows that in a case such as this, where all agree that the allegedly defamatory statements related to official conduct, the judgments for libel cannot constitutionally be sustained.

APPENDIX C

NEW YORK TIMES CO. V. UNITED STATES, 1971

The following are excerpts from a decision by the Supreme Court. Footnotes have been omitted.

NO. 1873
SUPREME COURT
OF THE UNITED STATES
403 U.S. 713
ARGUED JUNE 26, 1971
DECIDED JUNE 30, 1971

Together with No. 1885, *United States v. Washington Post Co. et al.*, on certiorari to the United States Court of Appeals for the District of Columbia Circuit.

SYLLABUS

The United States, which brought these actions to enjoin publication in the New York Times and in the Washington Post of certain classified material, has not met the "heavy burden of showing justification for the enforcement of such a [prior] restraint."

No. 1873, 444 F.2d 544, reversed and remanded; No. 1885, U. S. App. D. C., 446 F.2d 1327, affirmed.

Appendix C

PER CURIAM We granted certiorari in these cases in which the United States seeks to enjoin the New York Times and the Washington Post from publishing the contents of a classified study entitled "History of U.S. Decision-Making Process on Viet Nam Policy." Post, pp. 942, 943.

"Any system of prior restraints of expression comes to this Court bearing a heavy presumption against its constitutional validity." *Bantam Books, Inc. v. Sullivan*, 372 U.S. 58, 70 (1963); see also *Near v. Minnesota*, 283 U.S. 697 (1931). The Government "thus carries a heavy burden of showing justification for the imposition of such a restraint." *Organization for a Better Austin v. Keefe*, 402 U.S. 415, 419 (1971). The District Court for the Southern District of New York in the New York Times case and the District Court for the District of Columbia and the Court of Appeals for the District of Columbia Circuit in the Washington Post case held that the Government had not met that burden. We agree.

The judgment of the Court of Appeals for the District of Columbia Circuit is therefore affirmed. The order of the Court of Appeals for the Second Circuit is reversed and the case is remanded with directions to enter a judgment affirming the judgment of the District Court for the Southern District of New York. The stays entered June 25, 1971, by the Court are vacated. The judgments shall issue forthwith.

So ordered.

MR. JUSTICE BLACK, with whom MR. JUSTICE DOUGLAS joins, concurring.

I adhere to the view that the Government's case against the Washington Post should have been dismissed and that the injunction against the New York Times should have been vacated without oral argument when the cases were first presented to this Court. I believe that every moment's continuance of the injunctions against these newspapers amounts to a flagrant, indefensible, and continuing violation of the First Amendment. Furthermore, after oral argument, I agree completely that we must affirm the judgment of the Court of Appeals for the District of Columbia Circuit and reverse the judgment of the Court of Appeals for the Second Circuit for the reasons stated by my Brothers DOUGLAS and BRENNAN. In my view it is unfortunate that some of my Brethren are apparently willing to hold that the publication of news may sometimes be enjoined. Such a holding would make a shambles of the First Amendment.

Power of the News Media

Our Government was launched in 1789 with the adoption of the Constitution. The Bill of Rights, including the First Amendment, followed in 1791. Now, for the first time in the 182 years since the founding of the Republic, the federal courts are asked to hold that the First Amendment does not mean what it says, but rather means that the Government can halt the publication of current news of vital importance to the people of this country.

In seeking injunctions against these newspapers and in its presentation to the Court, the Executive Branch seems to have forgotten the essential purpose and history of the First Amendment. When the Constitution was adopted, many people strongly opposed it because the document contained no Bill of Rights to safeguard certain basic freedoms. They especially feared that the new powers granted to a central government might be interpreted to permit the government to curtail freedom of religion, press, assembly, and speech. In response to an overwhelming public clamor, James Madison offered a series of amendments to satisfy citizens that these great liberties would remain safe and beyond the power of government to abridge. Madison proposed what later became the First Amendment in three parts, two of which are set out below, and one of which proclaimed: "The people shall not be deprived or abridged of their right to speak, to write, or to publish their sentiments; and the freedom of the press, as one of the great bulwarks of liberty, shall be inviolable." The amendments were offered to curtail and restrict the general powers granted to the Executive, Legislative, and Judicial Branches two years before in the original Constitution. The Bill of Rights changed the original Constitution into a new charter under which no branch of government could abridge the people's freedoms of press, speech, religion, and assembly. Yet the Solicitor General argues and some members of the Court appear to agree that the general powers of the Government adopted in the original Constitution should be interpreted to limit and restrict the specific and emphatic guarantees of the Bill of Rights adopted later. I can imagine no greater perversion of history. Madison and the other Framers of the First Amendment, able men that they were, wrote in language they earnestly believed could never be misunderstood: "Congress shall make no law . . . abridging the freedom . . . of the press . . ." Both the history and language of the First Amendment support the view that the press must be left free to publish news, whatever the source, without censorship, injunctions, or prior restraints.

In the First Amendment the Founding Fathers gave the free press the protection it must have to fulfill its essential role in our democracy. The press was to serve the governed, not the governors. The Government's power to censor the press was abolished so that the press would remain forever free to censure the Government. The press was protected so that it could bare the secrets of government and inform the people. Only a free and unrestrained press can effectively expose deception in government. And paramount among the responsibilities of a free press is the duty to prevent any part of the government from deceiving the people and sending them off to distant lands to die of foreign fevers and foreign shot and shell. In my view, far from deserving condemnation for their courageous reporting, the New York Times, the Washington Post, and other newspapers should be commended for serving the purpose that the Founding Fathers saw so clearly. In revealing the workings of government that led to the Vietnam war, the newspapers nobly did precisely that which the Founders hoped and trusted they would do.

The Government's case here is based on premises entirely different from those that guided the Framers of the First Amendment. The Solicitor General has carefully and emphatically stated:

"Now, Mr. Justice [BLACK], your construction of . . . [the First Amendment] is well known, and I certainly respect it. You say that no law means no law, and that should be obvious. I can only say, Mr. Justice, that to me it is equally obvious that 'no law' does not mean 'no law', and I would seek to persuade the Court that that is true. . . . There are other parts of the Constitution that grant powers and responsibilities to the Executive, and . . . the First Amendment was not intended to make it impossible for the Executive to function or to protect the security of the United States."

And the Government argues in its brief that in spite of the First Amendment, "the authority of the Executive Department to protect the nation against publication of information whose disclosure would endanger the national security stems from two interrelated sources: the constitutional power of the President over the conduct of foreign affairs and his authority as Commander-in-Chief."

In other words, we are asked to hold that despite the First Amendment's emphatic command, the Executive Branch, the Congress, and the Judiciary can make laws enjoining publication of current news and abridging freedom of the press in the name of "national security." The Government does not even attempt to rely on any act of Congress. Instead it makes the bold and dangerously far-reaching contention that the courts should take it upon themselves to "make" a law abridging freedom of the press in the name of equity, presidential power and national security, even when the representatives of the people in Congress have adhered to the command of the First Amendment and refused to make such a law. See concurring opinion of MR. JUSTICE DOUGLAS, post, at 721–722. To find that the President has "inherent power" to halt the publication of news by resort to the courts would wipe out the First Amendment and destroy the fundamental liberty and security of the very people the Government hopes to make "secure." No one can read the history of the adoption of the First Amendment without being convinced beyond any doubt that it was injunctions like those sought here that Madison and his collaborators intended to outlaw in this Nation for all time.

The word "security" is a broad, vague generality whose contours should not be invoked to abrogate the fundamental law embodied in the First Amendment. The guarding of military and diplomatic secrets at the expense of informed representative government provides no real security for our Republic. The Framers of the First Amendment, fully aware of both the need to defend a new nation and the abuses of the English and Colonial governments, sought to give this new society strength and security by providing that freedom of speech, press, religion, and assembly should not be abridged. This thought was eloquently expressed in 1937 by Mr. Chief Justice Hughes—great man and great Chief Justice that he was—when the Court held a man could not be punished for attending a meeting run by Communists.

"The greater the importance of safeguarding the community from incitements to the overthrow of our institutions by force and violence, the more imperative is the need to preserve inviolate the constitutional rights of free speech, free press and free assembly in order to maintain the opportunity for free political discussion, to the end that government may be responsive to the will of the people and that changes, if desired, may be obtained by peaceful means. Therein lies the security of the Republic, the very foundation of constitutional government."

MR. JUSTICE DOUGLAS, with whom MR. JUSTICE BLACK joins, concurring.

While I join the opinion of the Court I believe it necessary to express my views more fully.

It should be noted at the outset that the First Amendment provides that "Congress shall make no law . . . abridging the freedom of speech, or of the press." That leaves, in my view, no room for governmental restraint on the press. . . .

There is, moreover, no statute barring the publication by the press of the material which the Times and the Post seek to use. Title 18 U. S. C. § 793 (e) provides that "whoever having unauthorized possession of, access to, or control over any document, writing . . . or information relating to the national defense which information the possessor has reason to believe could be used to the injury of the United States or to the advantage of any foreign nation, willfully communicates . . . the same to any person not entitled to receive it . . . shall be fined not more than $10,000 or imprisoned not more than ten years, or both."

The Government suggests that the word "communicates" is broad enough to encompass publication.

There are eight sections in the chapter on espionage and censorship, §§ 792–799. In three of those eight "publish" is specifically mentioned: § 794 (b) applies to "Whoever, in time of war, with intent that the same shall be communicated to the enemy, collects, records, publishes, or communicates . . . [the disposition of armed forces]."

Section 797 applies to whoever "reproduces, publishes, sells, or gives away" photographs of defense installations.

Section 798 relating to cryptography applies to whoever: "communicates, furnishes, transmits, or otherwise makes available . . . or publishes" the described material. (Emphasis added.)

Thus it is apparent that Congress was capable of and did distinguish between publishing and communication in the various sections of the Espionage Act. . . .

Judge Gurfein's holding in the Times case that this Act does not apply to this case was therefore preeminently sound. Moreover, the Act of September 23, 1950, in amending 18 U. S. C. § 793 states in § 1 (b) that:

"Nothing in this Act shall be construed to authorize, require, or establish military or civilian censorship or in any way to limit or infringe upon freedom of the press or of speech as guaranteed by the Constitution of the United States and no regulation shall be promulgated hereunder having that effect." 64 Stat. 987.

Thus Congress has been faithful to the command of the First Amendment in this area.

So any power that the Government possesses must come from its "inherent power."

The power to wage war is "the power to wage war successfully." See *Hirabayashi v. United States*, 320 U.S. 81, 93. But the war power stems from a declaration of war. The Constitution by Art. I, § 8, gives Congress, not the President, power "to declare War." Nowhere are presidential wars authorized. We need not decide therefore what leveling effect the war power of Congress might have. . . .

As we stated only the other day in *Organization for a Better Austin v. Keefe*, 402 U.S. 415, 419, "any prior restraint on expression comes to this Court with a 'heavy presumption' against its constitutional validity."

The Government says that it has inherent powers to go into court and obtain an injunction to protect the national interest, which in this case is alleged to be national security.

Near v. Minnesota, 283 U.S. 697, repudiated that expansive doctrine in no uncertain terms.

The dominant purpose of the First Amendment was to prohibit the widespread practice of governmental suppression of embarrassing information. It is common knowledge that the First Amendment was adopted against the widespread use of the common law of seditious libel to punish the dissemination of material that is embarrassing to the powers-that-be. See T. Emerson, The System of Freedom of Expression, c. V (1970); Z. Chafee, Free Speech in the United States, c. XIII (1941). The present cases will, I think, go down in history as the most dramatic illustration of that principle. A debate of large proportions goes on in the Nation over our posture in Vietnam. That debate antedated the disclosure of the contents of the present documents. The latter are highly relevant to the debate in progress.

Secrecy in government is fundamentally anti-democratic, perpetuating bureaucratic errors. Open debate and discussion of public issues are vital to our national health. On public questions there should be "uninhibited, robust, and wide-open" debate. *New York Times Co. v. Sullivan*, 376 U.S. 254, 269–270.

I would affirm the judgment of the Court of Appeals in the Post case, vacate the stay of the Court of Appeals in the Times case and direct that it affirm the District Court.

The stays in these cases that have been in effect for more than a week constitute a flouting of the principles of the First Amendment as interpreted in *Near v. Minnesota*.

MR. JUSTICE BRENNAN, concurring.

Appendix C

I

I write separately in these cases only to emphasize what should be apparent: that our judgments in the present cases may not be taken to indicate the propriety, in the future, of issuing temporary stays and restraining orders to block the publication of material sought to be suppressed by the Government. So far as I can determine, never before has the United States sought to enjoin a newspaper from publishing information in its possession. The relative novelty of the questions presented, the necessary haste with which decisions were reached, the magnitude of the interests asserted, and the fact that all the parties have concentrated their arguments upon the question whether permanent restraints were proper may have justified at least some of the restraints heretofore imposed in these cases. Certainly it is difficult to fault the several courts below for seeking to assure that the issues here involved were preserved for ultimate review by this Court. But even if it be assumed that some of the interim restraints were proper in the two cases before us, that assumption has no bearing upon the propriety of similar judicial action in the future. To begin with, there has now been ample time for reflection and judgment; whatever values there may be in the preservation of novel questions for appellate review may not support any restraints in the future. More important, the First Amendment stands as an absolute bar to the imposition of judicial restraints in circumstances of the kind presented by these cases.

II

The error that has pervaded these cases from the outset was the granting of any injunctive relief whatsoever, interim or otherwise. The entire thrust of the Government's claim throughout these cases has been that publication of the material sought to be enjoined "could," or "might," or "may" prejudice the national interest in various ways. But the First Amendment tolerates absolutely no prior judicial restraints of the press predicated upon surmise or conjecture that untoward consequences may result. Our cases, it is true, have indicated that there is a single, extremely narrow class of cases in which the First Amendment's ban on prior judicial restraint may be overridden. Our cases have thus far indicated that such cases may arise only when the Nation "is at war," *Schenck v. United States*, 249 U.S. 47, 52 (1919), during which times "no one would question but that a government might prevent actual obstruction to its recruiting service or the publication of the sailing dates of transports or the number and location of troops." *Near v. Minnesota*, 283 U.S. 697, 716 (1931). Even if the present world situation were assumed to be tantamount to a time of war, or if the power of presently available armaments would justify even in peacetime the suppression of information that would set in motion a nuclear holocaust, in neither of these actions has the Government presented or even alleged that publication of items from or based upon the material at issue would cause the happening of an event of that nature. "The chief purpose of [the First Amendment's] guaranty [is] to prevent previous restraints upon publication." *Near v. Minnesota*, supra, at 713. Thus, only governmental allegation and proof that publication must inevitably, directly, and immediately cause the occurrence of an event kindred to imperiling the safety of a transport already at sea can support even the issuance of an interim restraining order. In no event may mere conclusions be sufficient: for if the Executive Branch seeks judicial aid in preventing publication, it must inevitably submit the basis upon which that aid is sought to scrutiny by the judiciary. And therefore, every restraint issued in this case, whatever its form, has violated the First Amendment—and not less so because that restraint was justified as necessary to afford the courts an opportunity to examine the claim more thoroughly. Unless and until the Government has clearly made out its case, the First Amendment commands that no injunction may issue.

MR. JUSTICE STEWART, with whom MR. JUSTICE WHITE joins, concurring.

In the governmental structure created by our Constitution, the Executive is endowed with enormous power in the two related areas of national defense and international relations. This power, largely unchecked by the Legislative and Judicial branches, has been pressed to the very hilt since the advent of the nuclear missile age. For better or for worse, the simple fact is that a President of the United States possesses vastly greater constitutional independence in these two vital areas of power than does, say, a prime minister of a country with a parliamentary form of government.

In the absence of the governmental checks and balances present in other areas of our national life, the only effective restraint upon executive policy and power in the areas of national defense and international affairs may lie in an enlightened citizenry—in an informed and critical public opinion which alone can here protect the values of democratic government. For this reason, it is perhaps here that a press that is alert, aware, and free most vitally serves the basic purpose of the First Amendment. For without an informed and free press there cannot be an enlightened people.

Yet it is elementary that the successful conduct of international diplomacy and the maintenance of an effective national defense require both confidentiality and secrecy. Other nations can hardly deal with this Nation in an atmosphere of mutual trust unless they can be assured that their confidences will be kept. And within our own executive departments, the development of considered and intelligent international policies would be impossible if those charged with their formulation could not communicate with each other freely, frankly, and in confidence. In the area of basic national defense the frequent need for absolute secrecy is, of course, self-evident.

I think there can be but one answer to this dilemma, if dilemma it be. The responsibility must be where the power is. If the Constitution gives the Executive a large degree of unshared power in the conduct of foreign affairs and the maintenance of our national defense, then under the Constitution the Executive must have the largely unshared duty to determine and preserve the degree of internal security necessary to exercise that power successfully. It is an awesome responsibility, requiring judgment and wisdom of a high order. I should suppose that moral, political, and practical considerations would dictate that a very first principle of that wisdom would be an insistence upon avoiding secrecy for its own sake. For when everything is classified, then nothing is classified, and the system becomes one to be disregarded by the cynical or the careless, and to be manipulated by those intent on self-protection or self-promotion. I should suppose, in short, that the hallmark of a truly effective internal security system would be the maximum possible disclosure, recognizing that secrecy can best be preserved only when credibility is truly maintained. But be that as it may, it is clear to me that it is the constitutional duty of the Executive—as a matter of sovereign prerogative and not as a matter of law as the courts know law—through the promulgation and enforcement of executive regulations, to protect the confidentiality necessary to carry out its responsibilities in the fields of international relations and national defense.

This is not to say that Congress and the courts have no role to play. Undoubtedly Congress has the power to enact specific and appropriate criminal laws to protect government property and preserve government secrets. Congress has passed such laws, and several of them are of very colorable relevance to the apparent circumstances of these cases. And if a criminal prosecution is instituted, it will be the responsibility of the courts to decide the applicability of the criminal law under which the charge is brought. Moreover, if Congress should pass a specific law authorizing civil proceedings in this field, the courts would likewise have the duty to decide the constitutionality of such a law as well as its applicability to the facts proved. But in the cases before us we are asked neither to construe specific regulations nor to apply specific laws. We are asked, instead, to perform a function that the Constitution gave to the Executive, not the Judiciary. We are asked, quite simply, to prevent the publication by two newspapers of material that the Executive Branch insists should not, in the national interest, be published. I am convinced that the Executive is correct with respect to some of the documents involved. But I cannot say that disclosure of any of them will surely result in direct, immediate, and irreparable damage to our Nation or its people. That being so, there can under the First Amendment be but one judicial resolution of the issues before us. I join the judgments of the Court.

MR. JUSTICE WHITE, with whom MR. JUSTICE STEWART joins, concurring.

I concur in today's judgments, but only because of the concededly extraordinary protection against prior restraints enjoyed by the press under our constitutional system. I do not say that in no circumstances would the First Amendment permit an injunction against publishing information about government plans or operations. Nor, after examining the materials the Government characterizes as the most sensitive and destructive, can I deny that revelation of these documents will do substantial damage to public interests. Indeed, I am confident that their disclosure will have that result. But I nevertheless agree that the United States has not satisfied the very heavy burden that it must meet to warrant an injunction against publication in these cases, at least in the absence of express and appropriately limited congressional authorization for prior restraints in circumstances such as these. . . .

What is more, terminating the ban on publication of the relatively few sensitive documents the Government now seeks to suppress does not mean that the law either requires or invites newspapers or others to publish them or that they will be immune from criminal action if they do. Prior restraints require an unusually heavy justification under the First Amendment; but failure by the Government to justify prior restraints does not measure its constitutional entitlement to a conviction for criminal publication. That the Government mistakenly chose to proceed by injunction does not mean that it could not successfully proceed in another way.

MR. JUSTICE MARSHALL, concurring.

The Government contends that the only issue in these cases is whether in a suit by the United States, "the First Amendment bars a court from prohibiting a newspaper from publishing material whose disclosure would pose a 'grave and immediate danger to the security of the United States.'" Brief for the United States 7. With all due respect, I believe the ultimate issue in these cases is even more basic than the one posed by the Solicitor

General. The issue is whether this Court or the Congress has the power to make law.

In these cases there is no problem concerning the President's power to classify information as "secret" or "top secret." Congress has specifically recognized Presidential authority, which has been formally exercised in Exec. Order 10501 (1953), to classify documents and information. See, e.g., 18 U. S. C. § 798; 50 U. S. C. § 783. Nor is there any issue here regarding the President's power as Chief Executive and Commander in Chief to protect national security by disciplining employees who disclose information and by taking precautions to prevent leaks.

The problem here is whether in these particular cases the Executive Branch has authority to invoke the equity jurisdiction of the courts to protect what it believes to be the national interest. See In re Debs, 158 U.S. 564, 584 (1895). The Government argues that in addition to the inherent power of any government to protect itself, the President's power to conduct foreign affairs and his position as Commander in Chief give him authority to impose censorship on the press to protect his ability to deal effectively with foreign nations and to conduct the military affairs of the country. . . .

It would, however, be utterly inconsistent with the concept of separation of powers for this Court to use its power of contempt to prevent behavior that Congress has specifically declined to prohibit. There would be a similar damage to the basic concept of these co-equal branches of Government if when the Executive Branch has adequate authority granted by Congress to protect "national security" it can choose instead to invoke the contempt power of a court to enjoin the threatened conduct. . . .

It is true that Judge Gurfein found that Congress had not made it a crime to publish the items and material specified in § 793 (e). He found that the words "communicates, delivers, transmits..." did not refer to publication of newspaper stories. And that view has some support in the legislative history and conforms with the past practice of using the statute only to prosecute those charged with ordinary espionage. But see 103 Cong. Rec. 10449 (remarks of Sen. Humphrey). Judge Gurfein's view of the statute is not, however, the only plausible construction that could be given. See my Brother WHITE's concurring opinion.

Even if it is determined that the Government could not in good faith bring criminal prosecutions against the New York Times and the Washington Post, it is clear that Congress has specifically rejected passing legislation that would have clearly given the President the power he seeks here and made the current activity of the newspapers unlawful. When Congress specifically declines to make conduct unlawful it is not for this Court to re-decide those issues—to overrule Congress. See *Youngstown Sheet & Tube Co. v. Sawyer,* 343 U.S. 579 (1952).

MR. CHIEF JUSTICE BURGER, dissenting.

So clear are the constitutional limitations on prior restraint against expression, that from the time of *Near v. Minnesota,* 283 U.S. 697 (1931), until recently in *Organization for a Better Austin v. Keefe,* 402 U.S. 415 (1971), we have had little occasion to be concerned with cases involving prior restraints against news reporting on matters of public interest. There is, therefore, little variation among the members of the Court in terms of resistance to prior restraints against publication. Adherence to this basic constitutional principle, however, does not make these cases simple. In these cases, the imperative of a free and unfettered press comes into collision with another imperative, the effective functioning of a complex modern government and specifically the effective exercise of certain constitutional powers of the Executive. Only those who view the First Amendment as an absolute in all circumstances—a view I respect, but reject—can find such cases as these to be simple or easy.

These cases are not simple for another and more immediate reason. We do not know the facts of the cases. No District Judge knew all the facts. No Court of Appeals judge knew all the facts. No member of this Court knows all the facts.

Why are we in this posture, in which only those judges to whom the First Amendment is absolute and permits of no restraint in any circumstances or for any reason, are really in a position to act?

I suggest we are in this posture because these cases have been conducted in unseemly haste. . . .

Here, moreover, the frenetic haste is due in large part to the manner in which the Times proceeded from the date it obtained the purloined documents. It seems reasonably clear now that the haste precluded reasonable and deliberate judicial treatment of these cases and was not warranted. The precipitate action of this Court aborting trials not yet completed is not the kind of judicial conduct that ought to attend the disposition of a great issue.

The newspapers make a derivative claim under the First Amendment; they denominate this right as the public "right to know"; by implication, the

Times asserts a sole trusteeship of that right by virtue of its journalistic "scoop." The right is asserted as an absolute. Of course, the First Amendment right itself is not an absolute, as Justice Holmes so long ago pointed out in his aphorism concerning the right to shout "fire" in a crowded theater if there was no fire. There are other exceptions, some of which Chief Justice Hughes mentioned by way of example in *Near v. Minnesota* . . .

It is not disputed that the Times has had unauthorized possession of the documents for three to four months, during which it has had its expert analysts studying them, presumably digesting them and preparing the material for publication. During all of this time, the Times, presumably in its capacity as trustee of the public's "right to know," has held up publication for purposes it considered proper and thus public knowledge was delayed. . . .

Would it have been unreasonable, since the newspaper could anticipate the Government's objections to release of secret material, to give the Government an opportunity to review the entire collection and determine whether agreement could be reached on publication? Stolen or not, if security was not in fact jeopardized, much of the material could no doubt have been declassified, since it spans a period ending in 1968. With such an approach— one that great newspapers have in the past practiced and stated editorially to be the duty of an honorable press—the newspapers and Government might well have narrowed the area of disagreement as to what was and was not publishable, leaving the remainder to be resolved in orderly litigation, if necessary. . . .

The consequence of all this melancholy series of events is that we literally do not know what we are acting on. As I see it, we have been forced to deal with litigation concerning rights of great magnitude without an adequate record, and surely without time for adequate treatment either in the prior proceedings or in this Court. It is interesting to note that counsel on both sides, in oral argument before this Court, were frequently unable to respond to questions on factual points. Not surprisingly they pointed out that they had been working literally "around the clock" and simply were unable to review the documents that give rise to these cases and were not familiar with them. This Court is in no better posture. I agree generally with MR. JUSTICE HARLAN and MR. JUSTICE BLACKMUN but I am not prepared to reach the merits.

I would affirm the Court of Appeals for the Second Circuit and allow the District Court to complete the trial aborted by our grant of certiorari, meanwhile preserving the status quo in the Post case. I would direct that the

District Court on remand give priority to the Times case to the exclusion of all other business of that court but I would not set arbitrary deadlines.

I should add that I am in general agreement with much of what MR. JUSTICE WHITE has expressed with respect to penal sanctions concerning communication or retention of documents or information relating to the national defense.

We all crave speedier judicial processes but when judges are pressured as in these cases the result is a parody of the judicial function.

MR. JUSTICE HARLAN, with whom THE CHIEF JUSTICE and MR. JUSTICE BLACKMUN join, dissenting.

These cases forcefully call to mind the wise admonition of Mr. Justice Holmes, dissenting in *Northern Securities Co. v. United States*, 193 U.S. 197, 400–401 (1904): "Great cases like hard cases make bad law. For great cases are called great, not by reason of their real importance in shaping the law of the future, but because of some accident of immediate overwhelming interest which appeals to the feelings and distorts the judgment. These immediate interests exercise a kind of hydraulic pressure which makes what previously was clear seem doubtful, and before which even well settled principles of law will bend."

With all respect, I consider that the Court has been almost irresponsibly feverish in dealing with these cases. . . .

This frenzied train of events took place in the name of the presumption against prior restraints created by the First Amendment. Due regard for the extraordinarily important and difficult questions involved in these litigations should have led the Court to shun such a precipitate timetable.

Forced as I am to reach the merits of these cases, I dissent from the opinion and judgments of the Court. . . .

"The very nature of executive decisions as to foreign policy is political, not judicial. Such decisions are wholly confided by our Constitution to the political departments of the government, Executive and Legislative. They are delicate, complex, and involve large elements of prophecy. They are and should be undertaken only by those directly responsible to the people whose welfare they advance or imperil. They are decisions of a kind for which the Judiciary has neither aptitude, facilities nor responsibility and which has long been held to belong in the domain of political power not subject to judicial intrusion or inquiry." *Chicago & Southern Air Lines v. Waterman Steamship Corp.*, 333 U.S. 103, 111 (1948) (Jackson, J.). . . .

MR. JUSTICE BLACKMUN, dissenting.

I join MR. JUSTICE HARLAN in his dissent. I also am in substantial accord with much that MR. JUSTICE WHITE says, by way of admonition, in the latter part of his opinion. At this point the focus is on only the comparatively few documents specified by the Government as critical. So far as the other material—vast in amount—is concerned, let it be published and published forthwith if the newspapers, once the strain is gone and the sensationalism is eased, still feel the urge so to do. . . .

"Great cases like hard cases make bad law. For great cases are called great, not by reason of their real importance in shaping the law of the future, but because of some accident of immediate overwhelming interest which appeals to the feelings and distorts the judgment. These immediate interests exercise a kind of hydraulic pressure..." *Northern Securities Co. v. United States*, 193 U.S. 197, 400–401 (1904).

The present cases, if not great, are at least unusual in their posture and implications, and the Holmes observation certainly has pertinent application.

The New York Times clandestinely devoted a period of three months to examining the 47 volumes that came into its unauthorized possession. Once it had begun publication of material from those volumes, the New York case now before us emerged. It immediately assumed, and ever since has maintained, a frenetic pace and character. Seemingly, once publication started, the material could not be made public fast enough. Seemingly, from then on, every deferral or delay, by restraint or otherwise, was abhorrent and was to be deemed violative of the First Amendment and of the public's "right immediately to know." Yet that newspaper stood before us at oral argument and professed criticism of the Government for not lodging its protest earlier than by a Monday telegram following the initial Sunday publication. . . .

With such respect as may be due to the contrary view, this, in my opinion, is not the way to try a lawsuit of this magnitude and asserted importance. It is not the way for federal courts to adjudicate, and to be required to adjudicate, issues that allegedly concern the Nation's vital welfare. The country would be none the worse off were the cases tried quickly, to be sure, but in the customary and properly deliberative manner. The most recent of the material, it is said, dates no later than 1968, already about three years ago, and the Times itself took three months to formulate its plan of procedure and, thus, deprived its public for that period.

The First Amendment, after all, is only one part of an entire Constitution. Article II of the great document vests in the Executive Branch primary power over the conduct of foreign affairs and places in that branch the responsibility for the Nation's safety. Each provision of the Constitution is important, and I cannot subscribe to a doctrine of unlimited absolutism for the First Amendment at the cost of downgrading other provisions. First Amendment absolutism has never commanded a majority of this Court. See, for example, *Near v. Minnesota*, 283 U.S. 697, 708 (1931), and *Schenck v. United States*, 249 U.S. 47, 52 (1919). What is needed here is a weighing, upon properly developed standards, of the broad right of the press to print and of the very narrow right of the Government to prevent. Such standards are not yet developed. The parties here are in disagreement as to what those standards should be. But even the newspapers concede that there are situations where restraint is in order and is constitutional. Mr. Justice Holmes gave us a suggestion when he said in Schenck,

"It is a question of proximity and degree. When a nation is at war many things that might be said in time of peace are such a hindrance to its effort that their utterance will not be endured so long as men fight and that no Court could regard them as protected by any constitutional right." 249 U.S., at 52. . . .

It may well be that if these cases were allowed to develop as they should be developed, and to be tried as lawyers should try them and as courts should hear them, free of pressure and panic and sensationalism, other light would be shed on the situation and contrary considerations, for me, might prevail. But that is not the present posture of the litigation.

The Court, however, decides the cases today the other way. I therefore add one final comment.

I strongly urge, and sincerely hope, that these two newspapers will be fully aware of their ultimate responsibilities to the United States of America. Judge Wilkey, dissenting in the District of Columbia case, after a review of only the affidavits before his court (the basic papers had not then been made available by either party), concluded that there were a number of examples of documents that, if in the possession of the Post, and if published, "could clearly result in great harm to the nation," and he defined "harm" to mean "the death of soldiers, the destruction of alliances, the greatly increased difficulty of negotiation with our enemies, the inability of our diplomats to negotiate . . ."

INDEX

Locators in **boldface** indicate main topics. Locators followed by *b* indicate biographical entries. Locators followed by *g* indicate glossary entries. Locators followed by *c* indicate chronology entries.

Index

310

Index

Index

PROPERTY OF THE LIBRARY
YORK COUNTY COMMUNITY COLLEGE
112 COLLEGE DRIVE
WELLS, MAINE 04090
(207) 646-9282

M

PROPERTY OF THE LIBRARY
YORK COUNTY COMMUNITY COLLEGE
112 COLLEGE DRIVE
WELLS, MAINE 04090
(207) 646-9282